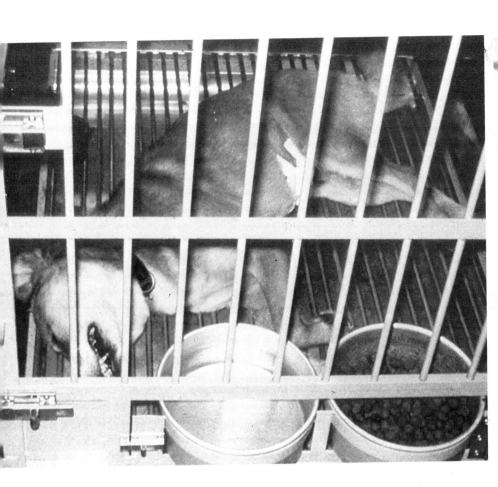

ILLUSTRATION 1.
Dog in cage…its stomach had been opened and acetic acid applied to the exposed tissue. Some days later an ulcer would develop which would then be treated by drugs. Tokyo, Japan.
Photograph by Jon Evans ©

Victims of Science

THE USE OF ANIMALS IN RESEARCH

Victims of Science

THE USE OF ANIMALS IN RESEARCH

Richard D. Ryder

NATIONAL ANTI-VIVISECTION SOCIETY LIMITED

First published in Great Britain 1975 by
Davis-Poynter Limited

Second and revised edition 1983 published
by the National Anti-Vivisection Society Limited (London)
51 Harley Street, London W1N 1DD
Distributed by Centaur Press Limited, Fontwell, Sussex

ISBN 0 905225 06 6

*The views expressed in this book are those of the author
Richard D. Ryder and are not necessarily those of
the National Anti-Vivisection Society Limited.*

'The day may come when the rest of the animal creation may acquire those rights which never could have been withheld from them but by the hand of tyranny . . . The question is not can they *reason?* nor can they *talk?* but can they *suffer?*'

JEREMY BENTHAM (1748-1832)

(Chapter 17 of "An Introduction to the Principles of Morals and Legislation". Footnote.)

'I rejoiced to think that I had accomplished a step towards obtaining the protection of the law for the victims of science.'

FRANCES POWER COBBE

(Autobiography, vol.2, p.262, 1894)

In memory of my mother, Vera Ryder (1899-1980), whose distress about mankind's mistreatment of the other animals I have tried to remedy

Contents

Illustrations

1. Dog in cage...its stomach had been opened and acetic acid applied to the exposed tissue. Some days later an ulcer would develop which would then be treated by drugs. Tokyo, Japan.

2. This kitten was photographed in a Polish laboratory during 1980, at the Nencki Institute of Experimental Biology, Warsaw. It is one of a batch of kittens used in "sight reversal procedures". Their eyes were bound shortly after birth and the bandages not removed until they were six months old. The result of the experiments proved that after the hoods had been peeled away the kittens never fully recovered their sight and the sexual life of the animals was either very seriously affected or non-existent. **(colour)**

3. Rabbit undergoing experimental surgery—if it survived this animal was destined for use in further experimental procedures. National University of Mexico. **(colour)**

4. Rat undergoing experiment for teaching of micro-surgery techniques, National University of Mexico. **(colour)**

5a. Pure strain mouse used for experimental purposes in Soviet laboratory under the direction of Dr. Vasilii Dushkin, senior researcher of Soviet Academy of Medical Sciences.

5b. Rodent breeding trays containing hybrid mice in Soviet Research laboratory forty kilometres outside Moscow.

6. Short-haired mongrel dog, picked up in a New York street, subjected to heart transplant operation in city hospital. Animal lies on floor of laboratory as there is no recovery room.

7. One of the many dogs used at the Department of Animal Experimentation, Hospital Clinico, Madrid, for research and the acquisition of manual skill. **(colour)**

8. A stray dog awaiting vivisection at the National University of Mexico. The dog had no run, and its cage was antiquated and rusty.

9. Rabbits undergoing drug tests. National Institute of Health, Tokyo, Japan.

10. This cat, incarcerated in a small cage, has an electrode implanted in its brain. By means of a battery the researcher can create an electrical discharge in order to ascertain at what anatomical point an electrical contact will stimulate fear, aggression and other behaviours (New York).

11. Picture was taken in a New York University training hospital. The protuberances on the shaved right hand side of the dogs' body (tumour implants) were produced as a result of an experiment from which the animal will die. The beagle cowered when approached and showed signs of great stress. The sides of the cage and floor are constructed from steel mesh. Nothing was included for the animal's comfort, not even a blanket.

Acknowledgements

I would like to acknowledge the considerable and courteous assistance I have received from officials of Government departments, commercial organisations, scientific establishments, animal welfare societies, and the authors of many books. I would like to thank especially my fellow members of the Animal Experimentation Advisory Committee of the Royal Society for the Prevention of Cruelty to Animals (RSPCA), the Committee's officials, FRAME, the British Union for the Abolition of Vivisection, the Scottish Society for the Prevention of Vivisection, the International Association Against Painful Experiments on Animals, the Animal Welfare Institute (Washington), the Institute for the Study of Animal Problems (Washington) the United Action for Animals Inc. (New York), Committee for the Reform of Animal Experimentation (CRAE), Lord Houghton, Clive Hollands, Meredith Lancashire, Dr Judith Hampson, Pauline Moroney, the late Dr Kit Pedler and my wife Audrey.

The author and publishers are grateful to the Home Office and Her Majesty's Stationery Office for permission to quote from The Cruelty to Animals Act 1876 and Returns under the Act, and to the Editor of the Daily Telegraph for permission to publish the letter which comprises Appendix C.

Lady Dowding, Jon Evans, Brian Gunn, Colin Smith and Sue Shakespeare of the National Anti-Vivisection Society, 51 Harley Street, London, and Eileen Ryan, Jon Wynne-Tyson and Angela Walder, deserve special acknowledgement for their assistance in the production of this second edition.

FOREWORD

RT. HON. MURIEL, LADY DOWDING
(President of the National Anti-Vivisection Society)

It has been said that cruelty is the worst of crimes. Increasingly one realises how true is that statement. And in my view there is no greater cruelty than that carried out in the vivisection laboratories of the world. Richard Ryder's book shows all too clearly the cold, callous, systematic and calculated cruelty of the animal experimental method and one reels with horror at the extent to which animals are exploited on the altar of science.

At its first printing 'Victims of Science' created a sensation. The publicity in the press, on the radio and television that this publication generated, caused many people to consider, perhaps for the first time, the moral decadence and hypocrisy of our civilisation which allows one tiny section of the community to deliberately inflict on living beings pain, suffering and distress in the often vain hope of alleviating human ills. The book forced open the eyes of many who had hitherto been unwilling to recognise the cruelty of vivisection and motivated many to join the campaign against this monstrous crime.

I was delighted therefore that the National Anti-Vivisection Society decided to finance the publication of the Revised Edition of 'Victims of Science'. It is a valuable and forceful weapon in the anti-vivisection armoury and I have the highest admiration for its author, Richard Ryder, whom I have known for many years as a valiant fighter for the rights of animals. His meticulously researched book strips away many layers of misconception about the practice of vivisection and exposes to public scrutiny the false claims of its apologists. Richard Ryder shares with the NAVS the conviction that the use of animals for research purposes is morally wrong and, at best, scientifically questionable. However it must be pointed out that the NAVS does not share all his prescriptions as to the process by which reform can be accomplished. For instance, the NAVS fervently believes that vivisection cannot be 'regulated' or 'controlled' and that only by amendments to the current legislation governing the use of animals, or new legislation, specifically banning certain types of procedures on animals is likely to bring any amelioration of the situation. Futhermore such measures would need to be seen clearly as only steps towards the final goal of abolition.

With that important reservation I thoroughly welcome this Revised Edition and pray it may hasten the day when the vivisection of animals is viewed by the community at large with the same horror as we now look back upon such obscenities as child-labour and slavery.

Muriel, Lady Dowding

FOREWORD

RICHARD ADAMS
(Author of "Watership Down" and "Plague Dogs")

"Out of sight, out of mind". This is the truth about the millions of live animals which are used to death every year in experimental tests in the western world. Most people don't think much about what they don't actually see; and of course those who profit financially from selling products — cosmetics, household cleaning agents, patent medicines, toothpaste and the like — which have been tested on animals, take care not to obtrude this aspect of their business on the public. Who wants to be haunted by blinded rabbits when they're spraying their hair?

"Don't tell me about it, I'd prefer not to hear", is a reply I have received many times when I have raised the subject of experimentation. Again, people have said to me "I couldn't read your 'Plague Dogs', I found the details too upsetting". (They were all authentic). In other words, "I know these things are done to animals, but although I use the products and benefit from the suffering, I don't want to have to exercise my responsibilities as a citizen of democracy by learning the facts and deciding whether or not I think there could or ought to be changes." Yet these same people, if faced with a problem in some other sphere of communal life — capital punishment, say — would react indignantly to the suggestion that it was best left to "the experts" and the bureaucracy. "Those who eat the pudding", they would say, "are both entitled and qualified to have opinions about it." Yes, we all eat puddings of one kind and another. Groups of us, however, are not force-fed with a new pudding until fifty per cent are dead, in order to decide whether it can be marketed to a public already well-supplied with puddings. Easiest to ignore so difficult and controversial a subject.

Quite plainly there is a moral dilemma involved in deliberately causing suffering to animals for the benefit of humanity. It may be justifiable: it may not; but a moral dilemma indisputably exists. Any honest-minded person admits that. So if there is a public moral dilemma, affecting us all and over which we are all entitled to make up our minds, why can't the facts be made public knowledge, and why don't more people demand that this be done?

The answers are first, that the experimenters and the bureaucrats, (with some justification), fear over-emotional and half-baked reactions from the press and from people who have not carefully considered all sides of the matter: and secondly, as I have said, that many people would rather not know the truth, because it upsets them and makes them feel guilty. Also, they suspect that it would be difficult to bring about any real change and they have too much else to see to and feel they can't spare the time. Besides, the animals aren't complaining are they? As Jane Austen remarked, "Those who do not complain are seldom pitied."

Over-sensitivity is one reaction. But another, also widespread, is the counter-charge that anyone who doesn't like the idea of animal experimentation is merely stupid and sentimental. "Bothering about a lot of animals, when human beings are starving or dying of disease — that's not only sentimental, it's irritatingly wrong-headed." In actuality, this is a relative question. No doubt compassion for human beings should precede compassion for animals: but does that mean that no compassion at all is left over for the animals? Does it mean that humans are morally justified in doing anything at all to animals? I suspect that the "stupid sentimentality" brigade would be quick enough to stop their children (or anybody else's) tormenting an animal if they actually caught them doing it. (And if they could actually see animals suffering in laboratories and experimental testing stations, they would no doubt want to ask those responsible "For what purpose is this being done? Is it really necessary?")

Surely there ought to be people ready to speak and campaign for animals since, although they can suffer, they cannot speak for themselves. Most people find distasteful the idea of simply using animals up and then throwing them away, as if they were boots or electric light bulbs. Different people, however, will form different views about precisely what is justifiable and what is not. At least, they will if they are put in possession of the facts and are ready to think about them.

During the past decade there has been a growing public interest in the whole question of animal experimentation and a feeling, gradually extending to more and more people, that it is time the business was brought into the open, the real facts were examined and a majority public view arrived at (as opposed to the views of the few who at present are the only people who know what is being done and why). It is towards the fulfilment of these aims that Richard Ryder has worked in writing this book. He has, of course, put forward his own personal views. (It would be a dull book if he had not). Nevertheless, his treatment of the subject is, in my view, accurate, balanced and fair, and he has the advantage of personal experience, as a result of which he is convinced that there is a lot wrong with the present situation.

There are today four principal spheres of interest in animal welfare: blood sports, commercial slaughter of wild life, factory farming and animal experimentation. In this country, there is a good deal of public concern about all four, but probably less information is actually known and available to the public in the latter sphere than in any of the other three. This book aims to improve that state of affairs and thus to help more people — ordinary members of the public — to form their own views. I hope that a great many people will have the courage to read it and that it will make the whole subject of animal experimentation much more widely known, thought about and discussed.

Are things satisfactory as they are or ought there to be changes? If so, what changes? That is what every reader of this book should consider. Make no mistake: if enough members of the general public wanted a change strongly enough to make their wishes felt, then that change would come about. It is unlikely to come about in any other way.

The question, as I see it, is "Can the amount of suffering involved to animals, used in tests and experiments, practicably be reduced?" To come to a worth-while view on that, one needs information. This book supplies it.

Richard Adams

Preface

The aim of this book is to provide documentary evidence of the way man mistreats animals for the purposes of research, and to suggest reforms. My intention is in no way to defame scientists, but to question their conventions.

The premise on which the book is based is that man's moral concern should spread beyond the boundaries of his own species to encompass the rights and interests of all suffering creatures.

I believe that animal welfare is a serious and technical subject, and one which deserves more attention in this age of greatly increased exploitation of animals. I have endeavoured to provide a reference-book for one part of this very large field, and I have made every effort that is humanly possible to ensure the accuracy of the information which I supply.

This shortened and revised edition has been brought up-to-date as far as possible.

RDR

ILLUSTRATION 2.
This kitten was photographed in a Polish laboratory during 1980, at the Nencki Institute of Experimental Biology, Warsaw. It is one of a batch of kittens used in "sight reversal procedures". Their eyes were bound shortly after birth and the bandages not removed until they were six months old. The result of the experiments proved that after the hoods had been peeled away the kittens never recovered their sight and the sexual life of the animals was either very seriously affected or non-existent.
Photograph by Jon Evans ©

1. Speciesism

Man is just an animal, one species among many species. He is certainly a very clever animal, but he is also an exceptionally destructive, aggressive and polluting animal. During the twentieth century the species of man has grown to overpopulate many areas of the planet and has begun to expand outwards into space, taking with it a potential for creativity as well as the capacity to spoil and to destroy. Man takes with him an advanced technology but only a primitive, intermittent and possibly declining morality. This clever and proud animal has already destroyed many other species; he now also has the power to destroy his own and, as more individuals gain this cataclysmic power, so the probability of total doom for his species grows. Man is, after all, still an animal — he has greater strength than the storm-gods of antiquity but he is still programmed for the jungle.

Whether or not moral schemes are based upon faith, enlightened self-interest or compassion, changes in moral outlook often have been based upon some extension of sympathy so that individuals (such as foreigners, slaves, those of other races) whose rights and interests had not previously been recognised or respected, gain this acknowledgement; they are, as it were, included in the moral in-group. In the nineteenth century the Western world extended its boundaries of compassion to encompass the poor and the enslaved. In some cases this increase in respect for the interests of others genuinely was based upon principle and compassion — it was not because of self-interest but in spite of it.

The first part of the twentieth century has seen the continuation of this trend with an increased recognition by the powerful races of the interests of the weaker ones. The time has now come to extend the borders of respect still further to include a concern for the sufferings of species other than our own.

It was in 1859 that Charles Darwin first published *The Origin of Species,* but it has taken time for its message of evolutionary kinship between man and beast to sink in and be acted upon. Most men intellectually accept their biological relationship with other animals without taking the logical step of acknowledging a *moral* relationship, that is to say treating animals as what they really are — our relatives.

If we examine the arguments used by slave-owners in the past to counter those of the reformers, we can see a striking similarity with the view expressed today by those who defend the exploitation of animals in factory-farms, the fur-trade, laboratories and elsewhere. The slave-owners discouraged travellers' visits to the plantations because they considered that such visitors were not experts and therefore tended to react emotionally to what they saw, not understanding, so it was said, the high-mindedness of such ventues nor the technical problems involved. It might be conceded that there were 'isolated' whippings and the mortality rate was rather high, but the average slaver could assure his 'ill-informed' or 'over-sensitive' visitor that he felt a deep compassion for his slaves and they reciprocated this with loyalty and devotion. After all, their living conditions were much better than in the jungle and, besides, these creatures had never known sophisticated pleasures and so what they did not know about they could not miss. The visitor must not judge slaves by his own standards — to believe that they could feel and suffer in a way similar to himself was to be merely 'sentimental'. Above all else, it would be stressed, slavery was necessary for economic survival.

Such arguments thrive to this very day in the mouths of those who have an interest in the exploitation of animals, although scientists should know better, for they often base the whole validity of biology on the assumption that man is indeed an animal like other animals, and that the study of animals will produce knowledge applicable to man. They cannot have it both ways; either men and animals are entirely different, in which case much of their work is invalid, or else men and the other animals are rather the same in which case animals logically deserve similar treatment and consideration.

There is hardly a scientist alive today who does not accept the basic Darwinian assertion that men and animals are on the same biological continuum. What reason can there be, other than a sentimental one, for not putting men and animals upon the same *moral* continuum?

For too long man has arrogantly exaggerated his uniqueness. Anthropologists differ in their opinions but many have labelled the great beetle-browed Neanderthal Man as being of a different species from modern man, and not even our linear ancestor. Nevertheless, this entirely different and now extinct creature practised ritual burial and had a brain larger than our own. It is therefore important to realise that it is not only modern *homo sapiens* who has been capable of displaying great intelligence — at least one other creature of the past demonstrates that man has had no monopoly on abstract thought. We may even be underestimating the intelligence and the cultures of other species extant today.

Some physical differences between species do, of course, exist. But science itself has produced progressively more evidence to suggest that major differences between men and the other animals are less than were once imagined; man now knows he is not the only toolmaker, he does not have the largest or heaviest brain or the largest brain-to-body ratio, he is not the only species with a language and although he cannot communicate in another animal's symbols, chimpanzees have learned to communicate in his own, inventing new and meaningful combinations of words in American Sign Language for the Deaf (see *Animals, Men and Morals,* p.79). In some environments man is not the best adapted species and in some special instances not the most intelligent. Certainly man is, on average, very clever, but he took thousands of years to develop his technology beyond the level of the simple stone-axe, and in some parts of the planet this development has only taken place within this century. Many of his apparent advantages over the other creatures depend upon his relatively recent discovery of how to pass on knowledge to future generations; but men isolated from civilisation, illiterate and reared in total ignorance of technology would probably survive, if at all, no better than other animals, practically tool-less and speechless for generations, without the discovery of fire or the luxuries of agriculture.

But how can such differences as exist affect the moral case? Can it seriously be argued that because man is cleverer than other animals he therefore has rights or interests that other animals do not have? Surely, a superior understanding entails greater responsibility rather than the opposite; just as an adult recognises a degree of responsibility towards an infant, so also should he towards animals. There seems no good reason why physical differences *between* species should effect such matters differently than do physical differences *within* species; there exist many individuals of the human species who, on account of injury to their brains or because of congenital dysfunctions are, permanently or temporarily, less intelligent, less communicative and less able to stand up for themselves than the average dog, cat or monkey. Yet, if a scientist presumed to experiment upon them, to poison them or electrocute them or inject them with diseases, he would rightly stand condemned. Similarly, many adult animals surely possess all the faculties, and more than those, of the human infant — but this does not justify experiments on babies.

All such physical differences are morally irrelevant. To be cruel to a weak creature but not to a strong one is the morality of the coward and the bully. If some creatures from outer space invaded Earth and proved to be stronger or vastly more intelligent than ourselves, would they be justified in ordering us to be vivisected? They might explain to us that, after all, they were very much more intelligent, that they doubted whether we really could feel pain, that they would keep us in perfectly clean and hygienic cages and that they naturally regretted having to perform severe experiments upon us but that it was, unfortunately, necessary for the benefit of their own species. One can imagine one of their scientists trying to justify himself in these terms — 'Please don't think I am a sadist. As a matter of fact I am very fond of humans and keep several as pets. I can assure you that I would be the first to criticise any experiments that were unnecessary or involved unnecessary cruelty. I agree that fifty million humans die in our laboratories every Earth-year, but most of these are in routine experiments that do not involve severe pain. You really must not allow your emotions to cloud the issue.'

The most important qualities that men share with the other animals are life and sentience. There is as much evidence to believe that another animal can suffer as there is to believe that another individual of one's own species can suffer. There is good evidence that pain is a function of the nervous system and that many animals have nervous systems very much like our own — so, is it not reasonable to assume that when a wounded animal screams and struggles that it is suffering in a way similar to that in which a wounded man can suffer? The capacity to suffer is the crucial similarity between men and animals that binds us all together and places us all in a similar moral category. Those politicians who still believe that politics have some remote connection with morality or who vaguely believe that their job has to do with increasing the total sum of happiness, should question why non-human animals should not be also represented by them? After all, the fully democratic politician already represents the interest of human citizens who do not vote — children, lunatics and lords — so why not also animals? Why should the animals in a state or a constituency or a country not also be accorded some status as citizens? The important question about animals, as Jeremy Bentham pointed out, is not 'Can they *reason?* nor can they *talk?* but, can they *suffer?*'

It used to be said that what distinguishes the species from each other is that they cannot interbreed; indeed such was once the core of the definition of 'species'. But this is no longer regarded as true, for lions and tigers, as an example, are known to be able to inter-breed and produce viable hybrids which are themselves capable of reproduction; and yet lions and tigers are still classified as being of separate species. Man is zoologically placed in the so-called Primate Order along with all the species of monkeys and apes, and although there are no well-authenticated accounts of man successfully interbreeding with any other species of primate, the possibility that this could happen still, at least theoretically, remains. Such an event would cause a bureaucratic upheaval! Would the ape-man off-spring be accorded all the rights of a citizen in the welfare state? Would the monkey mother receive maternity payments and free health-benefits, would the child legally be obliged to attend school at a certain age and receive the right to vote when majority is reached? If this ever occured the moral and legal reassessments provoked by the happy event would be greater than the zoological surprise, because many cases of interbreeding between primate species have already been recorded; undoubtedly, however, it would highlight the absurdity of mankind's current species-centred morality.

In recent decades the word 'species' has taken on almost magical undertones and many laymen seem to imagine that the zoologists can always draw some hard and fast line between the species which somehow might justify not only scientific but also moral discriminations. This is not the case and there is in fact no single criterion which distinguishes between all so-called species. The whole classification system is largely one of descriptive convenience and is chiefly based upon appearances. If one lot of animals look different from another lot then, arguably, they can be called a different species. Labels such as 'race', 'sub-species' and 'breed' still form the substance of controversies. To make matters even more confusing, there are even groups of animals which are reckoned to be of the *same* species but which apparently *cannot* interbreed.

I use the word 'speciesism' to describe the widespread discrimination that is practised by man against the other species, and to draw a parallel with racism. Speciesism and racism are both forms of prejudice that are based upon appearances — if the other individual looks different then he is rated as being beyond the moral pale. Racism is today condemned by most intelligent and compassionate people and it seems only logical that such people should extend their concern for other races to other species also. Speciesism and racism (and indeed sexism) overlook or underestimate the similarities between the discriminator and those discriminated against and both forms of prejudice show a selfish disregard for the interests of others, and for their sufferings.

Speciesism denies the logic of Evolution. Indeed, the Oxford zoologist Richard Dawkins, attacks the prejudice of speciesism on biological grounds *(The Selfish Gene*, Oxford University Press, 1976):

'Many of us shrink from judicial execution of even the most horrible human criminals, while we cheerfully countenance the shooting without trial of fairly mild animal pests. Indeed we kill members of other harmless species as a means of recreation and amusement. A human foetus, with no more human feeling than an amoeba, enjoys a reverence and legal protection far in excess of those granted to an adult chimpanzee. Yet the chimp feels and thinks and — according to recent experimental evidence — may even be capable of learning a form of human language. The foetus belongs to our own species, and is instantly accorded special privileges and rights because of it. Whether the ethic of "speciesism", to use Richard Ryder's term, can be put on a logical footing any more sound that that of "racism" I do not know. What I do know is that it has no proper basis in evolutionary biology.'

To those who retort that to grant that a group of individuals have 'rights' entails some reciprocal sense of 'duty' from that group, I would ask what duties are expected from a human baby, from a lunatic or from one who is in a reversible coma; but do we not respect the interests of such human beings?

It has already been said that the scientist, perhaps more than most men, has reason to know that men and the other animals have similar capacities for suffering. Why then does he, against both common-sense and compassion, so often insist that he has a right to do to other species what he would never do to his own? The answer is not that most scientists are sadists (although a few will be) in the simple meaning of the word. Both science and sadism are concerned with the lust for power, but only in this rather abstruse sense do most scientist and sadists have much in common. No, the straightforward answer is that the scientist does what is expected of him. Long past are the days when the scientist was the exceptional being, the genius, the eccentric, the unorthodox man who was a scientist because he *defied* conventions. In this scientific age, scientists are basically *conformers* who do not question what is expected of them. They are no more moral, no more sadistic, no more compassionate and have no more wisdom than any other group of reasonably well educated men. Like most men they seek security and success and in order to achieve these ends they know that it pays to toe the line.

Conformism is a powerful drive, often underestimated. Men were disinclined to believe Adolf Eichmann and other Nazis when they tried to explain their frightful actions by saying that all they were doing was obeying orders. Yet the alarming truth is that most men will do almost anything that is required of them as long as they believe that this is the norm of the group or the society in which they find themselves.

A psychologist, Dr. Stanley Milgram, once did an experiment in which he found that most ordinary volunteers were quite prepared to give potentially lethal electric shocks to other unwilling human subjects, even though these were screaming and begging to be released. (In fact no shocks were given and the screams were sham, but the volunteers did not realise this.) The important factor was that the volunteers found themselves being told to do apparently terrible things, in a laboratory setting where it seemed that such things were acceptable.

So it is when a young aspiring scientist finds himself in an animal-experimentation laboratory. He does not dare question convention; to be successful he must conform. His natural feelings of compassion for the laboratory animals and also any feelings of squeamishness are quickly suppressed. After a few months or years, he can no longer feel them, he is hardened, habituated, de-sensitised and unlikely to repent.

In my opinion, squeamishness and compassion are often spontaneous feelings. Squeamishness seems to be basically a fear of pain, death and disintegration, but it is not very much understood and perhaps it is underrated. What is important in the social sense about both these feelings is that they are responses to the sufferings of others through a form of identification.

Squeamishness, along with disgust, are two powerful feelings that have almost entirely been ignored by contemporary psychology — a science that may be noted by future historians for its stultifying obsession with the quantification of trivia and its brutal disregard for the subtleties and complexities of consciousness and behaviour. The facts that very many people are disgusted by disease and horrified by injury are surely most interesting phenomena in themselves. Are they learned behaviours or innate? Disgust (and hence avoidance) clearly has survival-value since it may well reduce the spread of infectious disease. Squeamishness also may lead the individual to keep away from the physically injured and so, by avoiding danger, to escape the other's fate. So strong has been the cultural suppression of squeamishness and disgust of disease — both feelings tending to be regarded as signs of weakness, unmanliness or irrationality — that their serious evaluation has never been undertaken. Yet the sheer power of these feelings and their frequency of occurrence poses some fascinating questions. Injury in the heat of battle, or when the individual is angry or in some other state of arousal, is less likely to provoke a squeamish response. It is the cold-blooded injury, to oneself or to another, which can wreak havoc with the autonomic nervous system and cause nurse, medical student or patient to faint at the sight of blood or bowel. With time and practice such reactions can be controlled by most medical personnel, but patients have less opportunity for desensitisation and, being in less than perfect physical health anyway, their squeamish reactions compounded with fear may even prove fatal.

Children (and adults) often find classroom dissections alarming, but they are encouraged to conceal their feelings, and few people, until they have grown used to doing so, find it easy to kill another creature, especially at close quarters. It is not the affectation of the city-dweller that makes him loathe to cut a pig's throat; rather, it is the reverse that is true — the farmer and butcher have learned to suppress their spontaneous revulsion with the job, and after many years grow callous and forget their earlier scruples; indeed they may even derive a certain pride from being able to do something that is naturally shocking for the uninitiated.

I have found that in a small group of adolescent female biology students, 55 per cent disliked dissecting a mouse and a third found such procedures made them feel sick or ill (Ryder, Paper read to the British Psychological Society, A.G.M., Exeter, 1977).

The power of squeamishness provides some evidence against those who claim that man, unbridled by conscience and culture, would emerge as a total carnivore and indiscriminate blood-letter. It also raises the question as to whether the widespread cult of cold-blooded dissection and vivisection is not a form of systematised perversion, tending to blunt or 'brutalise' the sensitivities of its practitioners.

Tenderness for animals is not the prerogative of so-called civilised man. Viewers of B.B.C. television in 1977 were moved to see that even cannibals can cry when separated from a pet pig. ('The World About Us', Jan. 23, 1977).

How much will the attitudes of callousness, the blunting of sensitivity and the disregard for the sufferings of animals that are being inculcated in the minds, not only of college students but, increasingly, of school children as well, affect the whole outlook upon life of future generations?

The striking quality of most animal experimenters that I have met is not that they are obviously peculiar or that they wear a cruel sneer, but that they at least *appear* to be so ordinary, so nice and so kind. Indeed I am not trying to claim that they are otherwise. What I am questioning is whether the *conventions* of the animal laboratory are right, not only for the animals who suffer but for the social health of humanity at large. Along with the increase in research upon non-human animals has been a sinister upward trend in experiments performed upon human-patients, as revealed in Britain by Dr. M. H. Pappworth in his book *Human Guinea Pigs* (1967). Dangerous and painful experiments have been performed upon humans and sometimes without their knowledge or consent. But it should not be imagined that such research has been done instead of research upon animals; in several cases known to me it has been in conjunction with experiments upon animals and by the same research-team. In other words, experiments upon human patients often spring from the ruthless mentality that is, in the first place, cultivated in the animal laboratory by conforming scientists.

Pain - a personal view

Pain, it can be said, is the quintessence of evil. All painful events are bad and all bad events are painful. The only possible justification for evil is that it brings a greater good, and the only justification for pain is that it creates a greater pleasure — a greater joy or happiness.

The dispute lies first in whether or not any pain will actually bring about a real benefit, and secondly whether such benefit, if it does occur, will outweigh the pain that accompanies its creation.

I believe that the only reality that we can be sure of is the universe of our own awareness. When through injury, anaesthesia or sleep our awareness is drastically reduced, reality slips away. Only from the stand-point of the conscious individual does reality have meaning. If, for example, I am rendered totally unconscious through injury then any events which occur while I am not aware, are not part of my reality but are only real to other observers who remain conscious.

If individual awareness is the only touchstone of reality and if awareness vanishes at death then it makes no sense to argue that events occurring after an individual death have any meaning to the individual who is dead. So also, it is spurious to argue that benefits of which I am unaware justify pain of which I *am* aware.

The problem of pain remains, and cannot be explained away by theology. Even the scientific theory that pain always has value in helping a creature to avoid danger, is no longer tenable; for it is now known that minor injuries can cause pointless and destructive agony, whereas cancerous tumours can grow to fatal proportions quite unfelt.

If pain forced upon an individual is to be justified convincingly, it must be in terms of the benefits accruing to the *same* individual.

Of course some individuals may suffer and others gain by it. Such occasions arise daily. But to jump from the sphere of consciousness of one individual to that of another individual is literally to leap from one universe to another. Benefits justifying pain can only be benefits if they occur within the same sphere of consciousness, that is to say within the same individual organism.

It is curious, but undoubtedly true, that consciousness is a function of the central nervous system. Just as an electric current emerges mysteriously from a coil of copper wire when it is rotated within magnets, so consciousness emerges from the pulsating blood and tissue of the brain. The basic physical properties of the human brain are well known and it is incontrovertible that the brains of other creatures are physically similar to our own. This being so, it is reasonable to assume that creatures of other species are conscious in a way similar to ourselves, and that they can similarly suffer pain and distress.

If all this is true, as I believe it is, one is again faced with the fact that pain forced unwillingly upon any individual creature can only truly be justified in terms of benefits consciously experienced by that *same* individual creature.

It is a fact that scientific research on animals is rarely justified in these terms. Attempts can only be made to justify it in terms of benefits to *other* individuals, and I believe all such attempts must fail. To argue that any species has more worth than any other species seems to me to be difficult to prove and I think one can dismiss such speciesist arguments as irrational prejudice. Thus to argue that the pain suffered by conscious creatures of one species is justified by benefits experienced by conscious individuals of *another* species because the latter species is better than the former, is double nonsense; first because one is arguing from one individual to another, and secondly because one is arguing as if, from the point of view of consciousness, the species were entirely different.

Pain cannot be directly observed except in oneself, but it is usually accepted that certain behavioural signs such as screaming and writhing are often indications that other humans can also suffer pain. Humans can, in addition, tell us (but only if we happen to speak their language) that they are suffering, but this does not apply in the case of a dumb person, nor an infant, nor does it rule out the possibility of lies being told. In general then, the grounds for believing that an individual of another species is suffering, are just about as strong as those for believing that another of one's own species is experiencing pain; this seems especially true in the case of 'higher' animals which are known to have nervous systems very much like our own.

In 1961 the eminent neurologist, Lord Brain, wrote:

'Since the diencephalon is well developed in (vertebrate) animals and birds, I at least cannot doubt that the interests and activities of animals are correlated with awareness and feelings in the same way as my own, and which may be, for aught I know, just as vivid.' (Presidential address to UFAW International Symposium on 'The Assessment of Pain in Man and Animals', 1961.)

In 1965 the British Government's Departmental Committee on Experiments on Animals under Sir Sydney Littlewood, reported that 'There is scientific evidence that all mammals have the physical structures which seem to be involved in the production of sensations of pain, and that these appear to work in the same way as in man' (*Littlewood Report* p.54). On this issue this Committee supported the findings of an earlier official report (*Committee on Cruelty to Wild Animals,* paragraph 36-42) which concluded that on behavioural, anatomical and survival grounds 'We are satisfied, therefore, that animals suffer pain in the same way as human beings' (paragraph 40).

There seems little doubt that the other animals suffer like ourselves, and I think that it is wrong that human beings should be the agents of so much of that suffering.

Speciesist Defences

The main speciesist defence of cruelty to animals is that mankind benefits — in terms of knowledge, economy or sport, for example.

In the particular case considered in this book, the defence of the exploitation of animals in laboratories usually takes the form of arguing that knowledge gained from such research will be of benefit to the human species. But such indeed was the argument put forward by some of the Nazi scientists tried for their experiments upon Jews, and with some scientific justification, for research upon human beings is more likely to produce results beneficial to humans than is research upon other animals.

I believe the speciesist case for animal experimentation is not acceptable. In the first place a large amount of the research which is done is trivial and the knowledge gained has no medical importance, as much evidence in this book demonstrates. Furthermore, a very great deal of research is after pure knowledge and there is no application for this knowledge in mind at the time of the experimentation. Knowledge, however important or practical it may seem, is itself essentially a *neutral* thing. Science gives men power to act destructively as well as constructively. Knowledge is not always good as Adam and Eve are alleged to have discovered, and as thousands of inhabitants of Nagasaki and Hiroshima also learnt. Knowledge about radiation, for example, can be used for the treatment of illness or for the destruction of life. Even new strictly medical knowledge can be, and is, evilly applied to torture *(New Scientist,* 15 November 1973, p.459) brainwash, extort, change, persuade, punish or annihilate, if it falls into the hands of the wrong people.

Those with genuinely humane motives are most likely to prolong life or alleviate suffering by bringing existing medical knowledge to bear in those parts of the world where men and women are suffering and dying because they cannot afford treatment. Yet many scientists prefer to spend their lives in laboratories causing untold suffering to animals in questionable medical research with a strong commercial motive; these researchers are not convincing when they plead that humanity is their over-riding concern.

It cannot be denied that out of all the millions of experiments performed upon animals, some useful knowledge has been gained. But equally it must not be forgotten that this knowledge often could have been acquired by other means and that many of the greatest discoveries of all have owed nothing to the use of laboratory animals and indeed might have been lost if animals had been used.

To impose suffering, allegedly in order to reduce it, and to take life, allegedly in order to save it, are self-contradicting claims. They are made even more dubious when one bears in mind that at the time of the experiment any benefits that might be accrued from it are merely hypothetical and uncertain. To attempt to justify the *certain* suffering of animals against some future, as yet *uncertain* benefit, seem to be an unwarranted gamble. Furthermore, the suffering imposed upon a laboratory animal is quite deliberate and *artificial,* in the sense that if the experiment was not performed then the suffering would not occur; but the suffering that it is hoped to reduce by doing the experiment is caused either by *natural* illness or by *self-inflicted* risks (e.g. through the use of a new cosmetic) — in other words the speciesist attempts to justify the deliberate infliction of suffering upon an innocent animal by claiming that the knowledge so obtained may perhaps, somewhere at some unknown moment in the future, relieve the natural or self-inflicted pains of his own species. This seems to be an entirely selfish, prejudiced and logically unsound argument.

Self-justification

I have myself experimented upon animals in Britain and in America. In many laboratories a guilty silence prevails. Some of the younger workers, those not fully hardened to the task, have to suppress their feelings of guilt and pretend that they do not exist. The question of whether it is justifiable to use animals in research is rarely, if ever, talked about. If someone is brave enough to broach the subject he is likely to encounter irritability and evasiveness — occasionally downright fury and contempt. But this latter reaction is rare and often conceals a conscience that is particularly uneasy.

Surprisingly, the argument that animals do not feel pain at all, or do so *less intensely* than humans, is still widely encountered among all those who have a vested interest in inflicting pain — for example blood sportsmen, bullfighters, farmers and, not least, experimenters.

When encountered in an intelligent person the motive for this argument can only be deception — of self or other.

As with the speciesist argument that one species is in a morally superior category to another, so also with the argument that animals are less sensitive to pain, one is left with a feeling that these are not the well-reasoned and cautious hypotheses worthy of scientists. In most cases these self-justifying arguments are mere rationalisation.

Animal Welfare

It is sometimes claimed that those who are concerned with animal welfare tend to neglect their own species or that those who are particularly fond of animals are emotionally ill or unable to relate to humans.

But it seems very rash to assume that friendships between individuals of different species are in any way unnatural or a sign of neurosis, for zoologists have reported comradely relationships occurring in their wild habitat between baboons and chimpanzees, and between one sort of monkey and another. In other words, relationships *between* species occur quite naturally and should not be regarded as the one-sided prerogative of frustrated, decadent or inadequate humans.

Isolated or lonely human-beings will sometimes show special affection towards animals, it is true, but this does not mean that there is anything artificial about such relationships. Nor does it mean that all 'animal-lovers' are neurotic; some will be, but many are quite normal people. It certainly does *not* mean that all neurotic people love animals — far from it, and indeed, cruelty to animals can sometimes be a sign of serious mental disorder and is often coupled with cruelty to humans. Four cases of men sentenced to prison for battering and killing babies were reported in the *Sunday Times* (4 November 1973) and two of these four men had had previous criminal convictions for cruelty to animals. In other words, men who are cruel to animals may tend also to be cruel to humans.

A study by L. T. Brown *et al.* at Oklahoma State University indicated 'that people who express little affection for dogs also tend to manifest little affection for other people', (*Psychological Reports*, 1972, 31, 957-958) and the psychiatrist Anthony Storr has pointed out that several psychopathic murderers, including the 'Boston Strangler', were extremely cruel to animals (*Sunday Times* 19 September 1976). 'What', asks Storr 'is the predictive value of extreme cruelty to animals? I suspect it to be highly significant'.

In my own clinical experience I have encountered disturbed individuals who have been violent towards humans and non-humans alike.

The corollary also appears to be true; namely, that men who are especially compassionate to humans are also kind to animals, and history produces some outstanding instances of great reformers who fought for the more considerate treatment of *all* life, non-human as well as human. St. Francis of Assisi was an early example. William Wilberforce and Lord Shaftesbury were more recent cases — Wilberforce being a founder member of the RSPCA and Shaftesbury being one of those who tried to get legal protection for animals in laboratories. Richard Martin was another whose humanity bridged the species-gap (see Chapter 13). So also was Angela Burdett-Coutts.

Indeed one can go further and say that animal welfare reformers have been especially far-sighted and have anticipated reforms in human society, often espousing causes long before they became fashionable.

Frances Power Cobbe, besides being an anti-vivisectionist, was also a pioneer social reformer and a colleague of Mary Carpenter; she was also one of the early champions of 'Women's Rights'. Lawson Tait, too, besides attacking vivisection was an eminent nineteenth-century advocate of women being allowed into the medical profession (see p.144). Maria Dickin, founder of the People's Dispensary for Sick Animals was, like Frances Cobbe, an early social worker and did much to alleviate the sufferings of her fellow humans.

The weight of such evidence tends to suggest that a concern for animals is not only a natural and a spontaneous thing, but can also be associated with a compassionate attitude towards other human-beings.

Speciesism is as great a prejudice as racism. Those of us who count ourselves as Socialists or Liberals, Humanitarians or Christians, should extend our ideologies to include the other species; the welfare of animal-citizens should be as much our concern as is that of other humans.

I believe our respect for others should include all sentients. To continue to exclude them from our morality is to be guilty of speciesism. If we accept that it is wrong to cause suffering to innocent humans then, logically, it is also wrong to do this to non-humans. There is no sound evidence for believing that other animals cannot suffer like ourselves, and indeed the evidence points the other way.

For these reasons I consider that animal welfare is a serious subject worthy of further research and deserving the support of governments and the respect of the community in an age when animals increasingly are being exploited.

The next great step forward in Man's moral evolution will be the full recognition of the rights and interests of the animal kingdom.

2. Some Facts and Figures: Worldwide

The number of animals being used in scientific research is very large. Exact figures on a world basis are, however, not available since most user-countries are not keeping records. In the United Kingdom, however, records were commenced in 1876 and have been elaborated and maintained by the Home Office since that time; these statistics are the best available longitudinal data and provide good evidence of the increasing use of animals in British laboratories. They may also give some indication of how experimentation in Europe and the USA must have expanded over the years. Since they are by far the best figures available in the world today, they are given in some detail.

British Statistics

It is important to realise that these Home Office figures* only cover experiments licensed under the Cruelty to Animals Act 1876, and so do not include those animals used in the scientific production of substances (e.g. vaccines, sera and anti-sera) since this is not deemed to be an experimental process; nor do they cover experiments upon invertebrate animals; nor do these figures include some experiments which are considered *not* to be 'calculated to cause pain', and there is an increasing trend to exclude behavioural experiments, such as those performed by psychologists, and also certain veterinary procedures. Only about 82 per cent of animals used in registered laboratories are counted under the 1876 Act (M.R.C. Survey of the Numbers and Types of Laboratory Animals used in the U.K. in 1972, published 1974).

Figure 1 shows the total number of British experiments upon living vertebrate animals which have been licensed under the Cruelty to Animals Act (1876). (Although under no statutory obligation to do so, the Home Office has in practice counted as one experiment each animal used in licensed research.)

Over the years an average of approximately ninety per cent of these experiments have been performed without anaesthetic, and about seventy per cent of those animals which are anaesthetised are allowed to recover from the anaesthetic. It can be seen from Figure 1 that there has been a rapid increase in the numbers of experiments licensed, especially

---

* A copy of the latest statistics under the 1876 Act may be obtained from Her Majesty's Stationery Office, 49 High Holborn, London W.C.1.

since 1920. The numbers of researchers holding Home Office licences permitting them to do research on living vertebrate animals has also considerably increased as shown in Figure 2.

Each year the Home Office publishes figures based upon returns filled in by the experimenters themselves. These figures are not audited and so they can be no more accurate than the honesty and diligence of the scientists allow. Until 1976 the figures gave little more than the total numbers of licensed experiments, experimenters, registered laboratories and certificates granted for work on dogs*, cats, equidae, and experiments without anaesthesia.

As regards the purpose for which experiments were being performed, the figures only gave the numbers of experiments for Cancer research (443,525 experiments out of a 1976 total of 5,474,739 i.e. 8.1 per cent), Diagnostic Procedures (90,231 experiments in 1976, i.e. 1.6 per cent of the total) and the mandatory Testing of Drugs (1,263,400 experiments in 1976, i.e. 23.1 per cent of the total). Added together, these three big medical uses had amounted to 62.02 per cent of all licensed experiments in 1920, but they accounted for only 32.83 per cent of all licensed experiments in 1976.

In other words, the proportion of experiments which definitely could be identified as medical had approximately halved over the years.

Much of the worldwide debate about animal experimentation during the 1970s has centred on this question — how many of the experiments are for genuine and worthwhile medical research?

As a result of a great deal of animal welfarist pressure upon the British Government, the format for the annual figure was radically altered, and the new statistics—giving at least three times as much information as the old format—were first published in December 1978. The latest give the figures for animal research carried out in 1981, which totalled 4,344,843 licensed experiments. (*Statistics of experiments on Living Animals*. September 1982. H.M.S.O. Cmnd. 8657).

In summary, the statistics confirm that a great deal of animal experimentation has little or nothing to do with medicine but is to do with behavioural studies (often involving stress, brain surgery or electrical and

---

* In 1972 71% of all the dogs were beagles, 9% were greyhounds, 20% were mongrels and other breeds. (M.R.C. Survey pub. 1974). About 30% of all the cats and dogs in 1972 came from casual dealers and the M.R.C. concludes that 'this high figure must be regarded as unsatisfactory since such animals may be discards from some other use or come from dubious sources'. 21,000 pigs and 33,000 sheep were used in Britain in 1972.

other forms of 'punishment'), the toxicity testing of cosmetics, detergents, toiletries and other luxury and inessential products, and agricultural research.

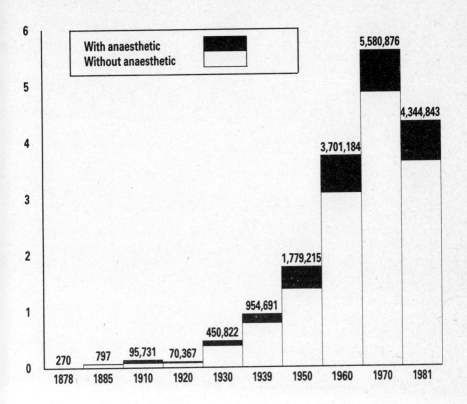

Figure 1. Total number of British licensed experiments performed on living animals each year (under Cruelty to Animals Act, 1876)

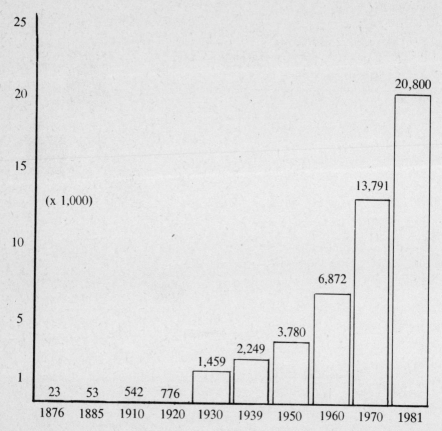

Figure 2. The numbers of persons licensed to experiment on animals in Great Britain.

One of the main aims of this book has been to draw attention to the many non-medical uses to which animals are being put in laboratories around the world. The routine toxicity-testing of various products accounts for the cruel deaths of countless thousands of animals internationally and constitutes the largest non-medical use. Behavioural research by psychologists, agriculturalists and others is another example.

Both these major non-medical uses are categorised in the new British Government figures which perhaps give some indication of their scale in other less well documented countries.

Table 2 of the 1982 Home Office Statistics show the number of British experiments performed in 1981 related to the study of various substances:-

	No. of Experiments
Plant pesticides including fungicides	30,634
Herbicides or substances modifying plant growth	12,861
Substances used in industry	69,199
Substances used in the household	14,250
Food additives	20,150
Tobacco and its substitutes	2,299
Cosmetics and toiletries	24,421
Injurious plants and metazoans	2,692
General environmental pollutants	45,848
TOTAL =	222,354

(6,423 of these experiments involved the application of substances to the eyes of the animals.)

These uses far outnumber the experiments carried out with a view to the treatment or prevention of cancer. (1981 Total = 118,128). Although some areas have shown reductions (e.g. the testing of cosmetics) other fields of research (e.g. testing smoking materials and experiments involving stress) have increased in recent years.

Table 8 gives information about behavioural studies performed in 1981.

	No. of experiments
Interferences with any of the special senses, or the brain centres controlling them	2,805
Interferences with the Central Nervous System (other than centres controlling the special senses)	16,754
Use of aversive stimuli, electrical or other:	12,144
Experiments conducted 'for inducing a state of psychological stress'	23,813
TOTAL =	55,516

The numbers of experiments performed for the testing of riot control devices or for weapon ballistic tests are not shown, unfortunately. But it is worth noting that 173,984 experiments were performed in Government Departments (is this really the sort of use to which taxpayers like to see their money being put?) and a large proportion of these were performed by the Ministry of Defence. This figure does not include 117,038 experiments carried out in Public Health Laboratories and 242,813 in the laboratories of quasi-autonomous non-government organisations (Quango's).

Just what proportion of all the experiments are for strictly medical purposes still remain a mystery. Not only is there a lack of any given definition of what is 'medical', but to make matters even hazier, one big category mixes together a lot of different areas or research ('medical, dental and veterinary'), and another large category is so vaguely worded that it would seem to embrace any animal experiment ever performed (the 'study of normal or abnormal body structure or function'). A mystery also surrounds the 519,411 experiments which do not come into any of these categories: they are simply described as being 'for other purposes'.

Within the genuine medical sphere itself there is very little information given as to the types of research being done. We do, however, learn that during the year 1981 there were 146,754 experiments involving exposure to ionising irradiation (mostly without any anaesthesia), 2,787 involving burning and scalding, (only 536 with anaesthesia for whole experiment), and 4,800 involving the infliction of physical trauma to simulate other human injury (Table 8). Mandatory drug-testing (including veterinary) appeared to account for less than one-fifth of all licensed experiments. (Table 4).

The new format also gives us more information about the types of animals used. Rodents, fish and birds still account for the majority. But there were 6,186 experiments conducted on primates during the year, 434 on horses, donkeys or crossbreeds, 8,016 on cats and 13,459 on dogs. One would like to know more about the animals used in the 74,504 experiments where the species is still unaccounted for (Table 7)—these include 1,781 mammals, 35,412 ungulates and 2,284 carnivores.

One of the most interesting figures is the apparent drop in the number of experiments carried out by commercial concerns. The 1977 statistics showed that 3,535,033 (64.6% of the total) were for commercial undertakings. With a slight change of wording, the 1982 returns give only 2,267,155 (52% of the total) as being carried out by commercial concerns. Has the U.K. commercial sector really collapsed as much as this? Whatever the truth of the matter, it still remains the case that most experiments are carried out commercially rather than by universities or hospitals.

One of the most worrying trends is the increase in the number of those holding licences to experiment. This has trebled since 1960 to 20,800 in 1981. In 1950 there were only 3,780, and in the year the Act was passed in 1876 there were 23. No information is given about the qualifications of all these new licensees. Many are, however, either students or technicians, and only a proportion will have medical qualifications; 56% of all licensees experimented on university premises but carried out only 19% of all licensed experiments.

All this research (4,344,843 licensed experiments performed in 527 registered laboratories during 1981) is supervised by only 15 Home Office Inspectors. The ratio of Inspectors to experimenters has dropped alarmingly over the years (see Figure 4). Each Inspector on average now has to control 1,386 experimenters and monitor over 289,000 experiments each year. In 1876, one Inspector had only 23 experimenters to keep his eye on.

The ratio of experiments performed to every one visit paid by a Home Office Inspector is about 644 to one.

The number of places registered for the performance of experiments (about 550) has remained more or less constant in recent years, but this has been due to amalgamations. One registered place may now cover many physically separate laboratories. An example is Oxford, where one registration covers twelve major medical and university departments (including those of Agriculture, Forestry and Zoology), some of these departments having several animal laboratories which contain a total of twenty-three different vertebrate species and use well over 50,000 animals each year. (An official list of the 527 British premises registered under the Cruelty to Animals Act 1876 can be purchased from the Home Office, Queen Anne's Gate, London S.W.1.)

The Act of 1876 was framed to control less than 300 experiments in one year; in 1876 there were 270. In 1981 nearly 20,000 times this number of experiments were performed. In 1876 there were twenty-three licensees compared with 900 times as many in 1981 (see *Littlewood Report*, p. 7 fn.).

Only approximately one quarter of *active* licensees publish any results of their experiments during a year. During the 1960s it was estimated that *three out of every four licensed experiments were never reported in any scientific journals because the results were 'inconclusive' or 'insufficiently important'.* (*Littlewood Report*, pp. 53, 166.).

On 1st August 1964, out of 8,748 licensees, 1,442 were technicians, 482 were undergraduate students and 6,824 were graduates (549 veterinary, 3,202 medical, 3,073 others). In other words, *little more than one-third (36.6%) of all licensees were medical, and the majority of researchers were experts in non-medical fields.*

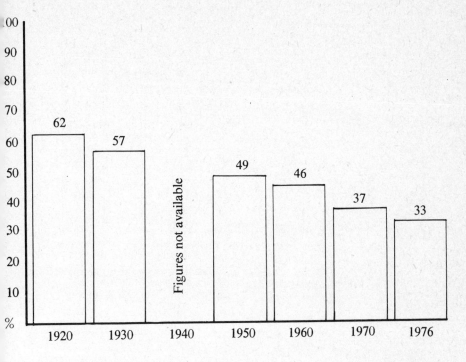

Figure 3. Percentage of the total number of U.K. licensed experiments (under 1876 Act) comprised by the combined medical fields of cancer research, diagnosis, and the mandatory testing of drugs, vaccines and sera.

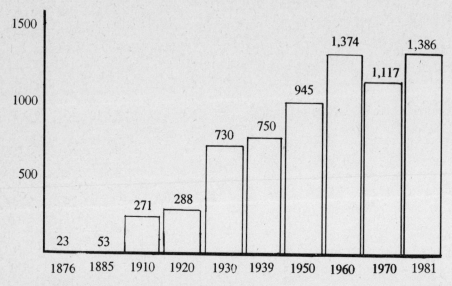

Figure 4. The numbers of licensed researchers for every one Home Office inspector in the U.K.

Denmark

In 1971, according to the Danish Ministry of Justice, 1,400,000 live animals were used in experiments, which is a high figure when it is borne in mind that the human population of Denmark is only five million. (IAAPEA, 1973.) Proportionately, this would be equivalent to about fifteen million animals being used in the U.K. whereas we know that it is actually about a third of this figure; rough allowances being made for the fact that the Danish system appears to include some categories not counted under the British law.

Estimates for the USA

Estimates of the numbers of living animals experimented upon in the USA range widely between twenty million and 200 million each year. A report published in the *Journal of Surgical Research* (June 1967) estimated an annual turnover for American laboratories of approximately 250,000 monkeys, 100,000 cats and 250,000 dogs. The number of monkeys used has dropped since then for special reasons. But there is no evidence that the figures for cats and dogs have dropped, indeed they may well have increased. If, therefore, the ratio for cats and dogs used to the total number of experiments is similar in the USA to that in the UK, then the American total of animals being used annually would be in the region of twenty-nine million or eighty million respectively. Another way of guessing at the American figure would be to prorate on the basis of human population levels. Using the UK levels this would suggest a total of around twenty million, but using the Danish figures it would approximate to nearly sixty million animals dying annually in American laboratories.

An estimate by Rutgers University puts the total at over sixty-three million, including:

Monkeys and apes	85,000
Cats and dogs	700,000
Rodents	45,000,000
Rabbits	700,000
Pigs and sheep	70,000
Frogs	15-20,000,000
Turtles, snakes and lizards	200,000
Birds	1,750,000

(Christian Science Monitor, 18 July 1973)

However extravagant these figures appear to be, they may still represent an underestimate.

Professor J. Clausen of the Institute of Preventative Medicine and Environmental Science, Odense University, Denmark has reckoned *(Progress Without Pain,* NAVS, 1973) that in 1965 the following numbers of animals were used in the American Pharmaceutical Industry alone.

Mice	23,200,000
Rats	9,900,000
Hamsters	900,000
Guinea-pigs	350,000
Rabbits	250,000
Dogs	93,000
Monkeys	60,000
Cats	33,000
Total	34,786,000

It is known that in the UK in 1965 there were 1,331,288 mandatory tests for the standardisation of sera, vaccines or drugs (Home Office Returns). If, but only if, this figure is comparable and equivalent to Professor Clausen's for the USA then the pro-rata figure for the total number of live animals used annually in American research amounts to the staggering figure of approximately 125 million. Hopefully, this is an over-estimate.

Other Countries

The Netherlands use over one million research animals annually (*Vet. Record* 29 May 1976).

In 1971 Australia used 850,000 animals for research, Canada 2,768,000, India 870,000, Israel 323,000 and Japan used some 19,000,000 in 1970 (which included 65,000 dogs).

Sweden used about one million animals in 1974, including 2,925 monkeys, 2,400 dogs and 4,900 cats.

World Estimates

Estimates for the world yearly consumption of laboratory animals are even more hazy. But on the assumption that there are at least three countries using a similar number as the UK (e.g. Western Germany, France, Italy) and that Russia probably approaches the Japanese level, then *the world total cannot be less than 100 million and may be more than three times that figure.*

The use of live animals for research began to be a regular practice in Europe during the mid-nineteenth century. It rapidly spread to America and during the present century almost every country in the world which claims to be developed or 'civilised' has followed the fashion. Animal laboratories are now found throughout Asia and Africa.

3. Behind the Figures

Research on animals used to be almost exclusively a medical affair, but nowadays an increasingly large number of *non-medical* fields also use animals; some of the largest and most obvious medical fields combined together have, over the years, accounted for only one third of all British experiments (see p.16).

Commercial examples of non-medical experiments are the oral toxicity testing of weedkillers, packaging materials, cosmetics and toiletries, food-dyes, flavouring-additives, detergents, floor polishes and anti-freeze liquids; in such experiments these substances are force-fed to animals to kill them (see pp.29, 33, 59).

Academic examples include research by zoologists, veterinarians (see pp.44-46), ecologists, agriculturalists (see p.44-52), forestry-experts and even anthropologists.

Out of twenty-eight British University Departments of Psychology answering a recent questionnaire, seventeen admitted that they use animals in research. Psychology is not a medical subject, nevertheless psychologists frequently operate on the brains of animals, cutting pieces out, coagulating, removing brain tissue by vacuum pump or electrically or chemically stimulating areas of the brain. Many psychological experiments involve the 'punishment' of animals; indeed punishment is a key concept in much psychological research (see p.52). As Dr. Keller Breland describes it, 'the typical laboratory experiment involving punishment or threat of punishment is conducted in a very restricted area — a closed box or small pen. Sometimes the animal is even strapped down. A light or buzzer signals the onset of a shock — the most common 'punishment' in such experiments. When the shock is applied, the animal tries to escape, but if he is boxed in or tied down, he cannot do so'. (Breland and Breland, *Animal Behaviour,* p.63).

Education

In the USA and in some other countries, the practice of allowing schoolchildren to experiment upon living animals is gaining ground. In the UK, no schoolchildren have, as yet, ever been licensed to experiment upon living vertebrates under the Cruelty to Animals Act, but they are often encouraged to dissect living insects and other invertebrate animals. Nobody knows the extent of an insect's capacity for suffering, and it can be questioned whether there is real need to use live creatures at all in drastic experiments of any kind when models and other alternatives already exist. Dissection of dead animals such as guinea-pigs and hamsters is also performed by British school-children and some examining boards insist on such dissections for children taking General Certificate of Education Advanced level examinations in biology and zoology. A survey conducted in 1970 by the Schools Council Educational Use of Living Organisms Project revealed that over forty species of living organisms were used in primary schools and over one hundred in secondary schools. The animals used are sometimes kept alive at the school for some months before being killed and can become, to some pupils at least, real pets. The methods of killing these animals is, in some cases, somewhat haphazard and may not be at all painless. (The psychological effects upon children of dissecting a pet they had become fond of, or of killing insects which they at least imagine have anthropomorphic faculties, could possibly be to blunt sensitivity and develop an exploitative attitude to living things in general.) Sometimes these school animals are inadequately looked after and, especially during vacations, animals have been left to starve.

Many university students experiment on animals. In 1964, one in twenty of all UK licensees were university undergraduates; one I met told me that the experiments he performed on animals were not original research but merely to teach himself what was already well known and available in basic text-books — it was, as he said, 'just a good way of learning'.

The Laboratory Rat

The word 'rat' conjures up horrors for some people, but the laboratory rat is far removed from its sewer-rat ancestors. Today's smart little white furry creature with pink nose and pink paws has been bred for over a hundred years to be friendly and long-suffering (in every sense of the word).

There are three main strains of the Norway rat which are now widely used for research: The Wistar rat — an albino; the Sprague-Dawley rat — an albino; the Hooded rat — basically white but with coloured head and shoulders, the colour ranging from cream to black.

Defenders of research often refer disparagingly to the rat as if it hardly counted as an animal at all, and those concerned about animal welfare hesitate to show compassion for a creature which has such a bad name. But the poor friendless laboratory rat ill-deserves its reputation, for it is an inquisitive and intelligent animal with a well-developed brain. If properly looked after it is active, playful and keeps itself remarkably clean and tidy. To dismiss a great deal of ruthless research as being pardonable because it was 'only performed on rats' is to miss the point; these creatures are as capable of suffering as dogs or cats or other such animals with whom the average human being more traditionally feels some bond of friendship.

The white rat, as much as any other single species or strain of animal, is the victim of science; millions die annually in laboratories throughout the world. They are not, however, mere machines — they are sensitive and sentient creatures.

Poison-testing of commercial products (toxicity-testing)

An increasingly huge area, probably already the largest field in which live animals are used for research, is the testing of new products for their poisoning effects.

In the 1950s drug companies began to employ a few toxicologists* who experimentally poisoned small numbers of animals using concentrated doses of test-chemicals. By the 1970s major producers of chemical products of all sorts (not just drugs) have enormous toxicology laboratories which may absorb a third of their total development resources and account for millions of animals annually.

A recent reference-book gives information about the poisoning-effects of hundreds of commercial products, much of the data based upon animal experiments. The products listed include insecticides, pesticides, anti-freeze chemicals, brake-fluids, bleaches, Christmas tree-sprays, church candles, silver cleaners, oven-cleaners, deodorants, skin fresheners, baby preparations, bubble-baths, bath-salts, freckle-creams, depilatories, eye make-up, crayons, fire-extinguishers, inks, suntan-oils, nail polish, mascara, hairsprays and rinses, zipper lubricants, paints, thermometers and children's novelties (Gleason, Gosselin, Hodge and Smith, *Clinical Toxicology of Commercial Products,* Williams & Wilkins Ltd., index). Eight pages of this book are consigned to a list of the names of cosmetics and toiletries showing their toxicity-ratings.

Acute Toxicity Tests — the LD 50

Almost any substance, if administered in a large enough dose, will kill. It has become fashionable to discover the lethal levels of an increasingly wide range of commercial products — and there seems no logical limit to what can be tested in this way.

A standard test is to force massive doses of the test substance down the throats of animals in order to discover at what dosage level half of the animals die within fourteen days. This is called the LD 50 test — where LD stands for Lethal Dose and 50 means fifty per cent (i.e. half of the animals).

Almost inevitably this procedure means that all the animals are being made severely ill, some taking perhaps two weeks to die, others just

---

* Toxicology is the science of poisons.

managing to survive. The amount of suffering caused by this is considerable.

Where not particularly poisonous substances are being tested, as in the case of food-additives, very large quantities must be forced into the animals by stomach tube, sometimes damaging them by causing internal rupture or other physical effects. As Professor A. C. Frazer has pointed out, in the context of testing food-additives:

'In some cases death in animals was caused merely by the physical properties (osmotic and pH effects, for example) of the large volumes or high concentrations that were given to them; these properties had no relevance to the low concentrations used in food technology.'

The LD 50 is often carried out upon several different species at a time. This is because of the notorious unreliability of generalising between one sort of animal and another (see pp.108-112). The traditional species chosen are rats, mice, rabbits, dogs (usually beagles), and monkeys. Cats are occasionally used instead of dogs.

Common signs of toxicity include unusual vocalisation, restlessness, paralysis, convulsions, irritability, lachrymation (tears), breathlessness, panting, diarrhoea, vomiting, tremors, jaundice and, of course, death.

Besides forcing animals to eat commercial products, toxicologists also inject them with poisonous doses, apply them to eyes or skin (see p. 34) or make the animals breathe the substances. The LC 50 is analogous to the LD 50 — it is the air concentration of the material which is found to kill fifty per cent of the animals, usually within fourteen days, and after the animal has been forced to breathe the poison for a period of time (usually four hours). (see G.E. Paget (ed.), *Methods in Toxicology,* Blackwell Scientific Publications, 1970, p.59.)

Chronic (long-term) Toxicity Tests

It is also considered necessary to make animals consume smaller doses of commercial products over longer periods of time. Rats and dogs are the most frequently used species. Of 134 studies of one month's duration or longer published in *Toxicology and Applied Pharmacology,* 43.3% were on rats, 38.1% on dogs, 6.7% on monkeys, 3.7% on mice, 3.0% on rabbits, 1.5% on chickens and guinea-pigs, 0.7% on gerbils (ibid., p.86).

In chronic toxicity testing the test-substance is administered daily over a number of weeks, months or even years. Signs of poisoning are observed and post-mortem analysis is made of the animals as they die.

While the animals are suffering whatever effects the poisoning causes them, they are often subjected to repeated and unpleasant investigations such as tests of lymph, blood or brain fluid.

These crude and cruel methods of testing are often criticised by toxicologists themselves as being almost pointless — 'In practice, they are of little use and are expensive in animals' is one such opinion — 'the main information they give is an indication of the size of dose required to commit suicide'. (Dr. S. B. de C. Baker in *The Use of Animals in Toxicological Studies,* UFAW, 1969, p.23.)

Despite the fact that animals are very expensive (see pp. 80-82) and that the alternatives are promising (see p. 121), little is being done to accelerate the development of these alternatives.

Much of the testing is not really scientific but is done to satisfy legal or bureaucratic requirements or to please the publicity departments of the safety-conscious firms concerned.

In a recent BBC television film, the head of a large chemical company was criticised for putting on the market highly profitable but possibly dangerous substances. He replied proudly that 'after all, we do spend much more on safety-testing our products than we do on marketing'. It is precisely so that executives can make comments like this that so much toxicity testing is being carried out — partly it has become a publicity stunt.

The scientists themselves are often more honest about this than are the business-men. One well known toxicologist writes (Paget, *op.cit.,* p.2) that producers are aware that public scrutiny must necessarily follow a failure in the evaluation of the safety of a drug:

'In these circumstances it is not surprising that the mere existence of a test will suggest to them that the test should be applied, not so much to determine whether the drug does or does not possess a particular property, but rather to provide a climate of assurance, either political or legal, should future events bring their actions into question.'

He goes on to say that 'although it all may give rise to a feeling of assurance, the scientific basis of safety testing is dubious, since all such tests are designed to demonstrate a negative, which, by definition, cannot be achieved'.

Most of the tests used were thought-up intuitively and it would be hard to substantiate their validity from any basis of scientific principle. The scientists are up against the unscientific demands of inflexible bureaucrats:

A real and powerful reason for the failure of many pharmaceutical firms to mount investigations of problems of toxicity employing techniques new to this field is that, should they obtain information of which the significance cannot be evaluated, they anticipate severe difficulties with the regulatory agency to which that information must be disclosed. They are often, therefore, placed in the anomalous and scientifically ridiculous situation of preferring not to obtain new information in case they are saddled with impossible requirements by a regulatory agency as a result. This attitude has certainly materially held up the development of techniques that undoubtedly in the long run will prove to be of use. (*Ibid,* p.5.)

Thalidomide: a lesson unlearned?

More than any other event, the thalidomide tragedy has stimulated the enormous increase in all forms of toxicity-testing; and yet there is no valid reason why this should be so, considering the ineffectiveness of current testing methods to detect the dangers of thalidomide.

In the first place it should be understood that thalidomide *was* tested on animals — and as rigorously as any product was, at the time of its production. As Dr. Paget puts it: 'It is commonly remarked, in fact, that the toxicity tests that had been carefully carried out on thalidomide without exception had demonstrated it to be an almost uniquely safe compound.' (*Ibid,* p.4.)

Secondly, it should be explained that, even *after* thalidomide's deforming effects have been discovered in humans, it still proved surprisingly difficult to reproduce similar effects in laboratory animals. (See Appendix C). Studies failed to produce thalidomide deformities in chickens, hamsters, dogs, cats, rats or monkeys *(Ibid.,* pp. 134-9). Only in a certain strain of rabbit did deformities similar to those found in humans begin to appear.

If the thalidomide tragedy taught us anything, *it demonstrated in a most cruel way that the traditional methods of toxicity-testing on animals are not only inadequate but actually misleading.* Yet they continue, and pregnant animals of many species are being heavily dosed with chemicals, the mothers often being killed during different stages of pregnancy so that their unborn offspring can be analysed.

Other examples of misleading findings in laboratory animals include the cases of insulin and cortisone, both of which have been found to produce deformities in commonly used laboratory species (*Ibid.,* p.132) and more recently practolol, where the adverse reactions have not been reproducible in any species of animal except man. (See p.160)

The commonest laboratory animal of all, the rat, proves to be especially misleading when it comes to testing for the deformity-producing effects of drugs. Meclazine (a travel-sickness drug) causes deformities in rats but not in humans, whereas thalidomide causes deformities in humans but not in rats.

Indeed, in the whole science of deformities laboratory animals have proved to be unreliable indicators (see p.109).

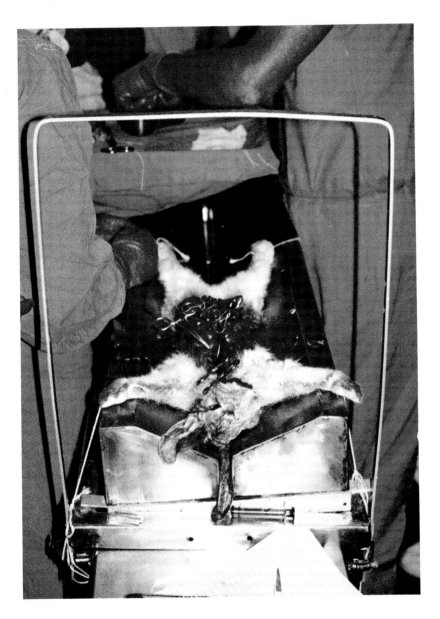

ILLUSTRATION 3.
Rabbit undergoing experimental surgery—if it survived this animal was destined for use in further experimental procedures. National University of Mexico.
Photograph by Brian Gunn ©

4. Non-Medical Research

We have seen that only one third of British research on animals historically has fallen into the combined total of those medical categories listed in the Home Office returns as Cancer Research, Diagnostic Procedures (defined as 'for the purpose of public health or directly for the diagnosis of disease in man or other animals') and the Testing of Medicinal Products (mandatory tests for the standardisation of sera, vaccines or drugs required under the Therapeutic Substances Act 1956 and the Medicines Act 1968).

Until 1978 the Home Office gave no further information about the purpose of the remaining 67% of experiments. Many of these, presumably, did not fall into medical or other clinical or therapeutic groups and it is known that animals are being poison-tested with the following products — cosmetics and toiletries, waxes, greases, rubber, dyes, paints, plastics, toothpastes, household detergents, floor-polishes, fire extinguishers, packaging-material, soap, weed-killers, insecticides, non-nutritive food-dyes and flavourings. A large proportion of experiments on animals performed anywhere in the world are no longer for a strictly medical purpose. Examples of experiments which are not strictly medical are discussed below.

The testing of non-therapeutic cosmetics and toiletries

Bubble-bath liquids, face creams, deodorants and other toiletries are all being tested on animals. A number of British companies have stated that their toilet preparations or their ingredients are tested on animals for eye and skin irritation or for toxicity (poisoning).

Figures supplied by the Central Statistics Office for June 1973 reveal that new cosmetics and toiletries come onto the British beauty market every week to satisfy the demands of over twenty-one million female buyers.

The manufacturers' professional association, the Toilet Preparations Federation, has stated that the use of animals in the testing of cosmetics is 'extensive' in the United Kingdom (personal communication) and in 1981 there were 24,421 such experiments on animals which were 'calculated to cause pain'. Furthermore, Government sources have confirmed that cosmetic and toiletry products have been force-fed to animals in order to discover the dosage-level which kills half of the test sample.

Cosmetics-testing takes three main forms — eye-damage tests, skin-damage tests and feeding tests.

Eye and skin damage testing usually follow methods which were developed by Dr. J. H. Draize in the USA (J.H. Draize, 'Dermal Toxicity' in *Appraisal of the safety of Chemicals in foods, drugs and cosmetics 46-59*. Food and Drug Officials, US 29 13009, Austin, Texas, 1959) for the purposes of the Federal Hazardous Substances Labelling Act (US Food and Drug Administration, 1964a). The Draize methods have been the quasi-official tests of the American Food and Drug Administration for many years and have become standard tests in the UK. Nevertheless the reliability of these procedures has been questioned, principally because the scoring systems they employ are based entirely upon subjective judgements made by observers. Moreover, considerable differences have been reported when substances are tested by different laboratories (A. B. G. Buxton, 'A Method for the Objective Assessment of Eye Irritation' in *Food Cosmet. Toxicol.* Vol. 10, pp. 209-17, Pergamon Press, 1972). The validity of extrapolating results from rabbits' eyes to those of humans has frequently been doubted and the large variations found between the reactions of individual rabbits makes all such procedures even more dubious scientifically (Gaunt and Harper, *J. Soc. Cosmetic Chemists,* 15, 1964, pp. 218, 226).

When testing for eye-damage by the Draize method, very concentrated solutions of commercial products are instilled into rabbits' eyes and the damage is then subjectively scored according to the size of the area injured, the opacity of the cornea, and the degree of redness, swelling and discharge of the conjunctivae. Substances which are found to cause blistering or gross destruction of the cornea are not scored according to the scale, but are simply classified as severe irritants. The use of monkeys has sometimes been advocated for eye-damage testing with cosmetics. Like man, and unlike rabbits, they do not have a nictitating membrane (inner eyelid) *(Food Cosmet. Toxicol.,* 10/5 1972, p. 708).

A measurement of *skin-damage* was also standardised by Dr. Draize. The hair is first removed from an area of the animals' skin. The test-material is then applied to the skin and covered with a piece of gauze held in place with adhesive plaster. The trunk of the animal can then be wrapped in a plaster of Paris bandage to keep the test-patch in position. The skin is examined after twenty-four hours and seventy-two hours and after longer periods if desired. and the damage is scored according to an arbitrary scale (G. P. Somers, 'Testing Drugs for Dermal Toxicity, *J. Soc. Cosmetic Chemists,* 15, 1964 pp. 385-94). Instead of using plaster of Paris, the animals can be immobilised in restraining-devices to prevent them dislodging the patch of irritant (A. B. G. Lansdown, 'An appraisal of methods for detecting primary skin irritants', *J. Soc. Cosmetic Chemists,* 23, 1972, pp. 739-772).

By such methods, any part of an animal may be subjected to irritancy testing or tests of poisoning through the skin. Eyes and eye-lids are known to be generally sensitive but, as Dr. G. F. Somers points out: 'in addition to the eye, tests may also be carried out on the penile mucosa of the rabbit, and in the vagina of the rabbit, guinea-pig, rat, monkey or dog'. *(Ibid.,* p. 387.)

For materials which are to be used either in the mouth (such as breath-sweeteners and toothpastes) or in the vagina (such as deodorants), scientists claim that the dog vagina gives valid results for testing mucous membrane damage (Bernard Idson, 'Primary Irritation Testing', *Toxicology and Applied Pharmacology,* Supp. 3, 1969, pp. 84-89).

Various modifications of the standard Draize patch-tests have been tried. By pre-testing the skin with formaldehyde it is made more sensitive to the test irritants. By injecting dyes into the test animal, the extent of tissue damage can be more readily observed.

Patch tests are usually employed for single applications of test-materials. Where repeated applications are required, it is more convenient not to cover the skin, but to restrain the animal to prevent it scratching or licking off the test-irritant, and to apply direct. Applications can be repeated at frequent intervals for periods of a year or over.

The skin of laboratory-animals can be prepared by abrasion or by tape-stripping. In this latter method, adhesive tape is applied by rollers to ensure that complete adhesion is achieved. The tape is then rapidly removed. Repeated applications of the tape allow the stripping of successive layers of skin down to the required level (A. B. G. Lansdown, *op.cit.).*

In another technique the elasticity of the skin can be measured after the application of test-materials. Rings of skin are cut from rats' tails using parallel razor-blades. The force required to rupture the ring of tissue is then measured *(ibid.).*

Perhaps the simplest method of measuring skin-irritancy is to immerse guinea-pigs in solutions of the test-substance, keeping them immersed for a total of twelve hours. This guinea-pig immersion test is also used as a test of systemic toxicity, since absorption takes place, particularly through the rectal mucosa.

In the testing of their effects upon skin, cosmetics and toilet preparations have been classified under the headings (i) hair and eye cosmetics, (ii) face powders, creams and lipsticks, (iii) nail cosmetics, (iv) anti-perspirants and deodorants (v) depilatories, (vi) perfumes, sunburn preventatives and (vii) special creams and lotions.

Testing for toxicity (i.e. to find out how poisonous a substance is) is usually done by means, of the *LD 50 test*. Any cosmetic-product which also makes a therapeutic claim must be tested in this way (and many other products, with no therapeutic pretensions, are also voluntarily tested). An example is a skin care soap containing a bactericide which has been orally administered, both in single doses and in repeated daily doses for up to three months, in rats, rabbits, dogs and apes. The acute oral LD 50 in mice and rats was approximately 4000mg/kg; this means that only when comparatively massive doses of Irgasan were forcibly fed to rats and mice, did the animals die (Ciba-Geigy pamphlet).

Feeding tests entail the forcing of cosmetics down the throats of animals by stomach-tube to see what dose will kill half of the animals (LD 50 test). Because most cosmetic products are not especially poisonous, it necessarily follows that if a rat or a dog has to be killed this way, then very great quantities of cosmetic must be forced into their stomachs, blocking or breaking internal organs, or killing the animal by some other physical action, rather than by any specific chemical effect. Of course the procedure of force-feeding — even with healthy food — is itself a notoriously unpleasant procedure, as suffragettes and other prisoners on hunger-strike have testified. When the substance forced into the stomach is not food at all, but large quantities of face powder, make-up or liquid hair dye, then no doubt the suffering is very much greater. If, for the bureaucratic correctness of the test, quantities great enough to kill are involved then clearly the process of dying itself must often be prolonged and agonising, all the animals being made very ill indeed, half of them just managing to survive, the other half eventually succumbing.

To make matters worse the LD 50 testing is a hit-and-miss affair. The toxicologist starts at totally lethal doses and works downwards. It is hard to imagine any man forcing — and it may indeed require physical force — massive amounts of cosmetic substances into struggling and choking animals, so that they die. Forcing water down the throats of their victims was one of the most feared tortures of the Inquisition and yet forcing toiletries down the throats of animals is regarded as a normal bureaucratic expedient.

When all is said and done and the last dying convulsions have ceased, what is the information gained by this clumsy and cruel prodecure? All that is obtained is a meaningless statement that a huge dose of product X has an average chance of killing a beagle or a retriever or a rat. This may satisfy the obsessional needs of some bureaucrat, but it has no real scientific value. In the words of a top Government toxicologist — 'it is only a crude measure'. Crude indeed.

An official study by the Royal Society of London, concluded by condemning the current practice of toxicology as being 'swamped by routine tests of limited value and governed by regulations rather than by rational thought'. *(Long Term Toxic Effects,* Royal Society, July 1978.)

Examples of Experiments

(1) At the Unilever Research Laboratory Colworth/Welwyn, Colworth House, Sharnbrook, Bedford, UK, commercial products have been tested for eye irritancy using New Zealand white rabbits:

'No anaesthetics were used for this process but the rabbits were restrained in canvas sleeves during instillation and for fifteen minutes thereafter. The materials instilled into the eyes were predominantly shampoos submitted to this laboratory for safety assessment, but a number of other materials (notably toilet soaps) were also applied.'

Damage to the eyes caused by these shampoos and toilet soaps was then measured. This was done by measuring the thickness of the cornea of the eye. Five measurements were made on each occasion of observation.

'Anaesthesia was not found to be necessary but the rabbits were restrained in canvas sleeves and an assistant steadied their heads during observation and held the eyelids apart when necessary.'

The author of the above claims that his method of measuring eye-damage in rabbits is superior to the standard Draize method. Having tested 'about 100 different cosmetics materials' on 'some 600 rabbits' he states that 'it has been found that most of these products cause some temporary corneal swelling. This swelling may be quite substantial with formulations containing active detergents at more than a few per cent (two per cent or so). This is true of all shampoos so far examined by application to the eye in undiluted form'.

He points out that 'when a shampoo is applied to the cornea, swelling occurs rapidly and the tissue remains in a swollen state for two or three days'. Some cosmetic products can cause a more persistent reaction — 'in this laboratory we classify as "persistent" all reactions that continue longer than twenty-one days'. 100 rabbits' eyes judged to show persistent damage, were found to have had an average corneal swelling of 164.14 per cent of their normal size in the four days after treatment with the cosmetic (A. B. G. Buxton, *op. cit.* pp. 209-17).

(2) At the Huntingdon Research Centre, Huntingdon, UK, similar testing has occurred. In one study 180 New Zealand white rabbits had a total of ten different shampoos instilled into their eyes. It was noted that one sample *caused all the rabbits to struggle violently and three of the six rabbits "screamed" upon instillation of this product'.*

The same workers went on to study the effects of soap on rabbits' eyes:

'I think we all know how painful it can be if soap gets into eyes, and the irritation can persist for several days. We therefore prepared what was considered to be a fairly strong soap solution and applied it to the rabbit eye as described in our paper. There was an immediate reaction — the eye was closed and there was slight lachrymation.' (I. F. Gaunt, BSc, and K. H. Harper, BSc, PhD, ARIC, 'The Potential Irritancy to the Rabbit Eye Mucosa of Certain Commercially Available Shampoos', *J. Soc. Cosmetic Chemists* 15, 1964, pp. 209-30.)

(3) Other workers, also at the Huntingdon Research Centre, Huntingdon, UK, tested the skin irritant effects of a range of cosmetic ingredients on eight species of animals. The animals they used were mice, guinea-pigs, New Zealand white rabbits, beagles, piglets, miniature pigs, *homo sapiens* and baboons. When dealing with baboons, the authors recommended that the animals be immobilised in restraining devices throughout the trial period. (The method they employed was the modified Draize test.)

Greater accuracy could be obtained if all testing was performed on the skin of human volunteers. This has been successfully tried in the case of some washing products *(B. J. Indust. Med.,* 28, 1971, pp. 303-7) and there seems no good reason why it should not be applied generally.

One of the authors speaks of the concern felt by the Society of Cosmetic Chemists about the introduction of legislative controls affecting the marketing of cosmetics — 'the legislators need to spell out specific procedures and yet it is apparent that there is no test that is appropriate for the assessment of all new cosmetic and toiletry products' (R. E. Davies, K. H. Harper, and S. R. Kynoch, *J. Soc. Cosmetic Chemists,* 23, 1972, pp. 371-81).

It is established beyond doubt that many animals are being used in the testing of cosmetics and that such tests often entail a considerable degree of suffering for the animals concerned. In Britain, it is mandatory to test only those cosmetics which make therapeutic claims or which contain more than a certain level of some specified substances such as hormones or hexachlorophene; *the bulk of the cosmetics-poison-testing using animals is carried out voluntarily,* under no specific obligation except the general legal requirement to market only safe products.

Gross differences in the reactions between the species, between individuals of the same species, and in the results obtained from different laboratories, cast severe doubt upon the scientific validity of these tests. Toxicologists themselves are among the first to make this point.

Despite extensive prior testing on animals, the use of vaginal deodorants by the human consumer produced a number of unpredicted and unwelcome side-effects which forced the United States Food and

Drug Administration to the conclusion that all such products must carry a health warning.

Although experiences such as these demonstrate again that tests on animals do not necessarily hold good for the human animal, it is unlikely that this action by the FDA will cause the cosmetic companies to reduce their use of test-animals. The opposite result is more likely, for the commercial stakes are great. The *Times* (22 June, 1973) points out that in the USA alone vaginal deodorants account for 'more than $50m (about £20m) worth of business a year' and according to a report in the *Sunday Mirror* (3 March 1974) the annual British expenditure on cosmetics and toiletries comes to about £300 million.

It seems likely that large industrial manufacturers of cosmetics are less concerned with scientific validity than with legal respectability should they ever be sued for any damage alleged to have been caused by one of their products. In such an event a manufacturer would be able to appeal to the mercy of the court by pointing to the large number of rats, mice, monkeys and dogs that have suffered and died in their laboratories.

Alternatives to the use of animals are available. So also are safe methods for the testing of cosmetics upon human skin — the only truly valid technique. There is a strong case for the immediate utilisation and development of these methods.

The Fund for the Replacement of Animals in Medical Experiments (FRAME) states:

'In the field of cosmetic studies where many animals are used, we know of work reported as early as 1954 (Livingwood and Hu Ann, NY Acad. Sci., 58 1202, 1954) on the use of human skin for evaluating the irritant-producing capacity of topical medicines. We would be interested to know why this work does not appear to have been further developed.'

There is an increasing bureaucratic interest in the testing of cosmetics. An EEC Draft Directive has been discussed at Brussels which aims to change a danger list of sustances not to be used in cosmetics, into a positive list, which shows only the safe and fully tested ingredients which *are* to be allowed. Such a step is likely very considerably to increase the numbers of animals that will be poisoned to death in cosmetics-testing. Furthermore, the Council of Europe has also looked into cosmetics-testing and the overall view of the future is a gloomy one for the laboratory animals, unless alternatives are rapidly developed.

The ethical argument against inflicting pain in order to test cosmetics, is surely irrefutable. There is no case for arguing that ordinary cosmetics are medically necessary. It is utterly wrong that animals should be suffering and dying in their thousands, just for the sake of human vanity, bureaucratic tidyness and commercial profit.

A more marginal case is that of toothpastes which have been and continue to be subjected to long-term toxicity trials on dogs and other animals (e.g. *Journal of Environmental Pathology and Toxicology* 2:835-851. 1979).

Food additives

These are of three main sorts; preservatives, flavourings and colourings.

Green peas are coloured a brighter green to increase their saleability. White bread must be whiter than white to attract a certain type of buyer. Fish, traditionally smoked over wood-smoke, now has to be artificially coloured so as to be its expected brown or yellow.

In order to ensure that the human consumer is not poisoned by the unnaturally treated food he buys, Western governments have taken steps to ensure that food additives are extensively tested on laboratory animals in advance of marketing. International recommendations have been published over a number of years by the Joint FAO/WHO Expert Committee on Food Additives (these reports are obtainable from HMSO). In Britain, regulations have been laid down in the Food and Drugs Act, 1955.

The British Government is quick to admit that testing on animals has 'obvious limitations' in its applicability to humans:

'It would be impossible to arrive at a complete assurance of the safety of a substance unless it had been ingested in food by persons of all ages in specified amounts over long periods and been shown conclusively, by a careful medical follow-up, to have had no harmful results. A substance might also be considered safe as a result of an accurate knowledge of its metabolism. In practice few compounds at present fall into either of these categories...' (Memorandum on Procedure For Submissions on Food Additives and on Methods of Toxicity Testing, Part 11, Section 10, HMSO 1965. Issued by the Ministry of Agriculture, Fisheries and Food).

The Ministry of Agriculture, Fisheries and Food goes on to state that knowledge gained from the testing of poisoning effects (toxicity) on animals cannot confidently be applied to humans:

'Extrapolation to man from toxicity tests in animals has obvious limitations but for the time being, such tests are the main basis for toxicological prediction (Section 11). The conclusions reached about the likely hazards to man can be no more than tentative, and they may have to be reviewed later in the light of further evidence, and particularly that which comes to hand in practice and from experience with man (Section

12). There is no general agreement about the extrapolation of results from animal experiments to man (Section 27).'

Indeed the literature is full of examples of how species react quite differently to poisons. There are even instances where it has been quite clearly demonstrated that man and animals assimilate food additives in quite different ways. One such study shows how a food-flavouring substance called Coumarin was tested on rats and rabbits *(Nature,* February, 1969, pp. 664-5); the researchers reported — 'The differences in metabolic behaviour of man and rat which have been described emphasise the importance of human studies and the weakness of animal toxicity data alone as a basis for human assessment.'

Despite all this the British Government expects food companies to go ahead and test additives on animals in three ways:

(a) *Acute Toxicity,* both oral and parenteral (by injection), for rats and mice, and at least one other animal species preferably non-rodent.

(b) *Short-term* feeding for ninety days or for ten per cent of the animal's normal life-span.

(c) *Long-term* feeding extending for the whole of the animal's life.

The acute toxicity tests rely heavily upon the infamous LD 50 test (see p.29). Rats, mice and another species have to be force-fed doses of the test substance large enough to kill them. By clumsy trial-and-error methods, doses are juggled with in order to establish the largest single dose that animals can just tolerate without dying. Similarly, 'the smallest fatal dose' must be established (section 20).

The Government lays down that:

'Toxicity tests themselves should include a study of the largest single dose an animal will tolerate, the largest daily dose it will accept for a limited period of at least three weeks, and the effects of a daily dose given to animals for ninety days or longer.' (Part 11, Section 19.)

The Government urges experimenters to 'record the time course and characteristics of the poisoning with full details of behavioural changes and the pathological findings' (section 20).

Examples of Experiments

(1) Research published in 1978 indicates that scientists at the Huntingdon Research Centre, Huntingdon, Cambridge, U.K., have been force-feeding dogs and monkeys with the *food additive* monosodium glutamate (M.S.G.). The animals were force-fed MSG at varying doses, observed for five hours and then killed. During these five hours the animals were subjected to up to seven separate blood tests and some endured repeated puncturing at the base of the skull in order to draw off fluid from the brain. Half the monkeys and every single dog was made to

vomit and some did so repeatedly. (*Toxicology Letters 2* (1978) 299-303, and *Toxicology 2* (1978) 305-311.)

(2) Scientists at BIBRA, Carshalton, Surrey, UK, poisoned mice, rats and white rabbits with large doses of a *food-flavouring* substance called Trans-2-Hexenal. This substance is used in synthetic essences, particularly those with a fruit or berry flavour.

In the acute toxicity tests, the animals were starved for twelve hours and then either injected with the test-substance or were force-fed the substance by stomach-tube. Deaths occurred within forty-eight hours after dosing. 'Salivation, lachrymation and vasodilation were seen immediately after treatment. At the higher dose levels, death was preceded by convulsions.' LD50 values were calculated.

(3) Again at BIBRA, scientists tested a *food-flavouring* substance called Methyl-N-Methyl Anthranilate, which is 'used in a wide range of food-stuffs, especially flour and sugar confectionery'. They force-fed this to rats and found that 'all animals given 3.38 g/kg or more died'. Four hours after dosing the animals' hair was observed to stand on end and it was noted that there was a 'red-coloured nasal discharge in the last hours before death' (*Ibid,* Vol. 8, 1970, pp. 359-68).

These common methods of testing for the toxicity of food-additives are crude and inaccurate. They provide only approximate indications of how man is likely to respond to low dosage levels over the course of fifty or sixty years. The short-term administration of massive doses of an undiluted substance bears little relation to the actual way in which the substance is likely to be ingested by the human consumer.

Toxicologists themselves have become increasingly critical of the way in which official regulations dictate the testing of food-additives. An article in *Food and Cosmetic Toxicology* (Vol. 8, 1970, pp. 214-16) states:

'Toxicologists, however, are now looking more closely at these protocols and are questioning the sensitivity, interpretation, validity and even the necessity of some of the tests. The value of the acute toxicity test generally used for food additives is coming under particular scrutiny.'

This writer goes on to explain that the regulation testing procedures produce scarcely any information about the absorption, distribution and excretion of the test substance, and wishes such data was available.

LD 50 testing may have been of use, the writer thinks, in its original role in biological assay:

It is unfortunate, however, that this classical approach to drug toxicity has been transformed *in toto* to food-additive toxicology, the LD 50 being used as an indication of low, medium or high toxicity. This is a role it cannot fill with any degree of certainty. In many cases no abnormality is found in animals given doses just below the lethal dose. Death in these cases is frequently caused by some physical or chemical property of the large volumes or high concentrations given to the animals, properties that are irrelevant to the low concentrations used in food. We need to know the lowest dosage level which damages organs, not the completely irrelevant overdosage that the LD 50 represents.

If this is the case, one might ask, why are alternatives to animals not being tried? It is possible to culture organs and tissues. Such test-tube studies would involve no suffering and would allow the direct study of the effects of a substance upon particular living cells. The writer of the above article is saying that hundreds of the animals which are being killed by the crude LD 50 procedure are dying, not because of the poisonous effect of the test-substance, but because of the physical properties of the enormous volumes of substance being forced by tube into their stomachs, or by the rupturing and infection caused by massive injections into the abdomen. He explains that when it is found that a lower dose is required to kill an animal by injection than is needed by stomach-tube, this is often put down to the effects of greater absorption, but 'In a great many cases, however, the intraperitoneal LD 50 (i.e. injection dosage which kills half the animals) is lower than the oral simply because injection of the compound has caused a fatal peritonitis'.

He goes on to cite examples of the unreliability of the LD50 in the drug field and concludes:

'It is surely time, therefore, that we ceased to use as an index of the toxic action of food additives the LD50 value, which is imprecise (varying considerably with different species, with different strains of the same species, with sex, nutritional status and environmental conditions, and even with the concentration at which the substance is administered) and which is valueless in the planning of further studies.'

Other scientists have spoken of animals dying, not by the chemical poisoning of a product, but by being choked or 'clogged' to death by massive overdoses (Personal communications).

There are already signs that a swing towards *in vitro* test-tube methods is beginning. Dr. S. Metcalfe of Cambridge writes that 'appropriate cell-culture systems provide a useful additional method of sreening for toxicity'. He states that 'an advantage of *in vitro* systems is that they are amenable to a wide range of microscopic and biochemical studies in a short time'. *(J. Pharm. Pharmacol.* Vol. 23, pp. 817-23.)

Food-Packaging
Scientists at the Industrial Hygiene Research Laboratory (ICI), Cheshire, UK force fed rats and dogs with a substance used for *coating food*

wrapping-paper. This substance is an antistatic agent called polyoxyethylene-tallow-amine.

With three daily doses gastrointestinal haemorrhage was observed in the rats, and force-feeding by stomach tube established an oral LD 50 at 1.85 g/KG.

With the dogs, a daily dose of 120 mg/kg caused 'frequent vomiting and anorexia'.

Eye-irritation tests on rabbits produced 'extensive oedema (swelling) and haemorrhage (bleeding) of the conjunctiva . . . the entire cornea was opaque'. A similar substance produced irreparable damage to the entire eye-ball. (*Food Cosmet. Toxicol.* Vol. 8, 1970, pp. 249-52.)

Agricultural Research

Particularly distasteful are reports of suffering being inflicted in agricultural veterinary experiments, and veterinary surgeons are among those who most searchingly question the rightness of such research as practised by some of their colleagues. The veterinary profession does, however, seem to contain an element which is closely associated with the commercial exploitation of animals, in farming, the breeding industry, sport and the testing of commercial products on animals.

Non-agricultural veterinary experiments also occur. For example, ten cats and two dogs had limbs experimentally paralysed and then underwent further major surgery. This work, which claimed to have therapeutic objectives, was supported by the Royal College of Veterinary Surgeons. (*J. Small Anim. Prac.* 1976, 17.).

Reports of breeding experiments have become quite plentiful where artificial insemination, experimental abortion, Caesarian sections and the transplantation of the foetus from one mother to another have been performed. At Cambridge the search for increases in the supply of beef have prompted scientists to transplant fertilised ova from cows to rabbits, and such procedures are no longer even counted as experiments under the 1876 Act.

Much research is being carried out in the development of intensive or 'factory' farming methods. These include the administration of antibiotics, hormones and other drugs to farm animals in order to artificially increase their yields of meat, wool or other animal products. The effects on the human consumer of the residue of such drugs left in the animal's flesh at the time of slaughtering, are often unknown. Such residues must be tested for their toxicity and this work is reported to be extremely time-consuming and very expensive — another factor no doubt in the world-wide upward spiral in the cost of food.

The deliberate infliction of diseases followed by experimental treatments or by plain observation is another disturbing field of veterinary activity, whether or not it is carried out on a clinical pretext. An example is the experimental induction of abscesses, 'in some cases larger than an orange', in the udders of cows *(Vet. Record,* July 1951).

Perhaps still more common are the experiments of non-veterinary scientists, carried out in veterinary establishments or published in veterinary journals.

Examples

The Agricultural Research Council lists forty-one research establishments in Britain. In the U.S.A. are many more. At many of these (probably at most of them) animals are in regular use. Examples are the Animal Breeding Research Organisation, the Animal Diseases Research Association, and the Poultry Research Centre (all near Edinburgh), and the laboratories around Cambridge which include the Institute of Animal Physiology and the Unit of Reproductive Phsysiology and Biochemistry. In the Reading area there are the Institute for Research on Animal Diseases, the National Institute for Research in Dairying, and the Animal Virus Institute.

Most of the research at these establishments is aimed ultimately at increasing the efficiency of meat production and the development of scientific farming. Breeding experiments and nutritional research sometimes involve experimental surgery. Research into animal diseases and the toxicity testing of herbicides, fungicides, and pesticides is widespread.

(1) In 1979 a report was published of research at the Agricultural Research Council Institute of Animal Physiology at Babraham, Cambridge, U.K. in which pigs had electrodes inserted into their brains. Experiments were then carried out in which the brains of the animals were electrically stimulated, the electrodes being moved from one part of the brain to other parts, while the pigs' behaviour was observed. (*Physiology and Behaviour.* Vol. 22 pp. 723-730. 1979).

(2) A researcher at the Central Veterinary Laboratory at Weybridge reports on the experimental poisoning of pigs. These animals were fed dried rhizome of bracken, became breathless and died within about six hours. Post-mortems revealed 'enlarged mottled hearts'.

Another group of pigs were kept for over three weeks on a wire grid in order to collect their faeces and urine *(Vet. Record,* 90, 1972).

(3) A pathologist in Glasgow infected kittens with lung-worm. Experimental forms of treatment killed the majority of the animals — 'and death was preceded by excessive salivation, impairment of locomotion and vision, muscular twitchings, panting, respiratory distress and convulsions'. *(Vet. Record,* December 1968.)

(4) Six researchers at two veterinary laboratories of the Ministry of

Agriculture, Fisheries and Food (The Veterinary Investigation Centre, Penrith and the Central Veterinary Laboratory, Weybridge) made twenty sheep blind by feeding them concentrated dried bracken in pellets over the course of more than a year. The sheep were regularly bled from their jugular veins in order to examine their blood. The poisoned sheep lost weight and it is clear from their extremely low platelet and leucocyte counts that they were very ill for many weeks, before being killed.

The sheep used in this experiment were Dorset Horn; a breed in which *naturally*-occuring blindness of this sort has never been reported. (*B. Vet. J.*, 128, 1972.)

In Britain, details of much agricultural research are, amazingly, obscured by the Official Secrets Acts. The M.A.F.F. performs about 100,000 experiments on living animals annually, at the cost of about £50 million. At the A.R.C. Institute of Animal Physiology at Cambridge, 'highly aversive shock' was administered to pigs in experiments publicly criticised by the RSPCA's expert Committee in 1975.

In my opinion, the veterinary profession should be exclusively concerned with the treatment of disease, the alleviation of suffering and the prolongation of a pleasant life in animals. Such research as has been cited above contradicts these objectives. Just as a medical doctor should put his patients' interest first, so also a veterinarian should put the interests of his animal patients before those of their human owners.

Depleting calves of salt (sodium) and injecting solutions into their jugular veins in research carried out at the Royal Veterinary College in London (*Proceedings of the Physiological Society* March 1979) or killing dogs with weedkiller (*Vet. Record* April 1972) are separate instances of research carried out by vets or on vets or on veterinary premises which ought to provoke thought among vets themselves.

Example number (4) quoted above illustrates the situation in which an animal of a species or strain not known to suffer from a particular disease or disorder naturally, has this ailment forced upon it artificially. Differences between strains and species already make questionable the validity of applying results to any animal other than those in the experiment. Why then is it necessary to artificially introduce a disorder into an unnatural host? If the experiment is to be done at all, then on grounds of scientific validity alone, the disease or ailment should be in members of the same class of animal in which the disorder naturally appears and needs to be treated.

(The worst case of this that I know of was that of a chimpanzee experimentally infected with the terrible disease of syphilis, which does not naturally occur in chimpanzees at all. This research was done in Denmark many years after the cause of syphilis and its effective treatment had been discovered *(Doktor,* 1958 7.))

Two of the above examples also raise the question of the responsibility of Governments for the spending of public money. If the electorate fully realised the extent to which their taxes are financing various research programmes on animals, would they entirely approve of this? In Britain, hundreds of thousands of experiments on animals each year are carried out on behalf of Government Departments (such as the Ministry of Defence and the Ministry of Agriculture, Fisheries and Food) and bodies such as the Medical Research Council.

Weed-killers

These have been extensively tested on animals. Nevertheless there have been a number of cases reported of accidental death, both in animals and also humans, resulting from ingestion of weed-killers.

Examples of Experiments

(1) Workers at the Industrial Hygiene Laboratory (ICI), Alderley Park, Macclesfield, Cheshire, poisoned rats with the weed-killer Paraquat, and reported that it caused lung haemorrhage *(British Journal of Experimental Pathology,* 51, 1970, p. 604).

(2) Another weed-killer, Diquat, was also tested in the same laboratory, using beagle dogs, rats, mice, guinea pigs, Rhode Island hens, Friesan cattle and albino rabbits. Diquat was found to be slowly poisonous, as animals sometimes took fourteen days to die after receiving a lethal dose. Despite these extensive tests, the scientists remained uncertain why Diquat acts as a poison, particularly when it is given in small doses — 'the symptoms following a smaller, though lethal, dose do not suggest an obvious mode of action to account for the deaths'.

The scientists found that the toxic symptoms following oral administration of Diquat were 'similar in all the species tested'. Diquat was force-fed to the animals by stomach-tube. After twenty-four hours the animals 'gradually became lethargic, showed some respiratory difficulty, lost weight and died between two and fouteen days after administration of the Diquat'.

Subcutaneous injection of Diquat lead to pupillary dilation and lethargy during the first twenty-four hours. 'Over the next few days respiration became laboured, body temperature fell slightly, and body weight was lost. Deaths occurred on days two to thirteen after injection; in all cases pupillary dilatation persisted until death.' Some animals were noted to have 'greatly distended abdomens'.

The experimenters tried many different dosage levels and report that 'a large injection of Diquat (four or five times the LD 50 dose) gave rise to subdued behaviour within a few minutes and laboured respiration within an hour. Muscular twitchings then occurred, leading to generalised convulsions and death within a few hours.'

Animals were also poisoned by having Diquat repeatedly applied to their skins. This caused scabbing, loss of weight, unsteadiness and muscular weakness. Some rabbits died after twenty applications.

One of the long-term effects of Diquat is the development of blindness due to cataract. Animals were daily fed small doses of Diquat and the formation of cataracts observed. Some animals were kept in total darkness for months, but it was found that this had no significant effect on the development of Diquat cataract.

Dogs which were partially or totally blinded in this way were fed Diquat, mixed with their food, for periods of *up to four years (B.J. Indust. Med.,* 27, 1970, pp. 51-55.)

(3) A veterinary surgeon, assisted by other scientists, poisoned pedigree beagle dogs with the weed-killer sodium chlorate. These experiments were performed at the Huntingdon Research Centre, Huntingdon. The dogs were force-fed the weed-killer by stomach-tube over a period of five days.

The scientists noted 'marked loss of appetite and body-weight with lassitude, vomiting and blood-streaked faeces . . . urine contained blood on day three. Death occurred on day four'.

A post-mortem on one female dog 'showed the mucous membranes to be blue, the blood was dark chocolate brown, the liver was dark brown, and all serous surfaces were blue-tinged'.

The experimenters concluded that 'the results would confirm generally the accepted low toxicity of sodium chlorate'. *(Vet Record,* April 1972, pp. 416-18.)

There are many accepted and well-tried methods of controlling weeds. The main motives for introducing new ones are military use ('defoliation') and commercial profit — on the principle that some of the public will always buy something new even if it is no more effective than older products.

Such motives do not justify cruelty to men or animals. The examples cited above indicate that both old (sodium chlorate) and new weed-killers (Diquat and Paraquat) are being tested on animals, including dogs which have been blinded and killed in this way. There is no doubt that such tests are causing severe suffering in laboratory animals.

The long-term risks of the new weed-killers cannot be tested by such methods. The effect that these chemicals may have over the course of forty or fifty years remains obscure.

Pesticides

Pesticidal chemicals are also tested on animals in order to establish lethal dose levels. Pesticides are administered to animals by mouth, by injection, by inhalation and by application to the skin.

Different laboratories have produced very different results. Marked differences between animals of different species and between individuals of the same species, make such tests unreliable.

Examples

(1) At Chesterford Park Research Station, Fisons Pest Control Ltd., Saffron Walden, Essex, six different pesticides were applied to the skins of white rats. The chemicals were held in contact with the skin by a sleeve of plaster. Most lethally-dosed animals died within seven days *(B.J. Indust. Med.,* 26, pp. 59-64).

(2) From the CIBA Laboratories at Cambridge comes a review of 'a promising new insecticide' called Iodofenphos, together with its poisoning effects on dogs, cats, mice, rats and rabbits (*Proceedings of Fifth British Insecticide and Fungicide Conference,* 1969).

The long-term accumulative effects of chemicals such as pesticides are still unknown, and cannot be discovered by tests on laboratory animals. New pesticides may be causing permanent ecological damage, from which the enviroment may never recover.

Nor do animal tests seem to stop the use of extremely poisonous materials. It is reported that a large quantity of wheat treated with the fungicide Methylmercury Dicyandiamide, was accidently eaten by peasants in Iraq and that thousands have died: many others have suffered irreversible brain damage. Products such as these are known to be poisonous but continue to be used mainly for commercial reasons (*Sunday Times,* 9 September 1973).

At a symposium on 'Animal Tests', (London, October, 1973) two hundred veterinarians and members of the Association of Veterinarians in Industry (c/o Agrochemical Division. CIBA-GEIGY (UK) Ltd., Whittlesford, Cambridge, UK) heard Dr. F. G. Brown of the Dow Chemical Company Ltd. describe the rising cost of testing pesticides on animals:

Year	Cost of developing and testing one pesticide (Dollars)	Unsuccessful products tested, per each success
1959	$1.9 million	800
1969	$4.0 million	5,000
1973	$10.0 million	10,000

The column on the right shows the number of chemicals produced and tested as experimental pesticides for every one *successful* pesticide actually reaching the market. In 1973 only one experimental substance out of every 10,000 tested proved to be both safe and effective.

It now takes about ten years from the time at which a substance is synthesized to the date at which it is first marketed. In the interim thousands of animals suffer and die.

Industrial

The field of industrial research is a large and ever-growing one. The underlying motive is commercial, since this field of study is not concerned with naturally-occurring disease but with the dangers of poisoning and death arising out of the production and use of new chemical, or other substances.

Nearly all the dangers of pollution are imposed upon man by man himself. Man is the most polluting animal the world has ever known. As commercial companies, driven by the profit motive, continue to increase their output of new chemical products, the risks of pollution become even graver.

The Home Office has stated that many products are tested upon animals in Britain, including household detergents and polishes, and in the U.S.A. it is known that the detergents Tide and Ajax have been extensively tested upon animals' eyes, causing lesions (*New York Post,* 5 July, 1973).

The cost of testing all these all these substances on animals is very considerable. In 1973 it was estimated to cost a manufacturer $2 million to develop and test a new chemical product which turns out to be a failure, and it cost about $6.4 million to develop and test a 'winner' (F. G. Brown, AVI Symposium, London, 1973).

Examples

(1) At Llandough Hospital, Penarth, Glamorgan, animals are made to inhale dust throughout the working week 'for periods of a year or more'. In some cases the animals are kept in controlled clouds of dust for twenty hours out of every twenty-four. Animals treated in this way have included 'mice, rats, cats, rabbits, and a small monkey'. They are then killed and the amount of dust in their lungs is measured.

(2) At the Institute of Neurology, Queen Square, London, baboons were fed acrylamide, a substance used in the manufacturing of paper and chipboard and as a grouting agent in the water-proofing of tunnels and foundations. The baboons were given oranges and bananas poisoned with acrylamide. The animals were afflicted with weakness and a lack of co-ordination so that they could lift neither hand from the floor of the cage without falling sideways. Their 'barks became hoarser and softer and all except B2 eventually became silent. Intoxication continued until

weakness and ataxia of the limbs was such that the animal was unable to rise from a lying position. Weakness of facial and jaw muscles was so severe that feeding by tube was required'.

This experiment illustrates the relentlessness of research: some baboons are made so wretchedly ill by repeated administrations of poison that they can scarcely move. Are they then put out of their misery? Not at all, the careful and deliberate poisoning continues; in the severely affected animals, too weak to swallow, it becomes necessary to give the further doses of acrylamide by injection or by forcing a tube into the animal's stomach *(J. Neurol, Neurosurg. Psychiat.,* V, 1970, p. 33).

(3) The same poisons, acrylamide, has also been tried on cats and found to provide ataxia, tremor, weakness, vomiting, defecation and convulsions (*B. J. Indust. Med.,* 23, 1964).

(4) Also at Queen Square, London, baboons have been poisoned with lead. They received repeated monthly injections of lead until they died, the average survival time being 120 days, the longest 265 days. Most animals developed convulsions, which were sometimes preceded by a cry. Several animals died during more or less continuous epileptic seizures. Some became 'very savage between fits'. Jaundice, bloody diarrhoea, pus and paralysis were observed. One infant female was seen to be dragging her hindquarters, a male became too weak to stand, but survived another three weeks partially or totally blind; a week before death this animal was examined in a restraining chair and still managed to withdraw limbs when they were pricked with a pin.

After all this, the author admits that 'the nature of lead palsy remains obscure, in spite of many observations on experimental animals. One problem is that lead produces different effects in different species. Punctate basophilia is found in the blood of lead poisoned guinea-pigs, rabbits and man, but not in cats and dogs' (*B.J. Indust. Med.,* 27, 1970).

So here is yet another example of inter-species variation which casts doubt upon the validity of animal research methods; each species reacts differently, so results cannot be confidently applied to man.

This project, like so many other studies, was paid for by the British tax-payer through the funds of the Medical Research Council.

(5) In one huge project by ICI at the Industrial Hygiene Research Laboratories, Alderly Park, Macclesfield, Cheshire, about 2,000 rats were made to inhale 109 different industrial chemicals. Tremors, gasping, intense eye irritation, staggering, emaciation, 'discomfort', pneumonia, haemorrhages, and convulsions were observed and recorded over experimental periods of about three weeks. Autopsies revealed congestion in lungs, livers and kidneys.

The author concludes by recommending 'more extended experiments on a variety of species' (*Ibid.*).

Also at these laboratories, dogs, rodents and monkeys were forced to inhale B.C.F., a fire-extinguisher agent; tremors and convulsions preceded death. (*Toxicology and Applied Pharmacology*, 24, 1973).

Behavioural Research (Psychology and Zoology)

Both psychologists and zoologists now extensively experiment upon animals. For example, the Regents Park Zoo in London, has two laboratories registered for the performance of experiments and employs some fifty research scientists and assistants. (*Wildlife*, July 1976).

Psychology is not a medical subject. But as the science of behaviour it is a major consumer of animals in pure research. Behavioural studies cause suffering in a number of ways, such as:

(i) *Deprivation of food,* water and selected nutrients.

(ii) *Stress* — the effects of prolonged threat or punishment.

(iii) *Sensory Deprivation;* this might mean rearing animals in total darkness, or depriving them of tactile or auditory stimulation, or the destruction of eyes, ears, or other sense organs.

(iv) *Social Isolation;* separation of infant animals from their mothers or solitary confinement of individuals, sometimes in small boxes or in dark soundproof chambers.

(v) *Brain Surgery;* deliberate damage or stimulation of parts of the brain in order to observe the effects upon behaviour.

(vi) *Punishment;* electric shock or other painful stimulation often in order to study the process of learning.

(vii) *Drugs;* psychologists also study the effects of drugs, drug-addiction and drug-withdrawal upon animal behaviour.

British Examples

(1) At Cambridge kittens were reared in total darkness and recordings were made of the electrical activity of their brains. Another kitten had its eyelids sewn up so as to allow no visual experience whatever. 'During the recording the kitten was paralysed with an infusion of gallamine triethiodide and anaesthetised by artificial ventilation with a mixture of nitrous oxide and oxygen.' This research was supported by the Medical Research Council (*Nature,* 241, 1973).

(2) In the Department of Psychology at the University of Hull, rats were given electric shock in order to observe the effect upon exploratory behaviour (*J. Exp. Psych.,* 24, 1972).

(3) A psychologist at the Institute of Psychiatry, Denmark Hill, London, removed parts of the brains of twenty-seven monkeys using a small-gauge sucker, and studied the effects upon visual discrimination

learning. The monkeys were tested in thirty trials a day for five days a week. The response boxes were 14.5 cm in length, 10.5 cm in width, and 10.7 cm in height *(Neuropsychologia,* 10, 1972).

(4) At University College, London, rats were subjected to inescapable electric shock to test the idea that high levels of fear reduce exploratory behaviour.

This researcher concluded that 'inescapable aversive stimulation, in this case electric shocks to rats' feet, consistently resulted in subsequent avoidance of the environment in which the shocks had been given' *(ibid.)*.

(5) Psychologists at Oxford castrated male rats and inserted electrodes in their brains to measure differences between the behaviour of males and females *(Zenith,* 10, 1973).

(6) Psychologists at Cambridge surgically damaged the brains of monkeys and observed that subsequently the animals 'stumbled around their cages, bumping into the walls and hitting their heads on protruding objects. If they had to steady themselves by catching hold of the wire, they reached too short, too far. or in the wrong direction, missed their target and fell; they appeared quite insensitive to hard pinches on one or both sides of their bodies and often let their limbs droop lifeless; they made no attempt to reach for food and showed no interest in it if it was put into their hands, although they took it greedily if it was pressed against their lips' *(J. Exp. Psych.,* 1969).

(7) Behavioural scientists as well as their more medically-minded colleagues have extensively studied experimentally-induced starvation in many different species. A British example is that of students at Sheffield University who studied the effects of 'semi-starvation and complete starvation' of rats *(J. Physiol.,* October 1968).

(8) Behavioural scientists at the Medical Research Council's Unit at Madingley, Cambridge studied the effects on infant monkeys of separation from their mothers.

Two twice-separated infants died before they were a year old and one long-separation infant died at four weeks and 'no definite cause of death was found'.

Some infants were eventually re-united with their mothers but the 'effects of separation were still apparent four weeks later!* (*Animal Behaviour,* Vol. 19, 1971).

---

*   It has been admitted (personal communication) that the zoologist who performed these experiments had not been fully licensed for them because the Home Office had considered them as being outside the Act.

(9) A psychologist at Cambridge partially blinded a monkey by cutting out those areas of her brain primarily concerned with vision. 'Six years ago, a monkey, Helen, had the visual cortex surgically removed — since then she has been able to recognise nothing' he writes. He goes on — 'our work was interrupted when we moved from Cambridge to the Oxford Laboratory. Helen moved with us, but I had a thesis to finish .and she was left to her own devices for about ten months — such devices, that is, as she could manage in a small cage'. He makes further observations on Helen's behaviours — 'Helen bumped into any and every obstacle, she collided with my legs and she several times fell into the pond' *(New Scientist,* 30 March 1972).

This case of the 'blind' monkey, Helen, provoked some historic correspondence in the pages of *New Scientist* which revealed a new attitude on the part of the scientifically-minded readers. One indignant correspondent wrote about the psychologist concerned:

'Either he is, on the evidence of his article, totally amoral in his pitiless (and seemingly pointless) inquisitiveness, or else I am a dangerously sentimental idiot' (6 April 1972).

Another reader expostulated:

'The animal was deliberately blinded wasn't it? What for? To help elucidate complex visual mechanisms, you say, possibly. Do you think that's a good enough reason to blind another creature? I'd just like to know' (13 April 1972).

The psychologist was obliged to defend himself:

'For my own part I find it hard to tolerate the attitude of those people who would if they had their way put a stop to all medical research on animals' (27 April 1972).

Which was again rebutted by one of the original correspondents who made the serious point that 'this particular experiment seems to me to prove beyond question that the scientist should not be free to choose his own experiments any more than the soldier is free to choose his own targets' (4 May 1972).

About a year after this interesting correspondence was published in the pages of *New Scientist,* poor blind Helen was killed and her brain was removed for analysis. To the embarrassment of the scientists concerned it was discovered that the experimental injuries to her brain were not quite those that had been intended. This discovery very much weakens their claim that the results of their experiment justified any cruelty that might have been involved.

Few psychologists have openly criticised the work of their colleagues. One exception is Dr. Alice Heim, who attacks 'the apparent callousness of much of the experimental work carried out on the lower animals' in her book *Intelligence and Personality* (Pelican, 1970). She writes:

> The work on 'animal behaviour' is always expressed in scientific, hygienic-sounding terminology, which enables the indoctrination of the normal, non-sadistic young psychology student to proceed without his anxiety being aroused. Thus, techniques of 'extinction' are used for what is in fact torturing by thirst or near-starvation or electric-shocking.

More recently, Dr. Heim has compared animal experimentation to the practices of Nazism.

The purpose of this section of the book has been to illustrate some of the many ways in which laboratory animals are being used in research which is not strictly medical. The defender of non-medical research may argue that it is still necessary. The toxicity testing of new household detergents and polishes, or the testing of toiletries, he will say is necessary in order to avoid any accidental injury to humans. But it is a dangerous principle to attempt to justify an evil on the grounds that another evil will thereby be avoided — such arguments have been used throughout history to excuse atrocities.

How trivial must a new product be before Governments and commercial interests refrain from forcibly pumping it into the stomachs of dogs and rats, monkeys and cats, in order to see how much it takes to kill them? After all, where should the line be drawn as far as safety-testing goes? Infants or adults who are mad or drunk or foolish or suicidal may try to eat almost anything. Should we therefore play safe by forcing *all* products down the throats of our laboratory animals to find out how poisonous they are? There is no logical point at which we need to stop. Some psychiatric patients are inveterate eaters of safety-pins; does this fact mean that safety-pins should be tested for toxicity on laboratory animals so that we can then know how many safety-pins kill the average beagle? Floor-polishes, bubble-bath liquids, lavatory-cleansers and anti-freeze additives have already been tested on animals, and we may already be proceeding to poison animals to death with coloured inks, glues, elastic bands, glazes, plastics, lighter fuels, lubricating oils, firelighters, methylated spirits, gasoline, moth-balls, paints, varnishes, dyes and other trivial household things (see pp.33).

In many cases new products are not necessary in themselves. We have adequate soaps, we have had them for centuries. So just how necessary is it that we should have new ones? We have adequate perfumes and face-powders, food-dyes and weed-killers; why must new ones be foisted on us? The answer is not the consumer's need but the manufacturers' desire for profits — in many cases there is no necessity except commercial greed.

It is grossly unfair that animals be made to suffer inevitable pain in order to reduce the future possibilities of men falling foul of their own self-imposed risks. But this is indeed what is happening. Profits mean pollution, and pollution means panic, and panic means pain — not for those who started the ball rolling but for the unfortunate animals.

The human risks are often only *hypothetical* but the pain to the laboratory animal is *real*. The risks are, in a sense, self-inflicted and so voluntary; but the suffering for the animals is forced upon them. The risks lie in the future and are *uncertain,* but the animals' pain is in the here and now and is a *certainty*.

This book is not very much concerned with the old debates about medical research, but there are just a few points to make. In the first place a good deal of medical research on animals has always involved a lot of cruelty and still does so today. Take for example, the continuing use of animals in smoking research — nicotine being injected into the brains of cats, and hundreds of beagles and rabbits being forced to inhale smoke hour after hour and year after year. Such 'medical' research still continues despite the fact that clinicians have known for more than fifty years that tobacco can cause cancer. How far, one must ask, have commercial interests infiltrated the medical establishment so that what parades under a medical banner is really a commercially-motivated search for alternatives to tobacco?

A medical research field which involves great cruelty is the deliberate infliction of burns upon animals. Although at the actual moment of burning the animals are usually anaesthetised, they must suffer the agony of their burns during the ensuing period of experimental treatment or other study. In 1970 a scientist at Queen's University, Belfast published details of his 'new "burning-iron" device for the experimental production of contact burns on laboratory animals' skin'. This might replace, he suggested, the older methods such as 'the use of naked flame, dipping the animal into hot water, contact with hot plates and irradiation and flash burns' *(Laboratory Animals,* October 1970). It seems odd that it is necessary to inflict yet more burns upon sentient creatures when providence provides so many tragic cases in the casualty departments of every hospital. Yet in 1981 there were 2,787 such burning and scalding experiments performed in Britain alone.

Another horrifying field which also excuses itself under a medical label is the transplanting of animals' heads and the maintenance of life and consciousness in heads without bodies and brains without heads. Professor J. R. White of the Department of Neurosurgery at Cleveland,

USA, has performed many such experiments with monkeys and baboons *(Sunday Times,* 9 December 1972). The isolated heads or brains of his monkeys lived on in his laboratory, totally unanaesthetised. Electrical recording equipment attached to them showed that they seemed fully conscious and reactive to sounds. Do we know what nightmare state could be experienced by a living isolated 'conscious' brain? One of Professor White's team gives as his opinion — 'probably like someone who awakes totally paralysed'. In the case of isolated monkey heads, they can continue to see, smell and call out; they can even attempt to bite their white-coated tormenters. *(Stern,* 10 1973.) Russian researchers, too, have specialised in this Frankenstein field and have proudly published photos of their two-headed dogs, both heads fully conscious and eating separately. One such 'preparation' lived for twenty-nine days, each head answering to its own name. In Britain, too, somewhat similar research has been carried out at the Medical School in Birmingham in which cats' brains have been isolated and maintained alive, still attached to the animal's body. These brains, which were unanaesthetised and apparently fully 'conscious' were then observed for their reactions to the injection of various drugs *(B.J. Pharmacol,* 14, p. 340). Reputedly, in the Clinical Pharmacology Department at Oxford University the isolated heads of animals have been kept alive and unanaesthetised.

The addiction of animals to 'hard' drugs is another speciality which seems to be unnecessary but once again calls itself medical. For decades the piteous effects of addiction and withdrawal have been well-known by clinicians. The human data is all too plentiful and available for study — and yet many scientists, even in Britain, earn their livelihood by addicting monkeys to morphine and heroin *(Daily Telegraph,* 19 April 1972, and *Nature,* 26 May 1972). At the Miles Laboratories near Slough addicted animals' symptoms were described as 'jumping, teeth chattering, irritability to touch or handling, diarrhoea, chewing, ptosis and body-shakes' *(ibid.).*

Very often the validity of much of this research can be questioned. Dr. M. B. Bayly quotes many examples of important medical advances which owe nothing to animal experiments and cites instances where animal-research has been misleading (see p.111). There can be little doubt that lives have been lost through the application of misleading findings gleaned from experiments upon animals, or from time being wasted in the laboratory by those who could be saving life at the bedside — such embarrassing occasions go unrecorded and are conveniently forgotten. In the examples of medical research I have cited, the validity of much of the work is certainly dubious — the species-susceptibility to drugs is very variable (pp.108-113) and in burn research the differences between the skins of species is quite notorious. Above all, in cancer-research the validity is very questionable indeed, for cancer tumours *of the human type* are never found in animals and animal-cancers often respond entirely differently to experimental treatments *(Lancet,* April 1972). Tobacco-smoke repeatedly has failed to cause lung cancer in experimental animals *(New Scientist,* 22 November 1973, p. 554).

Cancer-research raises another point. How much of it is really relevant to cancer? Scientists themselves are only too aware that in a number of cases projects that seem remotely removed from the subject are still labelled as Cancer Research in order to obtain funds. Some scientists jokingly refer to it among themselves as the 'Cancer Game'. There is no shortage of money for cancer research, only a shortage of ideas and a dearth of genius. Millions and millions of animals have died in cancer research this century with relatively little to show for it. A view put forward by Lord Zuckerman, until 1971 Chief Scientific Adviser to HM Government, is that a sudden increase in funds for cancer research could not be effectively used. Lord Zuckerman has pointed out that the shortage is not of money but of men and ideas: to buy a cure for cancer could 'encourage mediocrity and the routine pursuit of ideas which may long since have ceased to be fertile' *(Times,* 26 October 1972).

Spurious though some of this allegedly medical work may be, I have decided not to spend too long debating it. However false or frivolous the research, however expensive, or however cruel to the animals involved, it is of little use to remonstrate. The intonation of the words 'medical necessity' carries so much weight with the superstitious layman that the opposing argument is scarcely listened to.

So often one hears the medical vivisector solemnly defend his work on the grounds that it is for the betterment of humanity. It is time that men began to question such apparent high-mindedness. If such researchers are so keen to help their fellow mortals why are they hiding in laboratories, often wasting valuable qualifications in medicine and surgery? These scientists should be fighting the battle against disease and suffering out in the front lines where they could see the results of their labours. Many parts of the world have no medicine and no doctors. If the vivisector cares so much he should be out in the African jungles or in the South American slums treating curable diseases that are killing men because there are no doctors available, or aiding in the birth-control and sanitation campaigns of over-populated and underdeveloped countries.

In the so-called civilised world there is a movement away from wards and into laboratories. Research has boomed and now attracts all the prestige that patient-care once held. A doctor's merit is no longer rated on how many patients he makes better but on how many papers he publishes in learned journals. This has encouraged a great deal of trivial research and often there has been a decline in the standards of clinical care for patients. Indeed, in some instances, patients only really interest their doctors if their illnesses happen to fall in with a particular line of research.

The real motive for such research is quite simply personal ambition. Curiosity or the quest for knowledge runs this a poor second. A genuine and motivating concern to alleviate suffering through research is, in my opinion, not very common.

In a discussion on B.B.C. 'Woman's Hour' on 27th March 1974, the director of a commercial testing laboratory was asked what everyday products are tested on animals. He replied — 'Oh, a lot of cosmetics of course, as well as shampoos, lipsticks, face-powders and nail varnishes and so on, and a number of household products which may be hazardous, such as oven-cleaners, and various aerosol preparations'.

A brochure proclaims that his firm has tested 'adhesives, cosmetics, detergent raw materials, dyestuffs, food and food flavours, food additives and colours, paints ... plastics, printing materials, rubber, toiletries, waxes and greases'.

The safety testing of such inessential new substances on animals is dubious scientifically as well as morally — and especially when there are already many well tried and tested products on the market.

Some believe that in the UK it is obligatory under the Health and Safety at Work Act 1974, or other legislation, to carry out such tests. This is not so; and there are no stipulations in the 1974 Act which make animal (rather than alternative) methods mandatory.

There I leave all such medical fields of study, the spurious along with the genuine. The burden of my argument stands instead upon the evidence I have presented about the use of animals in research which *cannot* honestly be claimed to be strictly medical, and which now accounts for a large portion of all experiments being performed on living animals.

5. Para-medical and Pseudo-medical Uses

Weapons testing

The most secret use of animals is in the testing of weapons; radiation, chemical, biological, ultrasonic and photic as well as conventional explosive or ballistic weapons. In Britain, most of this research has been conducted at Ministry of Defence establishments such as the Microbiological Research and Chemical Defence Establishments at Porton, near Salisbury, Wiltshire. It has also been reported that the animals are used in hundreds for radiation experiments at the Atomic Energy Authority's laboratories at Harwell and Aldermaston.

During the Second World War the effects of high-explosive blast were studied, using monkeys, cats, rabbits, guinea-pigs, rats, mice and pigeons *(Lancet,* 24 August 1940). In 1943 the US Government spent $2 million on experiments on bats. Flame bombs were attached to the bats on a delayed fuse with the intention of sending the creatures into enemy cities to cause fires. Some thirty million bats were used for the development and testing of this weapon, but it was never used in battle *(Observer Magazine,* 28 October 1973).

After the war, during the test explosions of American and British atomic and hydrogen bombs, thousands of animals perished, some mercifully quickly, others lingeringly through the slow and terrible effects of radiation sickness. In one of the earliest of these tests an atomic bomb was exploded over a target area of seventy-five ships containing 4,500 experimental animals *(The Star,* 3 July 1946). And in the immediate postwar period, war-gases were reported to have been applied to the skins of dogs, goats and rabbits, causing blistering, gangrene and death *(J. Exp. Physiol,* 34, 1948). Such experiments certainly continue in the USA today. At Edgewood Arsenal in Maryland, de-barked beagle dogs were exposed to mustard gas and GB nerve gas in tests reported in 1973 *(Sunday Times,* 18 November 1973).

Many animals are still shot into space, where they are often left to die; presumably a proportion of such research has a military object.

British Examples

(1) During 1972, the Ministry of Defence used 129 sheep in tests of wounds caused by ballistic weapons. The sheep were anaesthetised and

then shot with high-velocity bullets in order to study the effects of new weapons *(Daily Mail,* 30 September 1972).

(2) At the Microbiological Research and Chemical Defence Establishment at Porton, three species of animal were deliberately infected with a 'new' disease. This disease had been accidentally found to be fatal to humans and so was, presumably, considered to have a weapon potential.

The animals developed a fever lasting six days — 'during this period the animals ate and drank very little, lost weight and remained hunched up and immobile in their cages'. In the monkeys 'the febrile stage continued until immediately before death which occurred six to nine days after infection'.

Pathological study revealed the spleen of the guinea-pig was 'sometimes three times its normal size' and 'brains were congested' (*B.J. Exp. Path.,* 1968).

(3) A scientist at the Royal Naval Medical School in Hampshire studied, in America, the effects of high energy proton radiation in 'several hundred young adult monkeys of both sexes'. In the first thirteen days after radiation, 211 monkeys died or were 'sacrificed'. The researcher reports that 'the animals were secured in a galvanised mesh or lucite cylinder and rotated at two rev/min while exposed. During exposure . . . they were in a sitting position with knees against the chest . . . the lower half of the animal was first irradiated, then the upper half'. *(Journal of Neuropathology and Experimental Neurology,* XXXI, No. 1, 1972).

(4) Nerve gases have been tested on animals in Britain *(Nature, 4* February 1972). Riot Control gases have also been tested. At Porton, animals were exposed to doses of CS gas 1,000 times greater than that needed to disperse a crowd, and for five hours each day over three months. This must have caused considerable suffering for it is known that even at lower dosage levels CS gas causes 'extreme burning sensation of the eyes and copious flow of tears, coughing, difficult breathing and tightness of the chest, involuntary closing of the eyes plus sinus and nasal drip, nausea and vomiting' *(Times,* 26 August 1969).

Arrangements are reported to exist between Britain, Canada, USA and Australia under which nerve gases and other biological weapons are developed in British establishments, such as that at Nancekuke in Cornwall, and then inflicted upon laboratory animals in other countries *(Sunday Times,* 1 November 1970).

It seems especially unfair that animals should be made the innocent victims of mankind's destructive lust. It can always be argued by those testing weapons that they are doing so for 'defensive' or even 'medical' reasons. But such arguments are only part truths, for whatever the pretext that any particular researcher gives himself for such experiments, the results he obtains will inevitably be available for use by the scientists of offensive warfare. The suffering that the human animal inflicts upon itself in the course of war is the responsibility of the human species alone, and there is no moral defence for the infliction of pain upon other species in the testing of such self-imposed iniquities.

There are reports from America that members of the extremely intelligent dolphin family have been trained by the US Navy to explode underwater mines and torpedoes (in the process, killing the animal itself). Furthermore, they have been equipped with harnesses fitted with knives and taught to attack under-water frogmen (University Federation for Animal Welfare, *Newsheet* No. 9, April 1973). Such animals may in some respects be more intelligent than men; certainly their brains are larger and reach volumes of up to 1,500 cubic centimetres.

Dr. John Lilly studied dolphins for twelve years and speaks of them as animals of 'intelligence, sensitivity, passion and affection'. He reports that they commit suicide from frustration in captivity and that this has made him abandon his scientific studies of them. For this reason Lilly advocates reforms in their treatment. Lilly says of dolphins: 'They are capable of understanding if spoken to, and can even mimic English. They can even say "I love you" and mean it; being intensely affectionate towards humans . . . If one is sick or injured it will commit suicide rather than endanger the group. Dolphins always hold an injured or sick fellow up to the surface to breathe. They are so sensitive they will do the same for a drowning man.' *(RSPCA Today,* 1973.)

Another disturbing feature of research on dolphins is their alleged sensitivity to conventional anaesthetics — which may have led experimenters to surgically operate upon them without anaesthetic. There are also reports of 'conditioning techniques in which subjects are denied food or given electric cattle-prod punishment in order to train them' *(Observer Magazine,* 3 February, 1974). Much of the American research on dolphins and whales is carried out at the Kaneobe Bay Naval Undersea Centre near Pearl Harbour.

Since Hannibal and his elephants, man has used animals as instruments of war. Dolphins and whales are his latest unpaid troops. To exploit such specially intelligent and friendly animals in this way seems morally questionable. The famous diver Jacques Cousteau, when he learnt of these experiments exclaimed 'No sooner does man discover intelligence, than he tries to involve it in his own stupidity'.

In Britain, 110,365 licensed experiments on living animals were carried out during the year 1975 by Ministry of Defence research establishments at Porton Down. This constituted about eleven per cent of the total number of experiments performed by or on behalf of Government departments and other official bodies. There were 533,835 licensed experiments on animals conducted in official laboratories during 1981 (including QUANGO'S and Government Departments but excluding the N.H.S.).

It is probable that in some other countries, notably America, the number of animals used in weapons testing is very much greater than in the UK. The choice of species differs from country to country, the Americans tending to use goats, the Swedes pigs, the British sheep, chickens and monkeys (IAAPEA, *Bulletin 6*, 1973).

Although it is often claimed that animals used in British weapons-testing invariably have been anaesthetised, this is not always the case and the Littlewood Committee reports that unanaesthetised animals have been used in blast experiments at or near Porton (paragraph 268). Furthermore, the treatment of bullet-wounds in the teaching of war-surgery will mean that experimentally wounded animals will, on occasions, be nursed back to health. This means that on recovery from any anaesthesia, the animals will have to suffer whatever pain their wounds cause them. In some cases the wounds are left open for a week (IAAPEA *Bulletin 6*, 1973).

In 1974 the United Action for Animals Inc. produced a document listing scores of experiments in which animals have been subjected to various forms or radiation. The document, entitled *Animal Models of Agony and Death: The Veterinary Killings,* contains several horrific photographs. Examples given include an experiment in Illinois where sixty-one beagles were radiated with Cobalt 60 gamma radiation. Half the dogs died within two or three weeks, symptoms including 'loss of appetite and weight, lethargy, vomiting, excessive salivation and diarrhoea, dehydration, depression, inflamed and rotting tonsils and throat tissues, mouth and skin haemorrhages, bloody faeces, bloody saliva, bloody vomit . . . rotting of the animals' tissue before they died led to early and rapid decomposition of their bodies'. This experiment was reported to have been published in *Radiation Research*, 35, 681, 1968.

In another example, dated 1973, beagles took three or four months to die. Similar symptoms are reported in pigs, hamsters, cows, mice, sheep and donkeys. Monkeys have also been used in Cobalt 60 radiation research (e.g. at the Los Alamos Laboratory, 1972, where individuals still alive after sixty days of radiation sickness were subjected to electric shock training schedules). Much of such research has a military purpose, overt or covert, and it all makes depressing reading.

Dental

Although the teeth of most experimental animals are very different from human teeth, animals are being used on a growing scale in dental research. Cats, rats, dogs and rabbits have certainly been employed. *(British Dental Journal,* October 1968).

Workers at the Turner Dental School in Manchester drilled holes in the teeth of thirteen beagle dogs. The pulps of sixty-eight teeth were exposed in this way, and were experimentally capped. After intervals of four or fourteen weeks the damaged teeth, together with some healthy 'control' teeth were excised, along with surrounding bone. In eighteen cases 'severe inflammation of the pulp tissue throughout' was reported. In thirty-one instances there was a 'massive infiltration of inflammatory cells'.

In the opinion of a dental surgeon, D. A. Sabel, LDS, RCS, of Farnborough, Hants, the dogs in these experiments must have suffered severely. For periods of up to fourteen weeks after the operation, life would have been extremely painful. During this period the inflammation caused by the experimental application of 'an obvious chemical irritant' was deliberately left untreated. Furthermore, in Mr. Sabel's view, these experiments were 'purely speculative — no one could get anything of great value from them'. In a letter to the journal which published the original report he wrote:

'I really must protest at the unnecessary suffering to dogs implied by the contents of the paper . . . In my opinion, deliberately exposing root canals and allowing infection to supervene and removing vital teeth thereby reducing masticatory efficiency certainly counts as cruelty. The experiment appears to have been of dubious value anyway and it may be that the licences for the carrying out of such procedures are too readily granted.' *(Ibid.,* 15 August 1972.)

Another dentist was of a similar opinion: 'Here is a voice of protest at the exploitation of the beagle dogs mentioned in an article last month, and all other sensitive creatures, for the purposes of trivial dental research' *(Ibid.).*

In the opinion of the RSPCA's then Deputy-Chief veterinary surgeon, Bill Jordan, these experiments were of very doubtful value. The workers were apparently studying the teeth of dogs in order to draw conclusions about human teeth. But as Jordan points out, dogs do not get tooth-decay — 'the pH of the dogs' mouth and the bacterial flora are different from man'. *(Ibid.,* 1972)

Pain Research

Much research is being done into the mechanisms of pain. Almost by definition this entails a great deal of suffering for the animals involved.

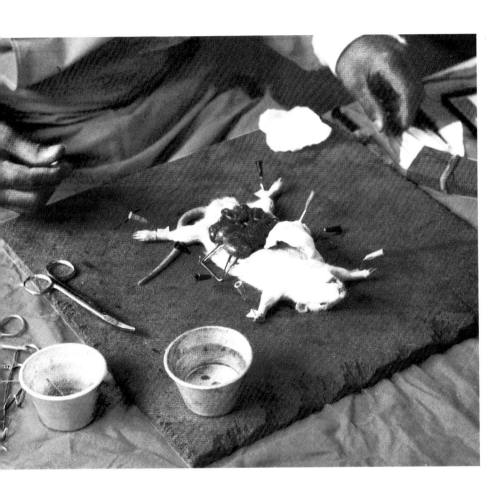

ILLUSTRATION 4.
Rat undergoing experiment for teaching of micro-surgery techniques, National University of Mexico.
Photograph by Brian Gunn ©

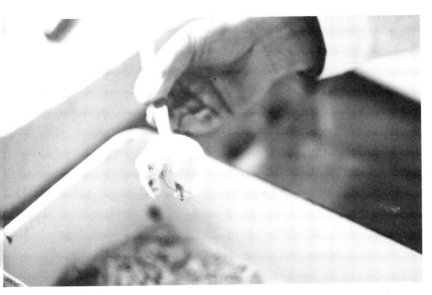

ILLUSTRATION 5a.
Pure strain mouse used for experimental purposes in Soviet laboratory under the direction of Dr. Vasili Dushkin, senior researcher of Soviet Academy of Medical Sciences.
Photograph by Jon Evans ©

ILLUSTRATION 5b.
Rodent breeding trays containing hybrid mice in Soviet Research laboratory forty kilometres outside Moscow.
Photograph by Jon Evans ©

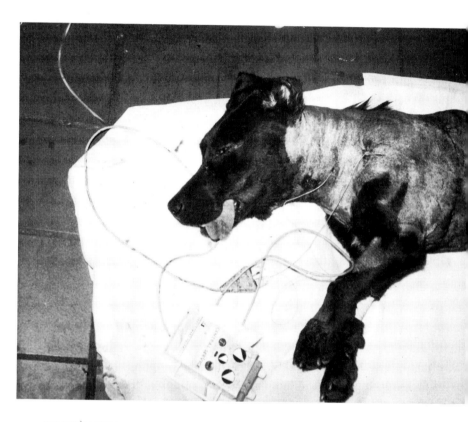

ILLUSTRATION 6.
Short-haired mongrel dog, picked up in a New York street, subjected to heart transplant operation in city hospital. Animal lies on floor of laboratory as there is no recovery room.
Photograph by Jon Evans ©

Some of this work is done with avowed clinical objectives, but much of it takes the form of pure research and is unlikely to have any immediate clinical application. Scientists of many different disciplines are occupied in the field, including psychologists and other behavioural scientists.

A grisly array of painful procedures is available for use:

Mechanical

This usually involves pinching or pressing tender points on the body of the restrained animal using metal pincers or alligator clamps. The tails and toes of cats and guinea pigs have been subjected to intense pressure and the responses noted — 'vocalisation, biting, struggling'.

Bristles have been pushed into the eyes of rabbits. Monkeys have been subjected to 'intense and repetitive pin-pricks and pinching of the muscles'. Such methods are said to produce 'intense pain'.

Electrical

Strong electric shock has been administered to animals via electrodes attached to scrotum, rectum and tail. Dogs have had electricity passed through the pulp of their teeth. The reactions are 'head jerk, chewing' and 'vocalisation'. Very high voltages lead to 'vocal response persisting after the cessation of electric stimulation'.

A French researcher reports applying shock directly to the exposed nerves of his experimental animals. He states: 'We have chosen the area of the trigeminal nerve which is the highest carrier of painful sensation; we have applied the electric shock directly to the trunk of the nerve' (Soulairac, Cahn and Charpentier, eds. *Pain,* Academic Press, 1968, p. 174). He describes how some of his animals were 'saturated with repeated strong stimulations'.

A Swiss scientist at Sandoz Ltd. has researched into pain by immobilising monkeys in a restraining chair with their heads clamped, and subjected them to intense electric shock through their tails. He observed 'baring of teeth with loud crying, pronounced agitation' (*Ibid.*).

Heat

Pain has been produced by radiant heat and by placing animals on hot-plates. When placed upon a hot-plate from which they usually cannot escape mice have been observed 'dancing, licking or blowing on forepaws'.

Chemical

The injection of phenylquinone into mice causes 'writhing behaviour' which continues for at least an hour after the injection.

Alloxan injections cause writhing in mice, rats, guinea-pigs and cats.

Injection of silver nitrate solution into the knee-joints causes inflammation and 'the reaction of the animal is manifested by squeaks and defensive movements'.

Kaolin injected in the paws of animals produces markedly painful inflammation and swelling.

Turpentine injected into the hindpaw of cats produces inflammation. Electrodes planted in the cats' brains record increased electrical activity and doses of strychnine further increased the evoked potentials.

Injections of yeast also cause painful swellings. Deliberate and sustained pressure on these swollen and inflamed areas have been found to cause 'vocalisation, struggling and biting'.

Injections of bradykinin produce intense burning pain and have been widely used in pain research.

Some American researchers record:

'In our experiments in unanaesthetised dogs, the bradykinin peptides were found to be far more potent in evoking the "pain" response, when injected into the splenic artery . . . We have obtained the same "pain" reponse by nocioceptive (i.e. by strong mechanical and thermal) stimulation of the skin of the nipple, prepuce and footpad as by chemical stimulation with intra-arterial injections of 2-4 mg of bradykinin into the spleen.'

They reported that their dogs reacted to intense pain by showing increases in blood pressure, respiration and pulse rates and by 'repeated vocalisation, struggling and biting behaviour' (*Ibid.*).

Abdominal pains have been experimentally induced by injections of acetic acid, hydrochloric acid and histamine. 'Intense pain' at the site of application has resulted from the use of mustard oil and croton oil.

Brain Stimulation

Although damage to the tissue of the brain does not produce pain in itself, it is possible to produce states of suffering by electrically stimulating certain brain-areas.

Stimulation of the amygdala in cats produces 'fear manifested by lying flat on the ground'. Stimulation of the hippocampus produces 'raucous and plaintive miaowing'.

Miscellaneous

Cutting off the blood supply (which creates 'ischemia') also causes pain and tourniquets have been used to this purpose. Furthermore, such procedures render organs more sensitive to other causes of pain. Some American researchers report 'We have found that ischemic sensitisation of mechanical electrical and chemical stimulation of the "pain" receptors in the spleen of the dog can be readily demonstrated by clamping the splenic artery' (Armstrong and Pardo (eds.), *Symposium on Pharmacology of Pain,* Pergamon Press).

Manipulation of the levels of certain chemical substances in the brains of animals has been claimed to produce a state of extreme sensitivity to pain, so-called hyperalgic behaviour.

Animals have been experimentally addicted to morphine. Withdrawal from this drug can be very painful and during pain-research in animals it has been found to precipitate 'writhing, squealing and teeth chattering'.

Examples

(1) A scientist at Reckitt and Sons Ltd., Dansom Lane, Hull, injected the pain-producing drug bradykinin into the arteries of unanaesthetised white rats. This is a standard procedure in the testing of new analgesic substances *(Pain,* p. 218).

(2) In the medical school at Birmingham, analgesics were tested on cats and rabbits whose brains had been separated from their spinal cords. After the operation, the anaesthetic was allowed to wear off, and electrical activity was recorded by electrodes implanted in the 'conscious' brains *(B. Med. Bulletin,* 21, 1965; *Pain,* p. 411).

Although there may be moral arguments against the use of human volunteers in research, they are weaker than those against the use of other animals. The main difference is that a human subject can indicate his willingness to participate, whereas an animal cannot do so. A further difference is that by understanding what is being done to him, by appreciating its scientific purpose and by anticipating possible monetary or social rewards, the terror and bewilderment can be reduced in the case of the human subject. An animal cannot fully comprehend why men in white coats are inflicting pain on itself, and the resulting bewilderment, which seems practically inevitable in any experiment using animals, almost certainly increases the total load of suffering.

Human volunteers have been used in carefully controlled pain research and the results obtained have been much more meaningful than those obtained from animals. How can a subjective state such as pain be accurately studied without the experimental subjects communicating to the experimenter what it is they are experiencing? To induce 'writhing behaviour' in a mouse may not be precisely the same thing as inducing pain. One can never be absolutely sure about it; the procedure lacks precision. Even if there is pain, the intensity, quality and duration of the experience itself remain unknown and may not entirely correlate with the observable response called 'writhing'. I may, for example, suffer pain for five minutes but only writhe for three; or, if the pain stops while I am writhing I may get it into my head that the writhing causes the relief and so I may continue writhing in the hope that I will prevent the recurrence of the painful experience. These sort of inaccuracies cannot be tolerated in science, if they can be avoided. One is not studying a visible phenomenon, such as an abscess; one is studying an invisible experience called pain, and the nearest we can get to these experiences in others is through the medium of language.

Those who try to justify painful experiments on animals often do so on the grounds that the findings of the research may have practical and beneficial effects for human-beings. In the case of pain-research they will argue that the deliberate infliction of pain upon an animal is justified because it may lead to the relief of pain in humans. If this is the objective, then it is the painful experience in humans that ought to be studied — not hypothetical correlates such as the writhing of mice.

Human volunteers seem to be available for such research, so why are they not more often used? Furthermore, the differences between the species is nowhere more apparent than in the field of pain-research. Some substances which are known to kill pain in men do not appear to stop pain in some other species — an example is methotrimeprazine which does not seem to have any analgesic effect upon experimentally induced pain in laboratory white rats *(Pain*, p. 218). Some narcotic painkillers produce increased activity in mice but have the opposite effect in rats. Morphine sedates the dog but produces frantic excitement in the cat. Other experimental analgesics seem to work as such in rats and mice but not in rabbits. As one researcher himself confesses, 'one of the difficulties encountered in studying the central action of potent analgesics (pain-killers), particularly the opiates in experimental animals, is the well known fact that they produce different effects in different species'.

So why do the drug companies, in their search for new pain-killers, continue to use animals? Many of them appear to plough on regardless of the opinion of the pharmacologists that inter-species differences render much of their research of very questionable validity.

A neurosurgeon in Holland has commented that 'a vast amount of information has been obtained, yet controversies concerning the interpretation of these findings seem to be as lively as they were at the beginning of the century. The gap between the clinician and the physiologist seems to be as wide as, or even wider than before. This pertains to sensation in general but to pain in particular' *(ibid.*, p.465).

Alas, much pain arises naturally as the result of injury and disease. Very careful ethical controls are necessary in all areas of clinical research, but nevertheless the raw data (i.e. pain) are available for study in almost every hospital ward.

H. K. Beecher of the Harvard Medical School urges the more intelligent study of pain as it occurs in everyday hospital practice. By doing this, the researcher would avoid the validity problems inherent in the experimental use of animals:

'Man is, of course, essential for definitive study of subjective responses. As a working hypothesis it seems necessary at present to carry the requirements further than this and to say that appraisal of therapeutic agents designed to modify subjective responses arising in disease or trauma are usually best studied where they arise spontaneously, when this is possible' *(ibid.*, p.205).

To those who counter this argument by saying that if animals are not available to use then the clinical researcher will start performing unethical research upon human patients, the rejoinders are first, that what is unethical for human subjects may also be unethical for animal subjects, and secondly, that evidence can be supplied that it is precisely some of those workers reared in the hard and callous techniques of vivisection on animals — and who have animals at hand in their hospital laboratories — who have, in some instances, gone on to perform unethical experiments upon their human patients.

In my opinion, research into pain should be limited to the human *volunteer* as subject, whether or not the pain is being experimentally induced or is the result of injury or disease.

6. Life in the Laboratory

General Conditions

Often before, and occasionally after, experimentation the research animals (if they survive) are kept in the laboratories for months and even years. Sometimes captured from the great arboreal freedom of their jungle homes, monkeys are closely confined in cages only three or four feet square. Usually they receive no variety of diet but only approved proprietary pellets. They may see no other living creatures except a white-coated technician on a brief daily visit. Very often the animal-room is without windows, being artificially ventilated by a machine which produces a constant unvarying drone. In order to facilitate cleaning, the animals live upon wire-mesh. They can never sit or lie down on a flat, soft or yielding surface. Little wonder that by the time they are needed for the knife or the needle they are so crazed or inert that they are no longer representative examples of animal life. Pyschologists who study the behaviour of thousands of such creatures annually, rarely make allowances for the fact that their pathetic subjects have been so deprived that they have become more like monsters than animals.

Actual cage-sizes advertised by one manufacturer are as follows:

Monkeys and Apes	2 foot 4¾ inches wide x 2 foot 3 inches deep x 3 foot high.
Rabbit cages	2 foot wide x 1 foot 6 inches deep x 1 foot 6 inches high.
Cat cages	3 foot long x 1 foot 9 inches deep x 1 foot 6 inches high.
Rat cages	11½ inches wide x 13 inches deep x 8½ inches high.
Dog pens	3 foot wide, 2 foot 9 inches long and 6 foot high.

Regardless of any experimental procedures being used, the animals must suffer on account of being solitarily confined in such small cages, devoid of exercise or interest.

Many people who have experienced close affectionate relationships with individuals of other species testify to the considerable potential for emotional and intellectual development that animals have. When properly cared for a pet dog or cat can develop great subtleties of behaviour that the laboratory animal never shows. Those who have been fortunate enough to closely observe unfrightened animals living in the wild are often struck by the complexity and richness of the life they lead. These positive pleasures the laboratory animal never knows; for him the same four white walls and the smell of disinfectant. As Professor Broadhurst enthusiastically describes it: 'It is now possible to rear and breed many smaller laboratory animals solely on a diet of tap-water and compressed food, not unlike dog biscuits or cattle cake. Some laboratories have automatic devices for delivering this food and water to the animals in their cages; sanitary arrangements may also be automatic. The animals have suitably sized wire-mesh floors in their cages so that droppings and urine pass straight through and are washed away from time to time . . . And so the laboratory animal is raised in these optimum conditions until it is needed for experimental purposes.' *(The Science of Animal Behaviour*, pp. 49, 50).

Such 'optimum conditions' are rather similar to those found in factory farms and seem to inspire similar arguments in support of them. Referring to the size of the cage the animals are kept in, Broadhurst comments: 'It is often thought to be too small, but with nocturnal animals such as the rat or mouse, which spend most of the day asleep — since it is their "night" — the size of the cage is immaterial after a certain point' *(ibid.*, p. 48).

These excerpts from a laboratory manual published by a well-known American university give some idea of what day-to-day life is like for many laboratory animals:

'There are two ways a frightened cat can be removed from a cage. One is with a snare. Hold the snare in your right hand and pull the cord tight. There will be coughing and fierce struggling. Try to keep the cat from choking to death as you pull the cat out by a snare. Always keep a safe distance between it and yourself.'

The manual further advises, and with complete composure:

'After feeding all the dogs in your area remove any dead dogs from the cages. Put the carcasses in the cold room then wash your hands.'

This bland callousness is one of the most disturbing qualities of some experimenters. They accept, almost without thought, that their murderous activities are perfectly ordinary. In the statistical sense they are unfortunately correct, for as we know, over five million laboratory animals are used every year in just one country.

Routine Procedures
Certain routine procedures may be carried out repeatedly on animals over the course of weeks or months. These are often taken for granted by laboratory personnel as being normal aspects of daily life. In published accounts of research, apparently innocuous references to the administration of anaesthesia, to the withdrawal of various body fluids or other

standard tests, give little hint of what in fact is involved. If looked at more closely it can be seen that even these simple operations must often entail considerable suffering for the animals concerned. A standard textbook on the use of laboratory animals, widely referred to throughout the English speaking world, is *Methods of Animal Experimentation*, W. I. Gay (ed.) (Academic Press, 1965), and this provides some interesting descriptions:

Withdrawal of Body-Fluids.

Technicians are instructed that blood samples can be obtained from mice by puncturing the tail or the heart or the jugular vein — 'samples may be drawn repeatedly from this site for several weeks if necessary' (p. 2). An alternative site for obtaining blood is from the eye:

Bleeding from the orbit. This technique is best performed under anaesthesia; however, *it can be done without its use* (my italics). The mouse is grasped by the back of the neck and held securely to a flat surface. A blunted 19 or 20 gauge needle and a 2 ml syringe or a special heavy-bore capillary pipette are used. The syringe or pipette is held horizontally and the needle or pipette tip is introduced into the lateral canthus* and pushed posterior to the eye, rupturing through the orbital venous plexus behind the eye. This usually produces rather profuse haemorrhage, and quantities of up to 1 ml may be obtained in this manner. Usually bleeding quickly stops when the collection instrument is removed; therefore, if only small quantities are desired this can be a survival procedure (p. 4).

In the case of dogs and cats, heart puncture is especially recommended, even without anaesthetic:

Blood Collection: heart puncture. This is best under anaesthesia; however, *anaesthesia is not essential* (my italics). The animal is restrained in left lateral recumbency and the right thorax is clipped, shaved, and a disinfectant solution applied. The fourth intercostal space is located (sometimes scribing an arc with the point of the animal's elbow helps to locate this area), and the point of strongest heart beat is palpated. Usually at least a one and a half inch needle is necessary, the gauge being dependent on the size of the sample. The needle is inserted through the fourth space into the heart. Total blood volume in the dog is approximately 80 ml/kg of body weight (pp. 8-9).

When puncturing the jugular vein, the technician is definitely advised against anaesthesia:

---

*   The corner of the eye.

Jugular venipuncture. Anaesthesia is not required for this technique. The animal is restrained in dorsal or lateral recumbency with the head extended. The vein is constricted with the thumb at the point of the thorax on either side. Holding the syringe with needle towards the thorax (bevel up) as near as possible in a plane parallel with the vein, the vein is entered with a 19-gauge, one and a half inch, needle. This vein has a tendency to roll with the needle, and it sometimes is easier to enter if a series of quick thrusts are used (p. 9).

A reason given for using anaesthesia for heart-puncture in birds is that it makes the operation 'easier'; the relief of suffering is not mentioned.

With cattle, blood can be drawn from the udder.

Urine is obtained by passing a rubber or steel tube into the bladder of the restrained animal.

Fluid from the brains of animals is usually drawn off from the base of the skull, a long needle being inserted under light anaesthesia.

Fluids from the abdomen and chest are similarly obtained using appropriate needles, sometimes with anaesthesia, sometimes without.

Infusion

It often happens that an animal must be force-fed exact amounts of substances which it would not normally eat. Such feeding procedures may occur daily for considerable periods of time. The usual way of doing this is by forcing a tube down the animal's throat and into the stomach. With cats the tube is passed either through the mouth or through the nose. Dogs are claimed to be docile victims:

The dog. Except in intractable individuals, the dog is easily intubated. An assistant restrains the animal on a table by reaching across the animal with his left elbow and bringing part of his body weight to bear upon the animal. His left hand then opens the dog's mouth by pressing on its cheek between upper and lower teeth and his right hand retracts the lower jaw (p. 35).

It is recommended that monkeys be held in a sort of judo-grip when they are being intubated — 'the rhesus-monkey is restrained by an assistant. This is done by holding the animal's arms together behind its back with one hand and immobilising its head with the other hand. It is desirable to have a second assistant to restrain the monkey's feet' (p. 36).

Injection

Injections are frequently given to animals. They can be subcutaneous (under the skin), intramuscular (into muscles), intravenous (into veins), into arteries, into the pleural or peritoneal spaces, into bone-marrow or into the brain.

Anaesthesia

Even the admission of anaesthetic can itself be traumatic, and animals can become terror-stricken during induction, as they begin to feel the first effects of the anaesthetic agent.

Anaesthetics are inhaled or injected. Either procedure may produce excitement and a violent reaction.

The usual route of injection is into a vein:

The selected vessel can be stabilized and prevented from rolling by placing the thumb parallel and adjacent to the vessel. Holding the syringe with the needle bevel down, insert needle into the skin parallel to the vein and direct the needle into the lumen of the vessel up to the hub. Should the patient move unexpectedly the needle cannot be readily dislodged (Armistead, 1959). Blood will appear in the barrel of the syringe upon slight withdrawal of the plunger.

In tough-skinned animals, e.g. cats and primates, a skin puncture for an intravenous injection should be made initially with a larger gauge needle, which is removed, and then the smaller gauge needle is inserted into the puncture hole. This will avoid bending, burring, and dulling the points of smaller gauge needles so necessary for an intravenous injection into very small vessels (p. 59).

For difficult or 'intractable' subjects, the anaesthetic can be injected straight into the animal's chest:

The preferred site for this injection is between the seventh and eighth ribs. Inject through the skin and subcutaneous tissue, penetrating through fascia, muscle, and parietal pleura. If the lung has been penetrated (it is difficult to avoid penetrating lung tissue) blood will frequently be aspirated into the barrel of the syringe. Slight coughing usually follows the injury to the lung. This is not a commonly accepted method of administration of an anaesthetic agent. However, occasionally it can be used in cats and primates that are intractable or struggle violently during the administration of a volatile or an intravenous anaesthetic (p. 59).

Research workers are advised to wear thick gloves when anaesthetising cats in order to avoid being bitten or clawed. Monkeys, too, have a reputation for putting up a fight and often have to be forcibly restrained before anaesthesia.

It is easy for any experimenter to say that an animal was anaesthetised, but it is not so easy to carry out anaesthesia in practice. In the field of human surgery expert anaesthetists are employed. Even so, human patients continue to suffer ill-effects from anaesthesia, and on occasion die of it. In the case of animals being used for research, the anaesthetic is not often administered by an expert. In consequence, the mere process of its administration often causes suffering.

Furthermore, there will be anxiety among the researchers that the inadvertent administration of too much anaesthetic will kill the probably valuable animal before the experiment has been finished. This leads to the temptation to give too little anaesthetic — enough to satisfy the Home Office rules, but not always enough to render the animal at all times totally insensible.

Another disturbing aspect of the anaesthetisation of research animals is that paralysing drugs are given at the same time as the anaesthetic. This creates a situation in which it is theoretically possible for an animal to be conscious without being able to move. To an innocent observer the creature would appear to be insensible to pain, when in fact it is not.

Anaesthesia is not a cut and dried all-or-nothing affair. There are stages of anaesthesia, and at lighter stages the animal may be sleepy and unable to control its limbs, but still able to register events. Even human surgery cases, under deep and expertly induced anaesthesia, surprisingly often manage to recall subsequently what happened during the operation (Hetherington, BPS Conference, 1970). Researches by two anaesthetists in Bristol, Dr. T. Wilton and Dr. T. McKenna, have revealed that a proportion of human surgery cases when apparently anaesthetised have in fact remained conscious and 'terrified'. Paralysing drugs have made them unable to indicate their consciousness to the surgeons. As Dr. Wilton says, 'many anaesthetists don't seem to be aware that this can happen' *(Sunday Times,* 9 December 1973).

Insufficient doses of anaesthetic administered for insufficient durations are not openly admitted to in journals. But some descriptions of the behaviour of 'anaesthetised' animals makes one wonder whether these creatures were really insensitive to pain.

In one British experiment recordings were being made from the stripped sinus nerves of 'anaesthetised' cats whose hindlegs had been strapped to a bicycle pedal and rotated at up to 100 revolutions per minute. The experimenters noted that 'the anaesthesia was not deep enough to abolish the reflexes and in the experiments, the movements imposed on the hind-limbs met with some resistance' *(J. Exp. Physiol.,* 1967).

If the cats were so lightly anaesthetised that they could resist the forcible rotation of their hindlegs, might they not also be able to feel the exposure and stripping of a nerve?

There is also an assumption in some researchers' minds that operations that would usually require deep anaesthesia in a human, only require partial, local or light anaesthesia in animals. A British example is where animals described as 'lightly anaesthetised' had pieces of their skulls sawn out. Would these same experimenters agree to such an operation being performed upon themselves under 'light' anaesthesia? *(J. Neurol. Neurosurg.,* 1972).

Also, researchers do not hesitate to use, on animals, anaesthetic substances which are never used on humans; an example is chloralose.

Another disturbing feature of the use of anaesthetics in research, is that substances are being used which may not be truly anaesthetic.

There are at least two drugs which are undoubtedly being used as animal anaesthetics, when it is uncertain that they really are. It is possible that they cause only paralysis without loss of feeling.

The manufacturers of one claim that it is an anaesthetic, and it has been used in cats for a variety of surgical operations. Although it certainly causes immobilisation it does not always stop reflex responses to painful stimulation.

One British veterinarian reports 'I cannot say that we have been totally impressed by the anaesthetic properties', and another considers that its use should be limited because of 'the persistence of reflex responses to painful stimuli and the difficulty experienced in assessing the level of consciousness of animals immobilised by the drug . . . the real demonstration of purposeful movements by an animal is the only real indication that anaesthesia is inadequate'.

Another drug has been in use for many years and is widely used as an anaesthetic for research animals. It is not, however, listed as an anaesthetic substance in main textbooks on anaesthesia.

The precise action of this drug is unknown but it certainly can produce unpleasant side-effects such as nausea and vomiting. It is believed to be a paralysing drug, but there is no definite evidence that it is a real anaesthetic.

In summary, it seems probable that surgical operations are being performed upon research animals which have been paralysed but not properly anaesthetised.

The claims of manufacturers and researchers that any substance is a proven anaesthetic, rather than merely a paralysant, should not be lightly accepted. The only convincing evidence that a paralysant is also an anaesthetic can be obtained from trials with human volunteers, and these are rarely performed. Human tests indicate that even the effects of paralysant alone, without any other form of stress being applied, can be most unpleasant. The relaxant succinyl-dicholine chloride was once given to conscious human volunteers who reported severe muscle pain throughout the body. A veterinary surgeon, L. W. Hall (*Vet. Record,* 5 March 1955, p. 191) comments — 'the feeling of terror which would probably be produced in animal patients can only be imagined'.

Restraint

The restraining procedure will vary with the equipment available, however, a net and squeeze cage will greatly facilitate handling. After the primate has been netted, place the net down flat on the floor. If possible grasp the animal at the small of the back through the net with one hand, pressing the whole body to the floor, and with assistance attempt to draw back both elbows behind the animal's back. In this arms-behind-its-back position with the front of its head facing away from the handler, the subject can now be presented for a parenteral injection (Gay, *op.cit.,* p. 90).

Some animals are held in restraining chairs for weeks at a time, often unable to move head or limbs. More often still, animals must be prevented from biting or clawing at experimentally induced wounds, sores or tumours. So-called 'Elizabethan' collars prevent dogs from licking any parts of their bodies. Other devices used include plastic or canvas jackets, masks, harnesses, slings, and frames. Plaster of Paris casts are also used to partially or completely immobilise animals, sometimes for long periods.

Pain-Relief

It is a strange fact that relatively little effort is made to alleviate post-operative pain in laboratory animals. The usual excuse given is that pain-killing drugs have side-effects that may delay recovery of the animal (p. 144) or otherwise jeopardise the research project. Yet pain itself will also affect the physiology of the animal and thus, the results of the experiment.

Euthanasia

It is difficult to kill an animal without causing it pain or fear. However, 'space in animal quarters in research institutions is usually at a premium, and it is self-defeating to keep an animal alive beyond its period of usefulness'. So regular and convenient ways of disposal must be devised.

It is recommended that cold-blooded animals such as frogs should be killed by having their heads crushed:

Turtles may also be killed by destroying the brain. The jaws are grasped with a forceps or hemostat sufficiently stout for the purpose, and the head forcefully drawn out of the shell, holding the body with the other hand. The head is brought to lie on a flat hard surface, and the skull is crushed by an assistant (p. 175).

Mice are killed by having their heads struck against a table edge. Dogs and cats can be shot, decompressed, electrocuted, or poisoned with cyanide, barbiturates or magnesium sulphate. They can be gassed with carbon monoxide or coal gas.

Many procedures which are supposed to be painless almost certainly are not and cause agonising deaths. Among these are poisoning with strychnine which causes repeated convulsions while the animal is entirely conscious. Carbon dioxide poisoning is known to cause severe headache in human subjects and will cause prolonged periods of gasping before death ensues. Ether and chloroform do not cause a rapid loss of consciousness but often produce desperate panic:

> Ether is an irritating agent, and when it comes in contact with exposed mucous membranes will cause smarting and burning. Animals subjected to these vapours will show the expected reactions; their eyes will water, excessive salivation will occur, and they will obviously be exceedingly uncomfortable. Unconsciousness does not come quickly, and usually the animal will first indulge in violent struggles in an attempt to escape, throwing itself against the sides and the top of the box, often times with sufficient strength to force open the lid unless it is securely latched (p. 189).

Exhaust fumes from an internal combustion engine are sometimes piped into gas chambers in order to kill animals. This causes painful burning and smarting of mucous membranes and eyes, unless the gas is previously passed through water.

Of course, mistakes can be made, and are made; as the handbook puts it:

> If an animal regains consciousness while mutilated, if it screams in pain or runs about blindly and uncontrollably, snapping and biting at anything in its path, including itself, this can hardly be called a 'well' death (p. 169).

If left out to be collected as ordinary refuse, the sight of the bodies of many dead animals — 'will certainly not enhance the esteem with which the research centre or school is held by the public' (p. 101). So laboratories are recommended to install an incinerator. This is the only hygienic and diplomatic way of disposal — 'Preferably once a day at the pre-arranged time, the accumulated corpses should be removed to the incinerator' (p. 191).

Like so many techniques of the animal laboratory, euthanasia methods appear to be humane as they are described in the text-book. But in practice accidents are bound to happen; a needle breaks, a hand slips, a leg is torn off, a terrified half-dead animal breaks loose and seeks refuge under a bench or on top of a cupboard.

Euthanasia is not often a subject that is taught. It is usually considered to be a skill that must be aquired — at the expense of hundreds of thousands of animals who die unclean deaths while the novice gets his practice.

A definition of euthanasia is rarely given. One hears of animals being swiftly disembowelled without anaesthetic, or pickled alive in formalin or immersed in liquid nitrogen — and all these deaths have been euphemistically described as euthanasia — but are they?

Germ-Free Conditions

More animals than ever before are being reared in germ-free conditions. This means they are born by Caesarian operation and then live their whole lives in stainless-steel or plastic containers called 'isolators'. In the case of rats and mice, the Caesarian operations have been performed without anaesthetic. Elaborate precautions are taken in such laboratories to ensure that the animals remain uncontaminated by germs, and the personnel feeding the animals and experimenting on them are dressed in clothing resembling space-suits.

The unfortunate animals may never meet another creature, will never see the sun or smell the open air. They are alone, surrounded by machinery.

Infectious Diseases

Animals which have been experimentally infected with diseases are similarly isolated, and often are only handled by technicians wearing gowns, rubber gloves and plastic hoods ventilated by airlines.

7. The Laboratory Animal Industry

There are three main ways in which business-men can make money out of the use of animals in the laboratory — other than by the actual manufacture of new chemical products. These are: animal breeding; supplying laboratory food and equipment; and testing products on behalf of clients.

There are a number of companies which supply feeding pellets, cages, and other laboratory equipment specifically designed for use in experiments with live animals. Among other instruments manufactured are clippers for the pre-operative shaving of small animals; test chairs for monkeys and apes; and 'a complete range of cremators for the destruction of animal bodies'.

Breeders

In recent years there has been an increase in the number of firms breeding animals specifically for laboratory purposes. Many of these breeders export animals internationally as well as selling on their home markets. Some breeders from the U.S.A. and Europe belong to the International Committee on Laboratory Animals (ICLA) which is based in Norway. In Britain, some thirty companies comprise the membership of the Laboratory Animals Breeders' Association, which describes itself as a 'non-profit making ethical trade organisation', and some sixty U.K. firms supplying laboratory animals are accredited and listed by the Medical Research Council; this scheme guarantees certain scientific standards, but provides no welfare safeguards.

By 1976, costs of food stuffs had begun to escalate, and prices were unstable. The approximate cost of each specially reared or imported laboratory animal in 1979 was as follows:

Species	Approximate Cost per Animal	
MOUSE (INBRED)	£	$
Newborn to 12 grams	0.84	1.70—
18-25 grams	0.96—1.30	2.50
Pregnant	2.74	5.50
Time Mated	3.74	8.00

Species	Approximate Cost per Animal	
	£	$
MOUSE (contd.)		
(OUTBRED)		
18-25 grams	0.30—0.34	0.60
Pregnant	0.92	2.00
Time Mated	1.53	3.00
Congenic, all types	1.77	3.60
RAT (OUTBRED)		
Dependent on weight and strain	0.91—1.76	2.00
Pregnant	2.72	5.40
Time Mated	3.31	6.60
(INBRED)		
40-60 grams (babies)	1.24	2.40
120-150 grams	1.63	3.20
250-300 grams (full grown)	2.75	5.50
GUINEA PIG		
Dependent on weight and strain	2.50—4.50	5.00—9.00
Pregnant	6.72	13.40
Time Mated	7.72	15.40
RABBIT		
Dependent on weight and strain	4.00—7.00	8.00—14.00
DOGS		
Beagles	120—160	240—320
Labradors	110—150	220—300
CATS	60—75	120—150
PRIMATES		
Rhesus (caught wild)	280—300	560—600
„ (home-bred) 1 kg.	320—350	640—700
Baboon Under 3 kg	140—150	—
„ 3-5 kg	170—180	340—360
„ 12 kg	—	340
Cynomolgus Under 2 kg	110	220
„ 2-3 kg	120	240
„ 3-4 kg	135	270

Most chimpanzees, orang-utangs and gorillas are now valued in thousands, rather than hundreds, of dollars.

		£	$
FERRET		2.00—2.50	4.00—5.00
HAMSTER		2.00	4.00
HORSE	From	210	420
DONKEY		100	
PIG	Dependent upon breed and weight	100—200	200—400

These are the approximate sale values of specially bred animals where some scientific control over breeding conditions is claimed.

Animals from casual dealers, many picked up off the street or stolen, or acquired from pounds, cost very much less. Dogs may cost as little as £8 ($16) and cats £5 ($10). Such animals may be suffering from disease and are recognised as being far from ideal subjects from the purely scientific point of view (1980 prices).

British breeders have exported (or re-exported) annually at least 50,000 animals (including hundreds of dogs, cats and monkeys) to laboratories abroad, sometimes where there may be no legal controls over experimentation. This trade is unlicensed and uninspected.

Testing Establishments

Testing products on behalf of clients is very much an expanding concern, and it is probably in this area of the laboratory animal industry that most profits are made. At least two firms fall into the category of commercial testing concerns which are not themselves big producers of chemical products. Other firms are also producers, while most have also been, or still are, breeders of laboratory animals. Large commercial testing laboratories, like Huntingdon Research, are American-based and have offices or laboratories in Europe and Japan.

The connections between Government and private industry are often obscure. In the laboratory animal industry this is no exception. Legislation encouraging companies to use animals for the testing of products means that the total turnover of animals remains enormous. This can mean costs for some companies but profits, perhaps for others. If new laws were to be passed which had the effect of increasing the number of dogs or monkeys which had to be used in safety testing then breeders would stand to profit. Suppose only 20 per cent of all animals used in Britain were dogs then this would represent a product worth over £100,000,000 each year; or suppose that some new regulations meant that 20 per cent of all animals used had to be monkeys, then this might mean that a few breeders would be in a position to share a £200,000,000 annual animal market. It can be seen that potentially this is a lucrative business.

The vested interests certainly exist. But there are also interests of a non-commercial sort. Thousands of low-grade scientific and technical jobs depend upon the laboratory animal business, so also does the dubious prestige of scores of well-established professors and other researchers. The scientist, like many professionals, is unwilling to abandon old techniques. To do so sometimes entails hard work or the implication of error. Guilt about the massive abuse of animals is often at a semi-conscious level among scientists and technicians. To admit, after years of work and the sacrifice of thousands of animal lives, that the venture was ill-conceived or unnecessary, is to risk painful awakenings for many uneasily slumbering consciences.

Many thousands of animals die caught in the cross-fire between belligerent industrial giants, battling to prove that a new product is safe or effective or that an old one is, after all, unreliable and not as indispensable as is a new and more expensive one; or vice versa. After the Second World War, a new group of artificial sweeteners, the cyclamates, were introduced onto the world market. Because they cost five times less than sugar and had thirty times the sweetening-power, they were a great commercial success and by the mid 1960's the sugar industry felt severely threatened. The American Sugar Manufacturer's Association set about financing research. The British sugar industry sponsored research at the Huntingdon Research Centre. By 1967 the British Sugar Bureau, a public relations organisation set up by the sugar industry, were pressurising members of parliament about the dangers of cyclamate sweeteners. The Dutch and German sugar industries launched similar research and publicity programmes. In 1969, both the British and American Governments banned the use of cyclamates. For a short time the world sugar industry had earned itself a reprieve — but how many thousands of animals had perished painfully in the process?

When all is said and done, the expansion in the laboratory animal industry is an effect of the expansion of the chemical and drug industries. Thousands of new chemical products are synthetised annually as companies frenziedly try to keep up with or ahead of their rivals. Old products, however effective in fact, must be questioned in practice. New ones, or old ones in new disguises, must be sold to the gullible consumer. New demands must be created for products that are not really needed.

Sixty years ago the physician had available about half a dozen drugs — opium, iron, digitalis, potassium iodide, arsenic and gentian. By the 1970's that same doctor had at hand some 2,500 listed preparations. (A. M. Cooke, 'Then and Now', in the *Oxford Medical School Gazette,* Vol. XXV, No. 1, 1972). Similar booms are overwhelming and perplexing food manufacturers, horticulturalists, agriculturalists and the ordinary consumer.

Nevertheless governments do not make serious attempts to curtail the chemical industries. *Instead of questioning the real necessity for most of these profit-making products* they promote various face-saving shams. One of these is the massive use of animals in toxicity-screening. In this way millions of animals are condemned to die pointless and painful deaths in what is little more than a world-wide publicity exercise organised by profit-motivated industrialists, encouraged by politicians and bureaucrats.

Both thalidomide and methylmercury dicyandiamide were screened on animals. The first tragedy was worsened because rats do not react to thalidomide in the way that humans do, the second because a known poison was carelessly or unscrupulously handled.

The desire to relieve suffering or to otherwise help humanity are not the main motives behind the deaths of millions of animals in laboratories around the world. The main motive is not medical but commercial.

Research can be big business for the breeders, the commercial testers, and the equipment suppliers. Many breeders, cage manufacturers and commercial organisations belong to a world-wide network called the International Committee on Laboratory Animals (I.C.L.A.) (National Institute of Public Health, Postuttak, Oslo 1, Norway). The aim of I.C.L.A. is "the promotion of laboratory animal science all over the world". I.C.L.A. has spidersweb connections with Governments (e.g. via the U.K.'s Medical Research Council) and universities; its experts make extensive promotion tours throughout the countries of the developing world. Some I.C.L.A. members are also members of bodies such as the Research Defence Society (R.D.S.) which exist to publicise the "necessity" for animal experiments. The R.D.S. in turn, has received funds from breeders, drug companies and commercial testing laboratories.

8. Primates

Man, the celebrated Naked Ape, is just one species in the primate order (monkeys and apes), and he is using the other primates in an ever-widening range of research projects.

A report published in the *Journal of Surgical Research,* June 1967, estimated that about 250,000 monkeys were being used annually in American laboratories. During the period when polio-vaccines were being almost exclusively produced in living monkeys, the USA imported 1,500,000 of the rhesus species alone in the space of only six years from 1954 to 1960 *(Biologist,* Vol. XVII, January 1970).

Over ninety per cent of monkeys required for research are still being trapped in the wild *(Medical News,* London, 28 August 1972), and such is the trade in apes and monkeys that it has been reckoned that at least nine Asian and eight African primates species are threatened with extinction *(International Union for the Conservation of Nature Bulletin,* Vol. XII, p. 120). Claims have been made that some traders kill between four and nine chimpanzees for every one they successfully capture and sell for research *(New Scientist,* 23 April 1970, p. 167).

One study suggested that a minimum of 750 healthy chimpanzees are required annually for use in laboratories throughout the world, but when account is taken of the losses a total of about 5,000 chimpanzees each year are being drained from the dwindling wild populations of Africa. (c.f. *Sunday Times,* 18 Jan, 1976).

In some areas of India, Rhesus monkeys, once common, have now disappeared. In the province of Uttar Pradesh sixty-three per cent of the villages lost all their monkeys to research laboratories in the five years prior to 1960.

Concern has also been expressed by the International Primate Protection League (P.O. Box 9086, Berkeley, California 94709, and Regent House, 19-25 Argyll St., London W.1.) who claim that about 1 million primates are taken from the forests each year to provide some 200,000 for research (800,000 dying in transit or capture). It is estimated that there will be no viable free populations left by the end of the century.

A trapper of baboons in Africa admits that he kills those animals that may have TB, even before he gets a definite diagnosis from the Mantoux TB test — 'If we do get a reaction, the animal is destroyed, but on several animals showing a reaction, we have carried out further tests which finally have proved to be negative. However, the time and effort spent on proving the Mantoux Test right or wrong is just not worth-while', he confesses. Once trapped, the baboons are kept for several weeks in cylindrical cages six foot high and three foot wide. Baboons are very active animals and stand about five foot high on their hind legs, having bodies the same size as adult humans, so the stress of confinement and the discomfort due to lack of exercise can be imagined (*Journal of IAT,* June 1971, p. 66). Like so many exploiters of animals, this trapper displays a strange respect for the creatures he uses — 'baboons are interesting to watch — their intelligence is almost unbelievable. We have satisfied ourselves, from personal experience, that it is fatal to release a baboon from a trap if the trapping session is not over. The animal communicates with its companions and they won't come near a trap again. We have had cases where a free baboon has managed to lift the door of a trap and release the inmate . . .'

Disarmingly, the writer admits the suffering he causes — 'it is accepted that trapping any animal under any condition must cause stress, fright and discomfort', but then, one supposes, his gain out-weighs their pain.

At least twenty per cent of all baboons trapped in Africa are however, unsuitable for the laboratory through disease and injury, and with some other species and for some forms of laboratory use, the proportion of animals trapped in the wild which are usable is small indeed.

For this reason, a primate breeding industry has recently been created to satisfy the demand for uninjured and disease-free animals. The Medical Research Council had recently set up its own colony (*B. Vet. J.,* October 1972) and there have been at least two British firms breeding monkeys for research, one of these being Shamrock Farms (Great Britain) Ltd. Victoria House, Henfield Road, Small Dole, Sussex.

An International Symposium on 'Breeding Non-human Primates for Laboratory Use' was held at Berne, Switzerland from 28 June till 1 July 1971. Participants from America, Austria, Belgium, Britain, Germany, India, Italy, Netherlands and Switzerland heard papers on the special breeding of mouse-lemurs, marmosets, squirrel-monkeys, guenons, mangabeys, baboons, macaques, chimpanzees and other apes (*UFAW Report,* 1972, p. 31).

In Britain, dealers boast that 'We are now specialising in supplying animals for medical research. We can quote prices for any quantity on application. Shipments can be made to any part of the world'. This firm advertised in 1973 *twenty-five different species of monkeys and apes,* including bush babies, woolly monkeys, gibbons, chimpanzees (£350), orangs (£1,800) and gorillas (£2,500).

Plans are afoot to set up a European primate-breeding centre perhaps on an island off the Italian coast, and in 1974 Singapore University produced figures for a five-year programme envisaging the production of 1,000 young monkeys each year, costing about £30 each to produce, with a capital outlay of £250,000 over four years. In Holland, chimpanzee-breeding is already under way (*Ibid.,* p. 486).

Polio vaccines are now being produced more often in human diploid cell cultures than from living monkeys, and so this source of demand for monkeys has almost entirely disappeared. This welcome switch to tissue-cultures led to a decline in the numbers of laboratory primates being used during the late 1960's. However, there are signs that the demand for primates in other fields is expanding steadily. The closeness of monkeys and apes to the human species makes them desirable subjects for scientific use, and it seems that areas of research that have hitherto relied upon lower animals are going over to primates.

Evidence that the demand for primates is once again expanding is that in 1970 the USA imported 101,302 (including several hundred chimpanzees), a slight increase on the previous year. In 1972, more than 9,000 primates were imported into the U.K.; in 1974 this number rose to 12,523 (D.o.E. *Report on the Animals (Restriction of Importation) Act 1964,* for 1974), some for re-export. These import figures show increases despite the fact that both the UK and the USA are now breeding monkeys. The UK uses about 6000 primates each year in licensed experiments. In the past the main limiting factor preventing the more widespread use of primates has been the economic one; one monkey costing the equivalent of about 100 laboratory rats. But now, as the breeding industry expands, it is possible that the price of mass-produced primates will become more competitive. If this is so, then the swing to primates will accelerate. The breeding of primates is not proving to be easy. Because of the soaring demand and the dwindling supply from the wild, one U.K. dealer urges that in order "to derive maximum scientific benefit" from these animals "every effort should be made to re-use animals wherever possible" and he offers to buy back used primates for re-sale to other laboratories. (The house journal of Shamrock Farms (Great Britain) Ltd. May 1976).

Primates are already being used in a multitude of ways. They have been shot into space and left in orbit for long periods, they have been addicted to hard drugs, blinded, stressed, poisoned and deliberately infected with syphilis and gonorrhoea (*New Scientist,* 12 October 1972). The CIA have been interested in methods of so-called brain-washing and monkeys have been subjected to microwave stimulation for months on end.

One well-known experimenter with primates writes — 'having

worked with chimpanzees a number of years, I have no doubt that these animals are sometimes angry, resentful, jealous, remorseful, affectionate, happy or sad' and maintains that although there are some intellectual differences between them and men, 'there are no fundamental or qualitative differences between the emotions and motivations of man and the other primates' (Professor H. W. Nissen, *Human Biology,* Vol. 26, 1954, pp. 277-87). If this is so, then why should man continue to dictate gross fundamental and qualitative differences between the rights he recognises for human and non-human primates?

The similarity between the blood of humans and that of other apes is so close that gorillas undergoing surgery have successfully received transfusions of human blood.

Research on the brains of monkeys has also revealed asymetrical functioning like that of the human brain *(New Scientist,* 13 May 1976).

In recent years, chimpanzees have displayed their remarkable intelligence by learning to communicate in American Sign Language for the Deaf, and by using other symbols. They have, so it is claimed, invented new and meaningful phrases and shown a possible capacity for abstract thinking. Dr. Alan and Beatrice Gardner have reported that one young chimp, Moja, has drawn pictures of a bird, a cat and a strawberry.

Such nearness to human behaviour would seem to call for greater fellow-feeling and a deeper respect for the rights and interests of our primate relatives.

In 1981 the International Primate Protection League published a damning attack upon the use of monkeys in the so-called induction of depression. Sophisticated as well as crude forms of torture (e.g. inescapable shock, inescapable extremely loud noise and the total isolation of monkeys in "pits of despair" for weeks on end) were described. These "learned helplessness" experiments (naively considered to teach new understanding of psychological depression) as conducted at Wisconsin University deserve outright condemnation from all civilised men and women. (I.P.P.L. *Newsletter* Vol 8. No. 2. May 1981.)

9. American Experiments and Others

Although there is ample evidence that British research causes great suffering for animals both in medical and in non-medical fields (see pages 44-76), the evidence from outside Britain often appears to be even more disturbing.

EXAMPLES

(1) Researchers for Technology Inc, San Antonio, Texas constructed a pneumatically driven piston to strike an anvil attached to a special helmet called HAD I, producing impact to the heads of thirteen monkeys. When they found the blows were insufficient to cause concussion, they made a more powerful device called HAD II which they used on the same thirteen monkeys, and found that it caused cardiac damage, haemorrhages and brain damage from protrusion of plastic rings which they had implanted under the monkeys' skulls. Monkey number 49-2 was again subjected to HAD II six days later, and thirty-eight days later was struck multiple blows until she died.

Some of the animals who temporarily survived suffered subsequent fits and the researchers were impressed to find that after the experiments the monkeys' behaviour 'was distinctly abnormal. The usual post-acceleration behaviour in the cage was that of hanging upside down cowering in a corner' (UAA Bulletin).

(2) A Canadian psychologist at the Department of Psychology, University of Alberta, Edmonton, Canada, elicited vocalisation from sixteen Japanese quails by gradually lowering a concentric stainless steel electrode into their brains in 0.3 to 0.4 mm steps and electrically stimulating with an amperage of 300. He notes that 'electrical brain stimulation has elicited vocalisation in a number of avian species (crow, parrot, pigeon and chicken)' *(Behaviour,* 36, 1970).

(3) A scientist at the California Institute of Technology is well-known for his 'split-brain' experiments in which he has divided the brains of living animals into two entirely separate yet functioning pieces.

In one such experiment he 'split' brains of seven Rhesus monkeys and confirmed a finding with split-brained chimpanzees that there is no transfer of skills from one hand to the other. It is rather as if there were two animals with the same body. *(Journal of Comparative and Physiological Psychology,* 1960).

(4) A psychologist gave electric shocks to sixteen dogs and found that his 'high-shock group' acquired 'anxiety' faster *(Ibid.)*.

(5) A psychologist from Hartford, Connecticut, points out that monkeys which have had a part of their brain cut out (the amygdala) will sometimes eat faeces. In this study he used eight pre-adolescent Rhesus monkeys. After opening their skulls under anaesthesia he removed their amygdalas 'using a small-gauge sucker' in order to observe 'these dietary changes' *(Ibid.)*.

(6) Psychologists at the University of Wisconsin separated sixty-three Rhesus monkeys from their mothers five to nine hours after birth and housed them in individual wire-mesh cages measuring fifteen inches by eighteen inches by twenty-four inches *(Ibid.)*.

(7) A Psychologist at Wisconsin University placed 571 hybrid mice in a large chromatography jar and sounded a five inch electric bell generating 102 decibels of noise for ninety seconds. 'Records were made of the incidence of wild running, tonic, clonic and lethal seizures.' 181 of the mice died *(Ibid., 1969)*.

(8) Psychologists at Pittsburg gave electric shocks to the feet of 1,042 mice. They then caused convulsions by giving more intense shocks through cup-shaped electrodes applied to the animals' eyes or through pressure spring clips attached to their ears. Unfortunately some of the mice who 'successfully completed Day One training were found sick or dead prior to testing on Day Two' *(Ibid.)*.

(9) Psychologists at the universities of Pittsburgh and Michigan described the 'Copulation of Virgin Male Rats Evoked by Painful Peripheral Stimulation'.

They prevented the animals from biting at the electrodes delivering the shock by surrounding them by other electrified wires — 'several contacts with the protective wire were sufficient to discourage future attempts' *(Ibid.)*.

(10) A psychologist placed monkeys in restraining devices and gave them electric shocks every twenty seconds during six hour experimental periods. After twenty-three days monkeys began to die suddenly of stomach ulcers *(Scientific American, 1958)*.

(11) A scientist at Holloman Air Force Base noted that 'six monkeys in restraint chairs for thirty days developed oedema and psoriasis of the feet and legs, and decubital ulcers in and around their ischial callosites'. Nevertheless he concluded that 'long-term behavioural studies requiring continuously restrained primates are feasible' *(Journal of Experimental Animal Behaviour, 11, 1, 1968)*.

(12) A scientist in Leningrad reports that 'healing of burns on the skin proceeded substantially more slowly in dogs with experimental

neurosis (106 to 133 days after the burn)'. Similarly, healing of lacerations took forty to sixty days — 'the process of healing in the neurotic subjects was protracted, as bleeding and granulation developed followed by slow epithelialisation'. He has also exposed neurotic dogs to high levels of radiation. He found that seventy per cent of dogs 'with a weak nervous system' died as a result of radiation sickness (M. W. Fox and W. B. Saunders Eds., *Abnormal Behaviour in Animals,* 1968, Chapter 6).

(13) At the Tasman Vaccine Laboratory, New Zealand, cats were killed by infection. 'On arrival, the cats were identified, bled by cardiac puncture and immediately force-fed with 15ml of a twenty per cent suspension of virulent paneucopenia virus-infected kitten intestine. These animals were observed several times daily and port-mortem examinations were made on those found dead or destroyed *in extremis'* (*Vet. Record,* December 1968).

(14) Indian scientists paralysed monkeys by giving lumbar injections of pure Ox-Dapro — 'the three monkeys with flaccid areflexic paraplegia showed no response to either stamping on the tail or pin prick applied to the lower-limbs' *(Nature,* 6 May 1967).

(15) An Italian scientist observed fifty-seven puppies born of starved mothers. Twenty-eight of these pups died soon after birth and the survivors showed abnormalities such as 'atheroid movements of the head and neck and ataxic gait . . . one animal died during an epileptiform fit and two others were found dead or injured in circumstances also suggestive of fits'. Others 'often ran in narrow circles' (Fox and Saunders, *op. cit.,* Chapter 16).

(16) A scientist at the University of California prepared monkeys caught in the jungles of Thailand by placing them in neck restraint devices, cutting off their tails and extracting their canine teeth. Electrodes were implanted deep in their brains. Catheters were implanted in bladders for urine collection, into main blood vessels and into the heart. After behavioural training some of these monkeys were fired into space (*New York Post,* 8 July 1969). One of these monkeys, Bonny, died unexpectedly after an eight-and-half-day flight.

(17) American psychologists kept puppies isolated individually in small boxes for nine months and thus 'denied them any experience with the outside world'. Tubes were placed on their limbs and a collar around their neck to prevent tactile contact with their own body. The effects of this deprivation were studied *(Scientific American,* 1956).

(18) An American researcher kept animals awake by placing them in rotating drums. Those animals which survived were highly irritable and aggressive after thirty days without sleep (*J. Comp. Physiol. Psych.,* 1950).

(19) A researcher at Johns Hopkins Medical School, Baltimore, investigated the phenomenon of sudden death in animals and men. He did this by dropping rats into specially designed cylindrical tanks filled with water and noting how long it took them to drown. The rats either died promptly from 'hopelessness' — 'they seem literally to "give up" ' — or swam for up to sixty hours before finally drowning. It was concluded that cutting off their whiskers, 'destroying possibly their most important means of contact with the outside world', resulted in more sudden deaths (Reed, Alexander and Tomkins (Eds.), *Psycho-pathology*, Chapter 16).

(20) A scientist in Moscow applied hot water to the legs of cats while electrically stimulating the reticular formations of their brains and applying strychnine to cerebral cortex (*Fitziologicheskii Zhurnal*, 1967), and Russian scientists at Lugansk studied effects on evacuatory function of ten dogs subjected to three or four weeks of painful stimulation of spinal nerve roots and the sciatic nerve, using electric shock and ligatures with sharp beads (*Ibid.*).

(21) At Tokushina University, Japan, starved rats with needle electrodes in their necks and steel electrodes in their eyeballs were forced to run in treadmills for four hours at a time (*Nature*, 1968).

(22) A psychologist at Yale made a Rhesus monkey reject her young by electrically stimulating a part of her mid-brain. These electrical signals were relayed via a radio receiver on the animal's neck (*The Times*, 25 March, 1967).

(23) In Shanghai rabbits were subjected to intense heat in pain endurance trials to test the effects of acupuncture (*New York Times*, 5 March 1973).

(24) In Taiwan, the US Naval Medical Research Unit, Number 2, has in excess of 25,000 laboratory animals at any one time, including monkeys, hamsters, gerbils, pigs and goats. More than 250,000 mice were used by NAMRU investigators during the year 1971 (*JAVMA*, Vol. 160. 8, 15 April 1972).

(25) At the University of Arkansas pure-bred pointer dogs were given electric shock through shock-collars. Some dogs were especially bred for timidity and were found to 'freeze' when shocked. The more normal dogs, when under shock, were observed 'often rolling on their backs and howling' (*Conditioned Reflex*, Vol. 6, 1971).

Similar research has been carried out by psychologists at many other American Universities (*UAA Basic Research Illustrated*, 1973). At the University of Pennsylvania the shocked dogs were restrained in hammocks. At Harvard the dogs were observed 'yelping and shrieking'. At the University of North Caroline cats were shocked every fifteen minutes for sixty-six hours. At the University of Florida monkeys were immobilised in a restraining chair and shocked through their tails and at the University of Chicago (*J. Comp Physiol. Psych.*, 81, 2, November 1972) squirrel monkeys had drugs injected into their brains while being 'punished' by electric shock.

(26) Research veterinary surgeons at Wisconsin University attempted to experimentally reduce milk production in pregnant sows by giving them electric shock, inflaming their teats and forcing them to fight. Sixteen of the pregnant sows were loaded onto a truck and hauled over bumpy farm roads for one hour. Although two of the sows died after this experience, none of these measures significantly affected milk production (*American Journal of Veterinary Research,* 33, 11, November 1972).

(27) At the University of Michigan sixty-four monkeys were addicted to drugs by automatic injection into their jugular veins. When the supply of drugs was abruptly withdrawn, some of the monkeys were 'observed to die in convulsions'. Before dying some monkeys plucked out all their hair or bit off their own fingers and toes (*Psychopharmacologia,* 16, 30, 1969).

(28) American researchers exposed monkeys to 'five hours of hard rock music, constant machine noises such as those from power saws and pneumatic hammers, and random gunfire, to learn how animals reacted to noises played at the constant loudness of 100 decibels' (*New York Times,* 25 September 1972).

Experimental Neurosis and Stress

Since the days of the Russian psychologist, Ivan Pavlov, laboratory animals have been used in experiments designed to drive them mad. Most of these procedures depend on the simple principle of inflicting pain upon an animal from which it cannot escape.

This field of research today is based upon original studies made after the First World War. Pavlov had reported that one dog 'became quite crazy, unceasingly and violently working all parts of its body, howling, barking and squealing intolerably' (I.P. Pavlov, *Conditioned Reflexes: an investigation of the Physiological Activity of the Cerebral Cortex,* London, Oxford University Press, 1927).

American scientists continued such work. One, using electric shocks, provoked experimental neuroses in sheep and dogs. They became irritable, restless, sleepless, and isolated. One dog became quite rigid and 'allowed passive moulding of limbs into bizarre poses'. These disorders persisted in some cases until death 13 years later. (*American Review of Physiol.,* 1947).

Another studied the effects of prolonged restriction and isolated animals in small cramped cages. He shut a young bitch in a small cage and noted that she died four months later (*Psychosom. Med., Monogr.*

3). Using explosions, injections and electric shock to the genitals, he experimented on another neurotic dog over a period of twelve years.

Other workers have made cats and monkeys appear neurotic by subjecting them to electric shock, blasts of air and jets of water (*Journal of Nervous and Mental Disorders,* 1953).

Most of these studies in so-called experimental neurosis seem to be conducted in America and Russia (Fox and Saunders, *op. cit.*). Recently, the fashion has been to produce states of so-called helplessness in animals.

Crash Studies

Animals have been widely used in motor accident research. Usually the animal is strapped into a car seat and crashed at measured speeds. Most of this research is carried out in America, using bears, gorillas, orang-utans and baboons.

Although it is well known that seat belts can cause foetal deaths in pregnant women, it was reported in *Medical Tribune,* 5 September 1968, that a scientist received $103,800 from the US Department of Transportation in order to crash pregnant baboons on impact-sleds at Holloman Air Force Base, New Mexico.

At the 11th Stapp Car Crash Conference it was described how nine dogs were subjected to forty-eight impact tests at Chicago Medical School. Some dogs did not die until twelve hours later.

Similar experiments on chimpanzees are reported to have been carried out at the Northrop Space Laboratories.

The Federal Aviation Administration, Oklahoma City, carried out sixty impact experiments on baboons. The experimenters were surprised by the inconsistency of their results. For example, baboon No. 3598, crashed in three consecutive impacts at sixty and forty-five minute intervals, suffered a ruptured bladder and dura (outer membrane surrounding the brain), but no damage to organs previously observed to be vulnerable in other test baboons.

One test baboon died during surgery before impact-testing, but was used dead. It was found that 'the intrauterine pressures corresponded closely to those found in the living animal'. Nevertheless, instead of using dead baboons in further tests, the researchers continued to use live animals, and there is no mention of their being anaesthetised during impact. In such trials the baboons sustained hideous injuries. Uterine pressures were sometimes ten times that observed during labour, causing foetal death and rupture of the womb and bladder. (*The Prevention of Highway Injury,* University of Michigan, 1957).

In later research it is made clear that *the impact tests were conducted on fully conscious female baboons.* Pre-impact surgery and attachment to the sled was carried out under anaesthesia — probably for convenience — but then, just before test-impact, 'the animal was allowed to recover from anaesthesia to the point that it responded to stimuli and appeared fully awake (Figure 1)' (*American Journal of Obstetrics and Gynaecology*, 1 May 1968). 'Figure 1' is a photograph of an alert looking baboon strapped to the impact vehicle.

Some baboons who survived one crash were subjected to a second one later in the same day. One mother survived for eighteen hours after impact, another 'died in shock twenty-four hours post-impact.'

Some of the foetuses appeared to die as an effect of 'maternal shock' and were delivered by Caesarian operation after impact.

In September 1973 it was announced that motor manufacturers in Britain, Canada, Germany, Italy, France, Holland and Sweden had joined together to undertake further extensive crash research, using animals. This international project was launched under the auspices of NATO. A spokesman for Ford UK said that all Britain's manufacturers had urged the Government to provide funds (*Observer*, 8 September 1973).

The practice of vivisection began in Europe 2,000 years ago. Barely more than a century ago the habit spread to the American States. Since the Second World War it has spread insidiously across the face of the earth infecting all of Asia and especially Japan. Already it is in Africa (see the *Unesco Courier*, May 1973) and now there is scarcely a country in the world where an animal is safe from the probe or the scalpel.

10. Legislation

The British legislation is not only the most detailed but also the oldest and most tried legislation in this field. A full analysis of its provisions and operation may, therefore, supply lessons applicable internationally.

In the United Kingdom, captive and domestic animals are protected from cruelty by the Protection of Animals Act 1911 and its subsequent amendments. Researchers who wish to experiment upon captive animals avoid prosecution under the Protection of Animals Act 1911 by obtaining special Government (Home Office) licences.

These licences are issued under the Cruelty to Animals Act 1876 which controls experiments upon living vertebrates. Anything done lawfully under this Act is specifically exempted from the Protection of Animals Act 1911 (Section 1 (3)). In practice, *"The Cruelty to Animals Act 1876"* (see Appendix) *allows an experimenter, under certain circumstances, to inflict severe pain upon animals.*

The Act is in two main parts: the first part makes several *humane* restrictions, and the second part counteracts most of these restrictions by providing the experimenter with special *certificates*.

Properly equipped with licence and certificate, an experimenter may inflict severe pain without fear of prosecution.

Under *Certificate A,* an experiment can be performed without anaesthesia. This certificate should state that 'insensibility cannot be produced without necessarily frustrating the object of such experiments' (section 3, Provision 2). Since 1910 approximately ninety percent of all experiments have been performed without anaesthetic under Certificate A.

Certificate B is required 'if experiments are to be performed under anaesthesia but the animal is not killed before anaesthesia has passed off' (Form of Application, Home Office).

Certificate C allows experiments 'to illustrate lectures'.

Certificate E allows experiments on unanaesthetised dogs and cats, and *Certificate EE* allows experimental cats and dogs to recover from anaesthetic.

Certificate F allows experiments upon horses, asses and mules.

It is important to realise that only about 3 per cent of all experiments take place under licence alone. All the rest are performed under Certificate as well as licence.

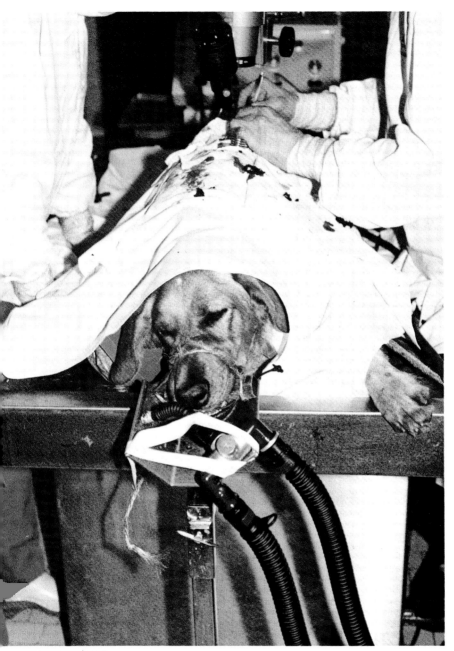

ILLUSTRATION 7.

One of the many dogs used at the Department of Animal Experimentation, Hospital Clinico, Madrid, for research and the acquisition of manual skill.

Photograph by Brian Gunn ©

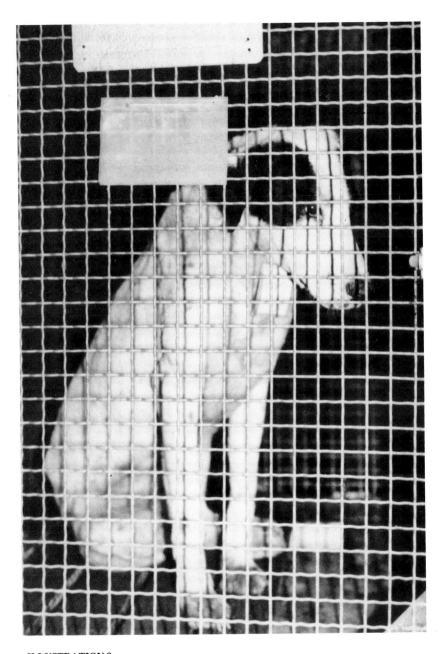

ILLUSTRATION 8.
A stray dog awaiting vivisection at the National University of Mexico. The dog had no run, and its cage was antiquated and rusty.
Photograph by Brian Gunn ©

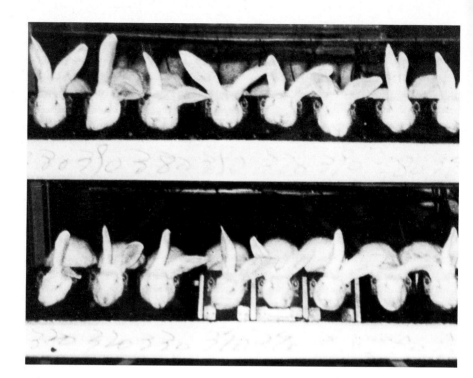

ILLUSTRATION 9.
Rabbits undergoing drug tests. National Institute of Health, Tokyo, Japan.
Photograph by Jon Evans ©

Section 8 empowers 'one of Her Majesty's Principal Secretaries of State' (in practice this appears invariably to have been the Home Secretary) to grant a licence for such period and on such conditions, not inconsistent with the Act, as he thinks fit, and to revoke a licence at his discretion. Section 12 empowers a judge to grant a licence to perform experiments essential for the purposes of criminal justice. (It seems that this only once occurred, in 1885). Section 11 requires an application for a licence to be signed by one or other of the presidents of thirteen specified learned societies (mostly medical) and also by a professor of physiology, medicine, anatomy, surgery, medical jurisprudence or *materia medica,* unless the applicant is himself such a professor.

Section 7 requires that the Secretary of State shall approve and register any place where experiments are performed for class instruction; and empowers him to require the registration of any place where other experiments allowed under the Act are performed.

Section 9 empowers the Secretary of State to 'direct any person performing experiments under this Act from time to time to make such reports to him of the result of such experiments, in such form and with such details as he may require'.

Section 10 requires the Secretary of State to cause all registered places to be visited from time to time by inspectors for the purpose of securing a compliance with the provisions of the Act, and empowers him to appoint inspectors.

Section 2 imposes penalties.

The Act does not bind the Crown. Unless the contrary is expressly stated or necessarily implied, the provisions of all statutes bind neither the Sovereign nor any body or persons acting as servants or agents of the crown. This means that Government bodies such as the Ministry of Defence and the Department of Health and Social Security are not bound by the Act, and so may experiment upon animals without licence and without their experiments being counted in the Home Office returns. The Home Office states that by *"an administrative arrangement"* all Government departments and research councils comply with all the provisions of the Act. This can be doubted in the case of the Ministry of Agriculture, Fisheries and Food.

The Act covers 'the performance on any living animal of an experiment calculated to give pain' (section 3). It does 'not apply in invertebrate animals' (Section 22).

(The Act does not define key words such as 'experiment', 'living' and 'pain'. The interpretation of these words, in practise, is left to the Home Office, and can be variable. With mounting criticism of the enormous numbers of animals being used in research, there may be increasing pressure brought to bear upon the official licensing authorities and the compilers of Statistics to exclude thousands of procedures using animals, on the grounds that such procedures are not defined as experiments or that any suffering they cause is not actually pain.)

Section 8 of the Cruelty to Animals Act 1876 states that there may be attached to any licence 'any conditions which the Secretary of State may think expedient for the purpose of better carrying into effect the objects of this Act, but not inconsistent with the provisions thereof'.

It should be noted that it is not necessary that any conditions be attached to licences. It is left to the discretion of the Secretary of State, who can add or subtract conditions as he sees fit.

The main licensing authority has been the Home Office, and over the years a more or less standard body of conditions has been evolved. The most important of these is Condition 3 which states: 'Unless otherwise provided below, the following conditions are to be observed in all experiments under any Certificate A (whether or not accompanied by a certificate E or F) or under any Certificate B (whether or not accompanied by a certificate EE or F):

(a) If an animal at any time during any of the said experiments is found to be suffering pain which is either severe or is likely to endure, *and if the main result of the experiment has been attained* the animal shall forthwith be painlessly killed (My italics RDR).

(b) If an animal at any time during any of the said experiments is found to be suffering severe pain which is likely to endure, such animal shall forthwith be painlessly killed.

(c) If an animal appears to an Inspector to be suffering considerable pain, and if such Inspector directs such animal to be destroyed, it shall forthwith be painlessly killed.

Conditions *3a, 3b* and *3c* are not at all humane, although at first reading they may appear to be. In fact they provide no real safeguard against suffering whatsoever, and actually condone the infliction of 'severe pain'.

In addition to the Conditions attached to licences, the Home Office issues 'notes for Guidance in Completing Forms of Application Under the Cruelty to Animals Act 1876'. These suggest that various procedures are acceptable without anaesthetic and these include administration of substances, withdrawal of body fluids, variations on diet, exposure to infections, exposure to radiation, electric shock and gases, needle biopsies and implantations (Notes, p.3). These notes also seem to suggest (Note 4, p.6) that provisions are made for experimenters who wish to paralyse an animal without giving it an anaesthetic of sufficient power to prevent pain. Provisions are also made (Note 9 (V), p.8) for a licensee who makes a request 'for amendment to or cancellation of any of the Secretary of States's special conditions on pages 2-4 of the licence'.

The Medicines Act 1968 obliges the manufacturers and sellers of medicinal (and other) substances to operate their business only under licence from the Government (Sections 6, 7 and 8). In issuing licences the licensing authority must take into consideration the safety, efficacy and quality of the products described (Section 19). The Government may direct that any substance deemed to be dangerous comes under the Act (Section 105). When finally implemented this Act repeals the Therapeutic Substances Act 1956 (Schedule 6).

The gradual implementation of this Act has led to a considerable increase in the mandatory testing of substances upon living animals.

So also should the *Health and Safety at Work Act 1974* which provides a general duty of care on the part of the employers. Proposals by the Health and Safety Commission (1977) are that importers and manufacturers of new substances for use at work should provide toxicological information on those substances to include acute and subacute toxicity tests, eye and skin irritancy, carcinogenicity, mutagenicity and teratogenicity.

Comments on the British Law and its Reform (see Appendix B.)

The first thing to emphasise is that the current administration of the 1876 Act seems to pre-suppose that all animal experiments are necessary; that is to say, there is no recent public record of the Home Office refusing a licence on the grounds that the proposed experiment is pointless, badly designed, repetitive or wasteful. The inspector's function has been merely to establish that 'the application is for a class of purpose permitted by the Act'; he is not required to evaluate the potential benefit likely to accrue from it. In other words, the principal loophole in this law, as in all equivalent laws in other countries, is simply that, although painful experiments are technically only allowed if they conform to the Act, *their necessity is rarely, if ever, questioned.* Only a small proportion of experiments can have more than an infinitesimal chance of being necessary in the sense that they will prolong human life; a slightly larger proportion may be called necessary in as much as they will be published and so may perhaps increase human knowledge, however academic and trivial; for the vast bulk of experiments, however, the only necessities are, I am afraid, curiosity, commercial profit and ambition.

It should also be stressed that the scope of the Act is unduly limited; it only covers vertebrate species and it excludes animals used for the production of biological substances such as vaccines, and for those procedures for which it is applicable it has been deemed to operate only from the moment an actual experimental treatment condition begins until experimental observation ends. That is to say, an animal may be kept in a small laboratory cage for months, or years, before and after an experiment without being covered by this Act. Before and after experiment animals are in theory protected by the Protection of Animals Act 1911, but as the Littlewood Report points out (Paragraph 273), 'the practice of excluding them from public view makes this protection of negligible significance'.

Furthermore, many experimental procedures (those not 'calculated to cause pain') also fall outside the scope of the Act. A zoologist or psychologist, such as myself, may confine any number of animals in laboratory cages in order to observe their spontaneous behaviour or their reactions to artificial, but not 'stressful' conditions without being controlled by the present Cruelty to Animals Act, 1876. This one source of possible confusion as far as the official Home Office statistics are concerned. It is left up to the Home Office to decide which applicants for licences are likely to perform experiments 'calculated to cause pain'. In practice the Home Office has defined this widely and included in this definition many procedures which may never have caused any real suffering at all. But as the numbers of experiments continue to rise, and with them the volume of public criticism, those responsible for issuing licences may come under political as well as administrative pressure to start excluding the less pernicious experiments from the licensing system altogether. Such experiments would be then unlicensed and so uncounted in the annual Home Office Returns. The progressive exclusion from licensing of the more humane experiments could lead some people to conclude that there was a real overall reduction in the use of animals in research, when in fact the reverse was true. So this is one way in which *a published reduction in the number of licensed experiments could be made to conceal an increase in the number of animals used.*

Another way in which this could happen lies in the discretion given to the Home Office as to how to define one experiment under the 1876 Act. Once again, in practice, the Home Office has played fair and counted one animal as one experiment. But there is no statutory reason why they should continue to do this. For instance, a scientist when he refers to one experiment he has done, may mean by this an experimental procedure he has applied to five, fifty or five-hundred animals. Each new substance screened by a drug company is tested on about 1,000 animals, but to the toxicologists concerned this could be referred to, quite properly, as a single experiment. So once again, there is opportunity here for the statisticians to conceal real increases in the number of animals used behind decreases in the number of 'licensed experiments' published.

To avoid such dangers it would be desirable for the law to clarify the definitions of procedures to be licensed and to establish firmly what constitutes a single experiment. As a general principle, statistics whose categories are defined at the mere discretion of their compilers, cannot be held to be reliable. The law should clearly and inflexibly lay down how such official statistics are to be constituted

As we have seen, the law brings four-fold pressure on the experimenter on a 'no-yes-no-yes' basis. First, it says, 'no, you must not do anything inhumane'; those are the Restrictions which on the face of it appear excellent. Then there is a 'yes' stage at which these restrictions can be avoided through obtaining various Certificates. The third stage provides for these Certificates to be partially counteracted by certain Conditions which are attached to the licence entirely at the discretion of the Home Office, and then fourthly come the Notes which tip off the licensee on how to avoid being bound by the Conditions. Those who defend the Act as it stands often point to the Conditions, maintaining that these protect the animal from pain, but a close reading of these conditions shows that this is only apparently true, for even if a licensee scrupulously follows the conditions (and if no Inspector is present, which is almost invariably the case) then an animal is only protected from suffering by being painlessly killed if it 'is found to be suffering severe pain which is likely to endure'. Clearly these terms are extremely vague, for even if the intensity of pain or its likelihood of endurance could be quantified no criteria are laid down stating what level of intensity is to be called severe or what duration is to be called endurance. Moreover, condition 3a reads: 'If an animal at any time during any of the said experiments is found to be suffering pain which is either severe or likely to endure, *and if the main result of the experiment has been attained,* the animal shall forthwith be painlessly killed'; that is, by implication the experimenter is allowed to cause enduring pain which is not severe and he is allowed to cause severe pain not likely to endure, so long as the main result of his experiment has not yet been attained. Let me repeat this: *under the British law a licensee can be allowed to cause severe pain (which is not likely to endure) so long as the main result of the experiment has not yet been attained.*

Furthermore, as has been pointed out, these conditions are attached only at the discretion of the Secretary of State and could be legally withdrawn at any time; indeed, each restriction includes the words 'unless otherwise provided', implying that the possibility of exemption from these conditions exists, and Note 9 (v) sent to licensees makes this quite clear. The same comments apply, as I have shown, to the conditions which only allows 'innoculations and simple venesections' without anaesthetic.

What is needed is a sweeping reform introducing meticulously defined legislation that produces real protection for the animals while simplifying situation from the point of view of the experimenter; at the moment the law is so complex that I have met some licensees who totally misunderstand their legal position under the Act.

Two further pieces of legislation seem to be required in order for us to avoid being hypocritical. The first is to prevent the export of laboratory animals to countries where their rights are even less respected. The second is the banning of agreements with other countries whereby experiments prohibited in one country are performed in foreign laboratories.

One of the largest importers of British animals, allegedly, has been Japan. Not only have British dogs been exported there for experiments, but even British race-horses have ended up in Japanese laboratories. One such horse, 'Gold Luck', broke a leg in a race in 1968. On 12 December he was presented to a Tokyo Veterinary Training School for experimental purposes. When seen in 1970 'Gold Luck' was emaciated, with pressure sores on his fetlocks and knees. He had large capped elbows. His coat was engrimed with dung and urine. According to one of the veterinary surgeons he had fallen in his box in the winter of 1969, and had broken his hip. This was untreated, and the horse was lame in his near hind leg as well as in his off fore leg. There was a large ulcer of about three inches in diameter over his hip joint. His hooves were overgrown and splitting. *(Magnet Magazine,* 14 November 1973).

A word should be said about publicity. As the Littlewood Report points out, most animal research is done in the public name and much is done at the public expense. Despite this, there appears to be a remarkable conspiracy of secrecy among experimenters which is actively encouraged by the Home Office. It is as if experimenters had uneasy consciences about their activities. It is customary for laboratory animals to be kept behind locked doors displaying notices such as 'No Unauthorised Person Allowed Beyond This Point'. That is an actual example. Furthermore, it is extremely difficult to obtain permission for the filming of experiments (which for teaching purposes would much reduce the wastage of animals) and it also has been usual for heads of laboratories to ban still photographs. As the Littlewood Committee points out, all this is a misinterpretation of the phohibition against 'any exhibition to the general public' (Section 6 of the Act).

About one fifth of experiments on living vertebrates are performed on behalf of government departments and are financed by public money. The taxpayer has little right of access to laboratories or to detailed information about these experiments. A strong case would seem to exist to allow certain persons, such as Members of Parliament, or officials of the RSPCA or other humane organisations, an absolute right of admission to certain laboratories.

Finally, *it must be questioned whether much of the non-medical research on animals (many examples of which are given in this book) is compatible with Section 3(i) of the 1876 Act as it stands:*

"The experiment must be performed with a view to the advancement by new discovery of physiological knowledge or of knowledge which will be useful for saving or prolonging life or alleviating suffering."

Can the poisoning of animals with non-therapeutic cosmetic products (pp.33-40) or the electrocuting of animals in order to observe effects upon behaviour (pp.52-53) be reconciled with this restriction? Even if the clever use of words may create an apparent reconciliation, can such tests honestly be considered to be compatible with the spirit of the law?

The Home Office Advisory Committee

This was set up (as a non-statutory advisory body) following the Royal Commission of 1906-1912 (see p.142), and its two principal aims appear to have been (a) "to prevent eminent scientists from feeling aggrieved because their own proposed experiments were disallowed by the Home Office on its own unsupported authority" and (b) *"to reassure the public* that proposals for undesirable or cruel experiments would be subject to critical scrutiny". (*Littlewood,* para 455. My italics.)

Throughout its history this has scarcely been an active body and an ex-member, the late Lord Platt, publicly questioned its efficacy. In the House of Lords on 14th May 1975, Lord Platt stated "I was on the Advisory Committee of the Home Office for eleven years and we met only five times and advised on nineteen cases". (*Hansard.*)

In answer to a Parliamentary Question raised by Sir Bernard Braine, M.P. (12th April, 1976) Dr. Shirley Summerskill of the Home Office, revealed that, in the ten years 1966-1975, the Committee met only on seven occasions (3 of these following the public outcries of 1975) and dealt with only 23 cases during this time — a period in which over 52 million licensed experiments were performed in Britain.

How can a Committee, with such a record of inactivity, be able to "reassure the public"?

The reform of this body was the main recommendation of the Memorandum sent to the Home Secretary in 1976 by Lords Houghton, Platt and others (see p.150).

The four main objectives for reformers should be:

(1) The reduction, and finally the total abolition, of those experiments upon animals which do not have a strictly medical purpose.

(2) Official backing for the development of non-sentient alternatives to animal experimentation. One way of setting up an effective system to this end would be to have a central body for the collation and distribution of information about humane techniques; this body would also direct research into the further development of such techniques through a network of units attached to existing research establishments. Furthermore scientists should be obliged to use humane alternatives wherever possible.

(3) All experiments causing suffering should be prohibited. All experimenters should be properly trained in the use of modern analgesic, anaesthetic, tranquillising and euthanasic methods. Pain affects the physiology of the animal anyway, and so is undesirable from the scientific point of view .

(4) The setting up of Government advisory and ethical machinery representing the interests of animal welfare and the general public, as well as those of the scientific community.

Legislation Outside the U.K.

It is staggering that some so-called civilised countries still have no legislation dealing directly with research on animals.

Only Denmark, Eire, West Germany, India, Rhodesia, Holland, Norway, Sweden and some British or ex-British colonial territories appear to have advanced legislation dealing with animal experimentation. As with the U.K., however, none of these countries seems to control the export of animals to other countries for laboratory use.

Norway, Sweden, India, Eire, Holland, West Germany require licensing of laboratories. Italy requires the licensing of experimenters. These same countries, and Denmark also, keep some official record of the experiments being made.

Canada has no federal law at all. The Canadian Council on Animal Care provides limited voluntary control, but dog-pounds in some provinces must hand over strays to laboratories.

In *Australia*, Victoria and Western Australia have detailed legislation but other parts of the country have only general restrictions on cruelty. The public have little right of access to laboratories but ethical committees are now being set-up.

In *Norway*, permission to experiment must be obtained from the Ministry of Social Welfare and wherever possible lower species of animals should be used. Under Act 73 of 1974, licenses are scrutinised by an ethical committee.

In the *Netherlands,* the law of 1st June 1976 enforces the use of lowest possible organisms. An Advisory Committee includes animal welfare representatives.

The *German* law of July 1972 is not a strong one but it has some good features. For example, it covers the accommodation and care of animals, taking into account what is suitable for each species and bearing in mind the animal's natural behaviour and its need for excercise.

This law covers only vertebrates, however. Experimenters do not need governmental approval to perform experiments which are 'already tried or nationally recognised methods and serve the prevention, diagnosis, healing or relief of illnesses, suffering, bodily injury or physical ailments of man or beast, the detection of pregnancy or gestation, or the preparation or testing of serums or vaccines' (Section 8, 6).

Official approval for all other 'operations or treatment which can involve pain, suffering or injury' must, however, be obtained, and will not be given if 'it is shown that the hoped-for results of the experiments could not be achieved by reasonable methods or techniques other than by animal experimentation' (Section 8, 4 1).

Furthermore, 'experiments on vertebrates which are ranked with the higher animals according to zoological classification are only permitted if experiments on lower vertebrates do not suffice the purpose. Warmblooded animals should then only be used if experiments on coldblooded animals do not suffice the purpose' (Section 9, 1 2).

So in these two respects at least, the German law is, in my opinion, better than the British one. *First, it makes it illegal to experiment on an animal when an alternative is available; and secondly, it encourages experimenters, when using animals, to use phylogenetically lower organisms.* (So also does Dutch law).

(To make the use of alternatives obligatory where possible was the essence of Douglas Houghton's unsuccessful attempt to reform the Cruelty to Animals Act in 1973. If he had succeeded, the British law would have caught up with the German one in this respect.)

Another requirement of the new German law which may turn out to reduce the numbers of higher species being used is that it is stipulated that 'on conclusion of an experiment each surviving hard-hoofed and even-toed animal, ape, monkey, lemur, dog, as well as each surviving cat and rabbit is to be presented immediately for examination by a veterinary surgeon. If in the opinion of the veterinary surgeon the continued life of the animal is only possible with suffering, the animal must be painlessly destroyed without delay' (Section 9, 6).

Clearly, having to present these higher species to a veterinary surgeon will lead to increased costs and so may provide an economic incentive against their use.

The *Indian law* (The Prevention of Cruelty to Animals Act 1960 [59 or 1960] Chapter IV) is based on the British 1876 Cruelty to Animals Act and is administered by a special committee which has the right to inspect laboratories and prohibit individuals or institutions from carrying on experiments. The Rules attached to the Act lay down regulations for the maintenance of animals before and after experiments. The format of the Indian law is simpler than that of the British Law, and does away with the latter's confusing triple system of Restrictions, Certificates and Conditions.

The *Danish law* of 31 March 1953 allows only Chiefs of State Institutes or trained persons who have obtained permission from the Royal Veterinary School or from the medical faculty of a recognised university to perform experiments on living vertebrates. Research can only take place in premises approved by these authorities. Exemption from the use of anaesthesia requires a special permit (Section 1 ii). As with the new German law, experimenters are constrained to use animals as 'primitive' as possible (Section 5). This law also requires that on recovery from anaesthesia an animal must be properly cared for and *treated with pain-killing drugs as required*. This latter stipulation is in advance of anything laid down by British law.

The *Swedish law* is a statute of 1944 (No. 771/1944) amended in 1966 (451 and 59) and 1972 (629). The experimenter must be a physician, vet, dentist, pharmacist or approved by the Veterinary Board. Restrictions regarding anaesthetics are similar to the British 1876 Act, which requires full details of the proposed research and its purpose, the location of the laboratory and its facilities. Records are required to be kept in considerable detail. A purchase-record must show the date of purchase, the number and species of animals bought, and in the case of dogs and cats, their sex, colouring and breed must be recorded and also the name of the dealer and his stated source of the animals. A research-record must show the date of the experiment, its purpose, the number and species of animals used, details of the anaesthetic, or if no anaesthetic is used then the reasons for this must be given with a description of other analgesic safeguards employed. The disposal of the animal after the experiment must be stated. All these details must be returned annually to the Department of Health. The law insists that, *wherever possible, alternatives to warm-blooded animals be used in educational demonstrations* and it stipulates that where possible *pain-killing or sedative drugs* should be used in animals which are unanaesthetised.

It should be noted that under the *Dutch, Danish and Swedish* systems, there is increasingly active supervision by central and local ethical committees which include animal welfare representation. The *Swedish and Danish* systems have further strengths, for example, the requirement that records must be kept showing the sources from which animals are obtained and the methods of euthanasia employed.

In 1979 the National Institute of Health issued new guidelines, the acceptance of which has a requirement for eligibility for NIH finding. These guidelines require that experimenters use *in vitro* techniques, computers and statistics means to reduce the use of animals.

In the *U.S.A.* the Act of 24 August 1966 was extensively amended by the Animal Welfare Act of 1970. This Act requires that each research facility shall submit on or before 1 February of each calendar year a report showing acceptable standards of care, the location of the facility, the number and types of animals used and the number of experiments conducted involving necessary pain or distress to the animals without the use of appropriate anaesthetic, analgesic or tranquillising drugs. *Two provisos, however, render this law practically meaningless;*

(1) Routine procedures such as injections do not need to be reported at all (Sec. 2, 28).

(2) 'Nothing in these rules, regulations, or standards shall affect or interfere with the design, outlines, guidelines, or performances of actual research or experimentation by a research facility as determined by such research facility' (Sec 2, 100).

In general, the controls operating under American law are less effective than those applied in some other countries. However, unlike the U.K. law, the 1970 Act does cover animals used in the production of vaccines and, furthermore, all laboratory reports are accessible to the American public under the Freedom of Information Act.

On 17 May 1979 the Swedish Government set up regional ethical committees to which all severe experiments must be submitted. These committees are composed equally of experimenters, animal care personnel and animal welfarists. The Government also pledged financial backing for the development of alternative techniques and decreed that most laboratory species should be purpose-bred rather than obtained from random sources or the wild.

There are signs that the whole area of animal welfare is becoming increasingly the concern of politicians. Moves are afoot in the U.S.A., Australia, U.K., Denmark, Holland, Finland, Czechoslovakia, and other countries, to improve the legal controls on animal experimentation. The Council of Europe has recently shown interest in this field and it is possible that before long great reforms will have taken place.

11. Examples of Invalidity

For many years the validity of applying results obtained from one species to another was questioned. Indeed, the old idea that human beings were entirely different to the other animals sustained the belief that research on animals could not produce results that would be clinically useful in the human case. Such extreme views are a thing of the past. Nevertheless there has been a revival in recent years of an awareness of species-differences.

The gross physiological similarities between all mammal species were sufficient validity for much of the early research into the basic principles of physiology and anatomy. But in the second half of the twentieth century, biological research has become more precise, more subtle and more concerned with detailed and intricate bio-chemical phenomena. This has led to the discovery of a number of differences between species which although in a sense of a minor sort, have major implications in practice.

Take for example the differences between species in the effectiveness of drugs. Dr. G. C. Brander of Beecham Research Laboratories illustrates this with the results of tests using a 'Product X'. Its effectiveness varied as follows:

Species	mg/kg of body-weight
Man	1
Sheep	10
Rabbit	200
Monkey	15.2

The variation is so great that there seems hardly any point in testing a substance on rabbits when the 'target-animal' is man (Association of Veterinarians in Industry, Symposium 'Animal Tests,' London, 1973).

With well-known differences in the effectiveness of drugs even between human beings of different races, it is hardly surprising that marked differences are found between animals of different species.

Another field in which there is marked inter-species variation is in the effects of radiation. It has been found that *responses to radiation vary by as much as a thousand times between one species and another* (*Nature*, 16 October 1973). Yet this finding does not reduce the amount of radiation-research being done on animals, but seems to have the opposite effect.

Major differences are now known to exist between the gut flora of different mammalian species, and nowhere do such inter-species differences raise greater problems than in the field of toxicology. We have seen how drugs, weedkillers, insecticides, food-additives and other industrial substances are force-fed to animals in order to establish their poisonous potentials (pp.29, 36, 41). Such toxicity testing is supposed to act as an effective safety-net to prevent poisonous products being released on the market, but its effectiveness has been questioned.

As one American toxicologist, Dr. Leo Friedman, writes:

The most uncertain aspect of safety evaluation is the relevance of animal data to human beings. Many examples can be cited regarding differences in species susceptibility. For example, only certain strains of rabbits, mice and rats have been shown to give teratogenic responses (deformations of the foetus) to thalidomide; in each case the doses required were considerably above those that resulted in teratogenesis in humans. On the other hand, substances with a considerable history of human use, such as epinephrine (i.e. adrenaline, as prescribed for asthma, and other conditions), salicylates (eg aspirin), certain antibiotics, and insulin are all well-known to cause malformations in laboratory animals but have not been shown to be teratogenic in man. (Leo Friedman, *Toxicology and Applied Pharmacology*, 16, 1969, p.498. My comments in parentheses).

So, in the classic case of thalidomide, normal animal screening methods are inadequate, for the simple reason that human beings react to thalidomide in a different way to most laboratory animals (see also pp.160-161 and 32 and Appendix C.)

In fact the differences in thalidomide susceptibility between species are very considerable. The dose producing changes in the human foetus is about 1 mg/kg per day, whereas the rabbit requires a dose thirty times this size before any ill-effects occur, and in the ordinary laboratory Wistar rat, no malformations to the foetus have been noted at any dosage levels whatever *(B. Med. Bulletin,* Vol. 26, No. 3, 1970). (The first thalidomide deformations were noted in 1961. After twelve years of the most intensive research upon animals, scientists were still unable to say how exactly thalidomide produces its terrible effects. —Phillip Knightley in the *Sunday Times,* 9 September 1973).

Dr. Friedman makes the point that 'We know that administration of *enough* of any substance in high enough dosage will produce some adverse effect'. So why, one may ask, is it so important to produce such adverse effects in animals with every one of the thousands of new chemical products being manufactured annually for the consumer market.

To reduce the invalidity inherent in toxicity testing enormous numbers of animals are sometimes used. Dr. Friedman illustrates the toxicologists' dilemma with the example — 'when an effect occurs in only one percent of the test animals, the effect will be entirely missed thirty-seven percent of the time if 100 animals are used in each test'.

There are five basic stages in the action of a chemical upon any living organism: absorption, distribution, excretion, metabolism and mechanism of action. There are, in other words, five stages at which the action of a substance may differ from one species to another; there are five points at which discrepancies can occur and accumulate. Even if these differences between species are very small, if they are repeated at every stage, then the total discrepancy can be a large one.

For the mathematically minded, Dr. David P. Rall gives as an example a substance which acts very similarly at each stage in two different species; it correlates 0.90 at each of the five stages. But small differences of this sort built up into a total overall drug response correlation between the two species of only 0.58 *(Environmental Research,* 2, 1969).

Dr. Rall gives as his opinion that 'a significant point in comparing laboratory animals and human data is, I am convinced, the undeniable fact that the clinical acumen of a skilled physician caring for an ill patient surpasses that of the most careful toxicologist studying a variety of animals in a toxicology study'.

In practice, of the five stages of absorption, distribution, excretion, metabolism and mechanism of action, it is the metabolism stage at which most variation between the species seems to occur. *(B. Med. Bulletin,* Vol. 26, No. 3, 1970). This can lead to remarkable effects giving one species protection against one substance while making it uniquely vulnerable to another. An illustration is the rat which is not teratogenically affected by thalidomide but is killed by a chemical called 7, 12 dimethylbenz (a) anthracene; this strange manifestation of acute toxicity does not appear in mice, hamsters, guinea-pigs or rabbits when they are dosed with the same substance.

Another example is a food-flavouring substance called coumarin. In rats it causes liver damage but it has been found that the route of coumarin metabolism in the rat is quite different from that in man. As a toxicologist points out: 'There appears, therefore, to be little justification for assessing the safety of coumarin as a food-additive in terms of the results of toxicity tests in rats.'

Yet another example is a well-known food-additive called butylated hydroxytoluene. In this case too, its metabolism in the rat has been shown to be quite different from that in man.

Years ago it was found that Digitalis shows different hypertensive effects in different species, and it has been alleged that the mis-application of animal research data to humans caused a clinical setback in the use of this drug (M. B. Bayly, *Clinical Medical Discoveries*, London, NAVS, 1961, p. 54).

It has already been noted (p.68) that in the case of the pain-killing drugs remarkable differences between the species can occur. Aspirin is extremely poisonous to some species and causes deformations in the foetuses of rats. Another classic example is that of morphine, which sedates most species but provokes 'maniacal excitement in the cat and mouse' (Gay, *op.cit.*, p. 70).

Perhaps the most disturbing inter-species difference of all is that penicillin is extremely poisonous to guinea-pigs, and it has been claimed that if it had been routinely screened on laboratory animals as all new drugs are today, then penicillin would never have reached the stage of a clinical trial, and its benefits would never have been enjoyed *(Clinical Pharmacol. Therap.*, 7, 250, 1966). Fleming's actual *discovery* of penicillin owed nothing to animal experimentation and he mentions *testing* penicillin only on a rabbit, a mouse and (probably one) man. Nevertheless, he claimed it was "non-toxic to animals in enormous doses". Partly on account of this claim, Florey decided to investigate penicillin further; fortunately, he chose to test it on mice, rats and cats, and not guinea-pigs. (*The Lancet,* August 24 1940). Man tolerates 1,000 mg., whereas guinea-pigs tolerate only 5 mg/kg/day of Penicillin G.

Dr. G. E. Somers gives as his opinion:

'If penicillin were to have been judged by its toxicity on guinea-pigs it might never have been used on man.' (Somers, *Quantitative Methods in Human Pharmacology and Therapeutics,* Oxford Pergamon Press, 1959).

Aspirin, streptomycin and chlorpromazine are all sensitising drugs which can produce allergic reactions in laboratory animals; if these three substances had been abandoned for this reason then three more valuable therapeutics would have been lost, (G. E. Paget (ed.) *Methods in Toxicology,* Oxford, Blackwell, 1970, p. 201). Chloroform, also, is especially toxic to male mice.

Not only, however, are there differences between species, there are also marked differences between laboratories, and these too are a source of invalidation. One study analysed results from twenty-five different laboratories in Britain, Canada and the USA in the testing of irritants upon rabbits' eyes and found 'extreme variation between laboratories'.

Some laboratories consistently recorded unusually severe scores and some consistently reported non-irritating scores. Certain materials were rated as the most irritating tested by some laboratories, and contrariwise, as the least irritating by others *(Toxicology and Applied Pharmacology*, 19, 276, 1971).

Another technical objection to toxicity testing on animals is that it cannot reproduce the effects that a chemical may produce over the course of a human life-time, nor can it necessarily pick up delayed long-term effects. As Dr. Friedman puts it:

'We still must learn how, with reliability, to associate effects, i.e. disease, seen in the human population with causes that have acted early in the life of an individual and are now gone, or which have been acting subtly by slow accumulation of a deleterious factor or effect' *(Ibid.)*.

A further point which throws doubt on the validity of animal research is that the animals cannot describe their experiences, including aches and pains which so often occur as the side-effects of drugs. For this reason, Dr. G. R. Boyes advocates the use of human volunteers — 'not only do trials on human subjects make it possible to assess the value of a drug in the prevention or treatment of disease, and also to determine the effective dose range, but they reveal side-effects such as nausea, headache, giddiness, skin rashes and other symptoms which cannot be determined from animal experiments' *(Pharmaceutical Journal*, 5 September 1953, p.167).

In the opinion of Dr. M. B. Bayly, the careful clinical study of humans is superior to experiments on animals as a method of advancing medical science. In his book he quotes scores of examples of the most important medical advances which were the results of sensitive and intelligent clinical observation, and in some cases, post-mortem analysis. When dealing with the diseases of the liver, Dr. Bayly quotes Dr. K. Blond as writing: 'Many years of my clinical studies were dedicated to experimental work on liver diseases . . . I based my conclusions on animal experiments. But there is not one conclusion arrived at in these experiments which I could not have perceived by correct interpretation of clinical observations.'

A paper in the *Lancet* (15 April 1972) throws doubt upon the usefulness of animals in the search for cancer cures:

Most of the (anti-cancer) agents now in use were first tested in tumour-bearing animals, particularly rodents with transplanted tumours. Clearly, however, this method has its limitations. As in human beings, there is a great variability in the response of different tumour lines to different agents. Since *no animal tumour is closely related to a cancer in human beings,* an agent which is active in the laboratory may well prove to be useless clinically. Clinical trials should always cover as many types of cancer as possible, otherwise potentially useful drugs may be lost.

A comment in the *British Medical Journal* for 28 October 1972 put the matter just as clearly when referring to cancer research on mice and rats — "it is difficult to see how experiments on strains of animals so exceedingly liable to develop tumours of these various kinds can throw useful light on the carcinogenicity of any compound for man".

Why then, with all this evidence against the validity of using animals for drug and toxicity testing (and for cancer research), are not more attempts made to develop valid alternatives?

Highly sensitive analytical techniques such as gas-liquid chromatography are available and have already made the determination of metabolic pathways easier, as has also the technique of labelling compounds with radioactive isotopes. It ought to be possible to develop such techniques so that they can be used safely in the human volunteer. Only then will the pit-falls of inter-species variability be avoided. All scientists, and toxicologists in particular, must finally agree with Alexander Pope that in most instances 'the proper study of mankind is man'.

It should never be forgotten that thalidomide was extensively tested upon animals (See Appendix C: Thalidomide does not produce its teratogenic effects in many ordinary laboratory species) and its dangers were not discovered, and that had penicillin been fully screened on animals, it might never have been used on men.

In 1976, it was revealed that I.C.I., the manufacturers of the heart drug Eraldin, had withdrawn the drug from the market the previous year following reports that some 500 patients had suffered eye-damage and other serious side effects. (*Daily Telegraph*, July 12, 1976). A spokesman for the manufacturers was reported as saying that seven years of testing, at the cost of nearly £1 million, had produced no side-effects on animals. However, the "dry-eye syndrome" which causes severe and chronic pain in humans (and probably animals also) is not easily detectable in subjects which cannot complain.

The far-from-perfect validity of animal experiments is quite evident.

12. Alternatives: An Outline

Over the years and often as a by-product of animal research, a number of techniques have been discovered which form alternatives to the use of living animals (see Dr. T. Hegarty, *Animals, Men and Morals,* London, Gollancz, 1971, p. 83).

Many of these techniques are more valid and cheaper than the use of animals. Research animals are, according to the Medical Research Council, both 'costly and inconvenient'. So-called safety-testing on animals has become a ritual to mitigate the dangers of legal liability for the manufacturers of new consumer products. Lawyers must find alternative rituals.

Like all men, scientists tend to be conservative. Moreover, the volume of technical and scientific information being put out daily is very great; there are reputedly over 6,000 medical journals in existence in the world and many thousands more in allied fields. In consequence scientists find it increasingly difficult to keep themselves up to date. This has meant that the alternative techniques to animals are not always being adopted or developed as rapidly as they might be.

In England, several organisations have been prominent in promoting alternatives; for example, the National Anti-Vivisection Society, 51 Harley Street, London, W1N 1DD, and the Fund for the Replacement of Animals in Medical Experiments (FRAME), 5b The Poultry, Bank Place, Nottingham. Both bodies advocate the better dissemination of information about alternatives and have urged the British Government to channel research funds into their further development. In Scotland, the Scottish Society for the Prevention of Vivisection, 10 Queensferry Street, Edinburgh, had advocated a similar policy. In the USA the United Action for Animals Inc, 509 Fifth Avenue, New York, NY10017, has promoted an interest in the subject, and in West Germany, the Salem-Forschung. (See *Bibliography of Selected Tissue Culture Experiments with regard to Replacing Animal Experiments* which contains some 2,691 entries in English. Published by Salem-Forschung (Dr. M—L Baasch) D8000 Munchen 70, Impeerstrasse 38, W. Germany).

There follows a brief and necessarily sketchy outline of some existing alternatives. Those seeking more technical information should contact NAVS, FRAME and Salem-Forschung and read their respective publications or those of the Lawson Tait Fund, the Humane Research Trust, the Dr. Hadwen Trust or other similar bodies.

Dummies

Several *crash test dummies* have been made in the USA and approved by the American Motor Vehicles Safety Standards Committee.

At Indiana University, a detailed model of the human head has been developed in order to simulate brain-damage caused in crashes *(R. Soc. Health Group News*, No. 45, May 1969).

In the UK, Ogle Design Ltd. have developed a dummy as required by the Motor Industry Research Association. This dummy is reported to give reliable results which correlate closely with the behaviour of a human body under impact (Searle and Haslegrave, *MIRA Bulletin* No. 5, 1969 and No. 5, 1970). This dummy is designed to have shoulders, pelvis and ribs which closely simulate the human skeleton.

At Wolfsburg in West Germany, the Volkswagen company have built their own dummies fitted with complex electronic equipment. Although expensive (about £8,000 each) these dummies can be used repeatedly in simulated car-crash tests. Dummies have been successfully used by the British Standards Institute in the testing of headrests in simulated motor accidents (*Drive*, Summer 1973, London, Automobile Association).

Several teaching dummies have also been developed. These are for the teaching of biology, nursing and medicine.

A sophisticated robot patient named 'Sim One' has been built by the University of California. This model can cough, blink, breath, vomit and 'die' as required. An even more complex computerised model named 'Sim One A' will bleed and show simulated reflex movements and autonomic activity (*Journal of the American Medical Association*, Vol. 208, 21 April 1969). Dr. George Sweeney of the Department of Medical Science, McMaster University, Hamilton, Ontario with Dr. C. J. Dickinson of St. Bartholomew's Hospital, London, has developed four computer simulation models to simulate circulatory, gas-exchange, renal, and pharmokinetic systems. In Sweeney's opinion these models are, for teaching purposes, superior to using animals, and running costs are low.

Less sophisticated dummies are already in use for the teaching of anatomy and biology in schools. These can take the place of the dissection of animals. Plastic and 'dissectable' models of animals are now available and with more support from school teachers no doubt will be further improved (see *Animals' Defender*, NAVS, March-April, 1973, p. 50).

Mathematical Models

These have now been developed for the study of the functioning of most organs and biological systems. They can be used for teaching, clinical diagnosis and pure research.

At the University of Pittsburgh computer simulation techniques are taught to medical students, and simulation experiments are performed on the absorption and metabolism of drugs.

A wave-form generator has been built to simulate various neurological phenomena and models to simulate fatigue, accommodation and neuromuscular phenomena were planned (Broughton and Lewis in *Lab. Pract.*,20,947,) as long ago as 1972.

The simulations of heart block and cardio-vascular defects have been described. (Bohn and Krovetz in *Simulation,* 10,117 March 1970).

Mathematical models can predict the efficacy of drugs and suggest ways of increasing therapeutic benefits. (Garrett et al., *Int. Z. Clin. Pharmic.,* 1, 1967).

It is important not to exaggerate the usefulness of such techniques as they exist today,but it is likely that there is room for a great deal of further development in the application of computer technology to the fields of diagnosis, treatment, research and education.

Tissue-Cultures

Tissue culture is the cultivation of living cells outside the organism. This is done by placing the cells in a nutritional medium. To put it very simply, pieces of living flesh can be grown and multiplied in the test-tube.

In 1885 Wilhelm Roux kept alive portions of bird embryos for several days in warm saline solutions. In 1898 human skin was cultured in amniotic fluid (L. E. Mawdsley-Thomas in *Progress Without Pain*, NAVS, 1973).

During the present century, slowly but surely, the various practical problems in growing cells have been overcome. Today there are two main categories of tissue-culture:

(a) *Organ cultures* in which small pieces of tissue are cultured so as to retain the function of the organ from which they are removed.

In the opinion of some biologists, organ cultures, to an even greater extent than cell cultures, have considerable potential for future development.

(b) *Cell cultures* in which dispersed cells are cultured in a medium allowing continuous growth. These can be sub-cultivated and can produce vast quantities of cells over the course of many years.

Cell-cultures can be from normal healthy cells or from tumourous cells.

One of the principal advantages over the use of animals is that it is possible to culture *human* cells, and these can be given by a living donor who need suffer no ill-effects from losing a few cells. The second major advantage of tissue culture techniques is that it is possible eventually to breed pure cells uncontaminated by hidden viruses. But when using animals, especially those trapped in the wild or bred under ordinary conditions, the possibility of contamination always remains present.

Such tissue cultures are already used in very many fields of study (A. N. Worden, 'Tissue Culture' in Boyland and Golding (Eds.), *Modern Trends in Toxicology,* London, Butterworth, 1973).

Here are some of the uses:

Teratology

The tendency of some substances, like thalidomide, to cause deformations of the foetus is all too well known. Exactly how this happens is not understood, and there are marked differences between animal species in their vulnerability. Cultures of human embryo cells are allowing scientists to study such processes under better control (Lash and Saxen in *Nature,* 232, 1971).

Toxicology

It is now well known that different species of animals show marked differences in their sensitivity to the poisonous effects of chemical products (see pp. 40-43). To some extent this can be overcome by testing on human cells cultures and this has been done for drugs, pesticides, tobacco extracts and other substances (Dawson, *Cellular Pharmacology,* Charles Thomas, 1972).

The skin-irritant properties of cosmetics or medicaments can similarly be tested using human skin techniques (Livingood and Hu Ann, *op.cit.,* see p.39)

Physiology

Culture of pancreatic tissue has allowed the study of an important peptide. Brain cell cultures have been used to determine the influence of hormones and drugs on development processes.

Vaccines

Cell cultures are widely used for the production and testing of safer vaccines. Most viral vaccines are now produced in cultures, whereas a few years ago they were cultivated in living animals. In 1973 it was claimed that ninety per cent of all vaccines manufactured in the USSR were produced in tissue-cultures. The new rabies vaccine is grown in human diploid-cell culture, and is considered safer than that obtained from living animals.

The first vaccine produced in a cell culture was the polio-myelitis vaccine.

One of the best cultures is WI-38 established in 1964 by Professor L. Hayflick at the Wistar Institute at Philadelphia. This is a clean and stable human diploid cell strain developed from embryonic lung tissue. Cultures of WI-38 have been used to grow vaccines against polio and

German measles. Stocks of WI-38 are distributed all over the world by the MRC, National Institute for Medical Research, Holly Hill, London, NW3 on behalf of the World Health Organisation.

A vaccine against German measles (Almevax, made by Burroughs Wellcome) was the first released for general sale in Britain which had been cultured in human cells.

A major problem in the production of vaccines in animals was that the vaccine might contain 'sleeping viruses'. Millions of people have been injected with a monkey-derived polio-vaccine subsequently found to be contaminated with a tumour virus designated SV40. Although cell cultures may also contain viruses, the advantage of them over animals is that a small number of cultures can be exhaustively screened over a number of years and when proved to be virus-free they can be industrially proliferated and kept alive indefinitely. Furthermore, cultures can be stored in deep freeze. As the late Professor S. T. Aygün said, 'it is possible to prepare enough vaccine to vaccinate the whole world from one original cell' (in *Progress without Pain,* p.39).

Viruses can be deliberately grown in cultures and anti-vival drugs can then be tested (*R. Soc. Health Group News,* 65, 1972).

Cancerology

Most cancer research continues to be done on animals, but this is unsatisfactory because each species has its own different form of cancer (p.58)

Human cancer cells can, however, be cultured and are in increasing use (Mitchell *et al., Lancet,* 7759, 995, 1972). Aygün has demonstrated that foetal cells can destroy colonies of cancer cells (*op.cit.*) and there are now *in vitro* studies of the regulation of endogenous tumour-virus in formation and the molecular biology of human cells (Walker, *Lancet,* 7765, 1379, 1972).

Cultures of diseased cells provide good material for the study of these diseases.

Leuchtenberger and Leuchtenberger have developed techniques for testing the effects of cigarette smoke in kidney tissue and embryonic lung organ cultures. (*Expl. Cell Res.* 62, 161, 1970)

The Study of Metabolic Inhibitors

Professor K. R. Rees has studied the anti-metabolite aflatoxin, in human cancer cell (HeLa cells) and monkey kidney cell cultures.
He writes:

'Thus, tissue cells in culture with their high rates of protein and nucleic acid synthesis coupled with the ease with which one may manipulate them to study the synthesis and breakdown of precursor molecules provided us with a system to obtain these results with aflatoxin

B₁. These analyses could not have been readily made in whole animals and I believe demonstrate the versatility of tissue cells in culture for the use of the investigations into the mode of action of anti-metabolites' (*Progress Without Pain*, p. 60).

Tissue Banks

The following organisations now commercially produce tissue: Flow Laboratories, Heatherhouse Road, Irvine, Scotland, UK. Foetal Tissue Bank, Royal Marsden Hospital, Chelsea, London, UK. Microbiological Association, Bethesda, Maryland 20014, USA. Associated Biomedic Systems Inc. 872 Main Street, Buffalo, NY, USA. Huntingdon Research Centre, Huntingdon, PE18 6ES, UK.

Lower Organisms

Water moulds and ochromonas have been used in the screening of anti-cancer agents (Volz and Beneke in *Mycol. Appl.* 30, 97, 1966).
Luminous bacteria have been used in the investigation of anaesthetics and the study of drug action (White and Dundas, *Nature*, 226, 456, 1970. Halsey and Smith, *Nature*, 227, 1363, 1970). *Eggs* can sometimes be used for culturing procedures. *Plants* have been used to study the effects of radiation and the effects on man have been extrapolated from these studies (*Nature*, 245, 460, 1973).

Radioactive Isotope Techniques

It is possible to 'label' chemical compounds with minute quantities of radioactive material so as to record and measure their action in the living organism.

Such techniques are now used in the diagnosis and treatment of diseases, the measurement of organ function and the investigation of immunity.

The development of improved equipment opens up prospects of the use of such techniques for the study of the metabolism of many different substances (Barnaby and Smith in *J. Scient. Instrum.*, 44, 499, 1967. Quimby et al., *Radio active nuclides in medicine and biology*, Lea and Febiger, 1970).

These procedures can be safely performed directly on the human body, thus obviating the need to extrapolate from animals.

Gas Chromatography / Mass Spectrometry

The application of these techniques to biological research is relatively new. Gas chromatography is a method of separating a mixture of substances. Mass spectrometry is a means of identifying substances. Used in conjunction, they now make possible the detection of minute quantities of substances in their journey through the body. In this way the action of new drugs, cosmetics, food-dyes and so on can be observed in the *human* body in such infinitesimal dosages that toxic effects can be noted well before they become dangerous (*Drug Research Report,* 11 (32), 6, 1968). There is a growing feasibility of combining human tissue-culture screening techniques with the testing of chemicals at low and safe levels in man to produce an effective and valid method of toxicity-testing, and such steps have been recommended as being sometimes better and safer than the use of animals by Nobel Prizewinner Professor U.S. Von Euler of the Kavolinska Institute, Stockholm.

The overwhelming technical advantage of most of the methods outlined is that they help avoid the dangers of extrapolating from animals to men.

Tissue cultures allow the study not just of animal tissue but also of *human* cells, both healthy and diseased ones, and more precise tools of study (such as gas chromatography, mass spectrometry and radionuclide techniques) allow the safe and direct study of the action of substances in the *human* body.

The use of animals is usually expensive and often unreliable. By 1972 the Medical Research Council could admit to 'the clear advantages of economy, convenience and accuracy afforded by tested alternative methods'. (Letter to a Member of Parliament.)

In 1975 a consulting firm, Foster D. Snell Inc., judged that testing cost would range from $15,000 to $800,000 per product. In an article by Dr. R. Lewin (*New Scientist* vol. 69, pp. 168-169) the cost of a carcinogen test for a single chemical in a single species at a single exposure level, was put at $100,000 over the course of 3 years. Whereas the Ames Test (a pre-screening "test tube" technique using bacteria to measure the mutagenic capacity of test substances) should cost, exclusive of overheads, in the region of only $100 to $300 for each compound, and takes only three days. (Ames, B.N. et al., *Mutation Research,* 31. 1975) (RSPCA Research. 1977 prices).

The costs of alternative materials can be very much cheaper than animals. Flow Laboratories Ltd., for example, can supply a 16 x 125 mm test tube of primary human cell culture for only 45 pence, and a 120 cc flask of culture for £17.50 (1975 prices). Some tissues are, however, available from hospitals or the U.K. Medical Research Council (MRC-5) for which only handling charges are made (RSPCA Research).

What is now needed is an organised drive to develop these alternatives further and to ensure that they are used wherever possible. As observed, Governments spend many millions on research annually — it surely would make economic sense to spend a small proportion of this sum on the development of these cheaper methods.

In 1976, I.C.I scientists reported some important evidence to show that several cheap and humane procedures constitute an accurate method of screening substances for carcinogenicity. (Purchase et. al., "Evaluation of six short term tests for detecting organic chemical carcinogens and recommendations for their use", *Nature*, vol. 264. Dec. 16th 1976). They concluded that their results "clearly establish that the Ames Test and the Cell Transformation Assay are both able to detect a high percentage of a wide range of carcinogens while also generating an acceptably low level of false positives". In plain words, the safety of products (i.e. concerning carcinogenicity) can be tested by using humane test-tube methods.

In 1978, the late Professor D. H. Smyth published the results of his survey of humane alternatives, carried out for the Research Defence Society (*Alternatives to Animal Experiments,* Scolar Press, 1978). He widened his definition of "alternatives" to cover "experiments on ani...als not causing pain or distress". Smyth called for a body to be set up to collate reliable information on the subject. Industry and government should spend money on investigating the literature, particularly with regard to toxicity testing, and projects should be funded to find an alternative to the Draize test, and to encourage the development of Immunoassay which Smyth described as "one potentially very useful alternative".

In 1979 a workshop was held in Montreal under the auspices of the Canadian Society for Prevention of Cruelty to Animals which published its findings the following year (*Report of a Workshop on Alternatives for the use of Laboratory Animals in Bio-medical Research and Testing:* CSPCA.). This workshop reviewed the field of *in vitro* methods, concluded that many offered great potential and urged Governments and research organisations to devote more funds towards the development and validation of these techniques.

While it would be wise not to exaggerate the applicability of non-sentient alternative techniques as they exist at the present time, it cannot be denied that the twentieth century has seen many instances of the rapid development of technologies from small beginnings. Within a life-time Man has learned to fly and has reached the Moon. In the matter of alternatives to laboratory animals we are at the beginning, but the potential is surely there — all that is needed is the political, commercial, legal or moral incentive. If scientists cannot mend their morals then the laws may have to provide that final impetus to *oblige* experimenters to develop humane methods — necessity has, after all, so often found itself pregnant with invention.

13. The Campaign for Reform

Two Frenchmen, one born just before the Revolution and the other just after, seem to have carried some of the cold-blooded ruthlessness of those years into their laboratories. In the name of Liberty the scaffold in the Place de la Concorde had been drenched in blood, now in the name of science the laboratory work-bench became the altar upon which creatures suffered and were sacrificed.

François Magendie (1783-1855) was professor of medicine at the Collège de France and was succeeded in the chair by his pupil Claude Bernard (1813-78).

Magendie was, according to Bernard, the founder of experimental physiology. He was, however, an experimenter in the hit-and-miss sense of the word and entirely lacked the modern concern for precision and the control of variables. John Elliotson, afterwards professor of medicine at the University of London, attended some of Magendie's demonstrations in Paris and was appalled at the clumsy savagery he witnessed — 'Dr. Magendie, who cut living animals here and there with no definite object, but just to see what would happen'.

Magendie seems to have used enormous quantities of animal subjects including some old Army horses which had survived Waterloo. His fellow vivisector at the Académie Francaise, Marie-Jean-Pierre Flourens records that 'Magendie sacrificed four thousand dogs to prove that Sir Charles Bell was correct in the distinction he drew between the sensory and motor nerves; but later he sacrficed four thousand more to prove that Bell was wrong. I have also made experiments on this, vivisecting a large number of dogs, and I have demonstrated that the first opinion is the only true one' (H. Blatin, *Nos Cruautés,* 1867, pp. 201-2).

There exists an eye-witness account of one of Magendie's demonstrations, recorded by Dr. Latour:

> Magendie, alas! performed experiments in public, and sadly too often at the Collége de France. I remember once, amongst other instances, the case of a poor dog, the roots of whose spinal nerves he was about to expose. Twice did the dog, all bloody and mutilated, escape from his implacable knife; and twice did I see him put his forepaws around Magendie's neck and lick his face. I confess — laugh vivisectors if you please — that I could not bear this sight *(B.M.J.* 22 August 1863, p.215).

There is no doubt that Magendie's callousness was outstanding even for the age he lived in, and shocked some of his contemporary physiologists. John Elliotson wrote: 'In one of his barbarous experiments, which, I am ashamed to say I witnessed, he began by coolly cutting out a large round piece from the back of a beautiful little puppy as he would from an apple-dumpling.'

All of Magendie's experiments and nearly all of those carried out by his successors, including Claude Bernard, were of course entirely without any form of anaesthesia or analgesia. Moreover, each of these experiments and demonstrations continued for some time and the agonies of the subjects must have been not only intense but also prolonged. We know from Claude Bernard that dogs were cut open in preparation 'an hour or more' before the actual demonstrations took place. We also know that they were not destroyed immediately afterwards, but if still alive were available for further operations by students.

Bernard's famous description of science is an ironic example of a scientist's starry-eyed idealism:

'If I were to look for a simile that would express my feelings about biological science, I should say that it was a superb *salon* resplendently lit, into which one may only enter by passing through a long and horrible kitchen' *('une longue et affreuse cuisine')* (*Ibid*, vol. 1, p. 35).

Such purple passages were a speciality of Bernard, the failed playwright. His self-congratulatory writings resound grandly with words such as 'glory' and 'honour'. But these fine words ring hollow when one contemplates the screams of the thousands of animals slowly put to death in Bernard's blood-soaked laboratory — 'his long and horrible kitchen'.

If Bernard had ever had any feelings of compassion they were soon dispelled:

'The physiologist is not an ordinary man: he is a scientist, possessed and absorbed by the scientific idea that he pursues. He doesn't hear the cries of the animals, he does not see their flowing blood, he sees nothing but his idea, and is aware of nothing but organisms which conceal from him the problems he is wishing to resolve.'

Dr. George Hoggan worked under Bernard and he subsequently wrote in his famous letter to the *Morning Post,* 2 February 1875:

We sacrificed daily from one to three dogs, besides rabbits and other animals, and after four years' experience I am of the opinion that not one of those experiments on animals was justified or necessary. The idea of the good of humanity was simply out of the question, and would be laughed at, the great aim being to keep up with, or get ahead of, one's contemporaries in science, even at the price of an incalculable amount of torture needlessly and iniquitously inflicted on the poor animals . . . I think the saddest sight I ever witnessed was when the dogs were brought up from the cellar to the laboratory . . . they seemed seized with horror as soon as they smelt the air of the place, divining, apparently, their approaching fate. They would make friendly advances to each of the three or four persons present, and as far as eyes, ears and tail could make a mute appeal for mercy eloquent, they tried it in vain.

Just as Bernard had succeeded his master Magendie, so Bernard was succeeded by his pupil Paul Bert (died 1886) who carried on the tradition of ruthless vivisection which is so much a character of the physiology studied and taught in nineteenth-century Paris. Paul Bert's contributions to science were less noteworthy than his predecessor's. But he earns an infamous niche in the history of vivisection and its opposition, thanks again to the witness of Dr. George Hoggan before the first Royal Commission on Vivisection set up in 1875. Dr. Hoggan read a translation of Paul Bert's experiment on a curarised dog and he commented as follows:

In this experiment a dog was first rendered helpless and incapable of any movement, even of breathing, which function was performed by a machine blowing through its windpipe. All this time, however, 'its intelligence, its sensitiveness, and its will, remained intact; a condition accompanied by the most atrocious sufferings that the imagination of man can conceive' *vide* Claude Bernard in *Revue des Deux Mondes,* 1 September 1864, pp. 173, 182, 183, etc. In this condition the side of the face, the side of the neck, the side of the foreleg, the interior of the belly, and the hip, were dissected out, in order to lay bare respectively the sciatic, the splanchnics, the median, the pneumo-gastric and sympathetic, and the infra-orbital nerves. These were excited by electricity for ten consecutive hours; during which time the animal must have suffered unutterable torment, unrelieved even by a cry. The crowning discovery made, to which the experimenter calls special attention, being that, at times, when thus tortured, *it urinated!* The inquisitors then left for their homes, leaving the tortured victim alone with the clanking engine working upon it, till death came in the silence of the night, and set the sufferer free.

In the cross-examination that followed, Dr. Hoggan confirmed that in his opinion the dog described in this experiment was in excruciating pain throughout the ten hours of the operation and afterwards until it died.

The other outstanding Frenchman whose work helped to earn France the reputation of being the country of vivisection was Louis Pasteur (1822-1895), whose life-long advocacy of germ-theory led him to experiment upon many animals, infecting them with various fevers, anthrax and rabies. Pasteur was not the only nineteenth century scientist who also performed experiments upon humans which would, by today's standards, be considered unethical.

Pasteur became famous for the development of his anti-rabies vaccine and although this continued for years to be controversial, he was created President of the Académie Francaise in 1882 and died covered in honours.

It was these four Frenchmen, Francois Magendie, Claude Bernard, Paul Bert and Louis Pasteur, who succeeded during the first two-thirds of the last century in turning vivisection into an everyday practice. Before their time, research upon animals had been on a small-scale and usually conducted furtively in order to avoid social ostracism. These men of the Paris School transformed what had been an occasional method, often reluctantly resorted to, into a scientific fashion and a ritual part of the training for medical and veterinary students throughout Europe and America.

In 1882, the Victoria Street Society estimated that in France there were 85 vivisectors, in Britain 45, Italy 51, Germany 29, Netherlands 8, Switzerland 6, Austria 7, Sweden 6, Denmark 3, Norway 1. But as the practice grew, so did the feeling against it.

It is probable that opposition to cruelty is as old as cruelty itself. Compassion may be an instinct as strong as any other.

It is known that Cicero and especially Plutarch both opposed the torturing of animals for sport or in the mistaken belief that this practice improved the taste of meat —'let us kill an animal', writes Plutarch, 'but let us do it with sorrow and pity and not abusing or torturing it as many nowadays are wont to do'.

Classical philosophers had taken differing views of the relationship of men to beasts. Aristotle (384-322 BC) had placed man at the head of the *Scala Natura,* above other animals intellectually, but in other respects similar to them. The majority opinion, and that taken by Heraclitus *(circa* 540-475 BC) and then the Stoics was, however, that men and gods were entirely separated from all other living creatures by their capacity for reason. Man alone among mortals was rational; the irrational brute creation behaved automatically and without reflection.

Heraclitus added the opinion that only gods and men possess souls, and with minor variations this arrogant view has persisted in Europe for many centuries. Reason, or perhaps consciousness, became associated with the concepts of 'free-will' and 'soul'.

From Assisi in the early thirteenth century, St. Francis (1182-1226) had preached mercy to all God's creation. He stands out as one of the first who vigorously administered to the human poor and sick and naturally extended this compassion beyond the boundaries of his own kind to all suffering creatures. But during the Christian era there were too few who championed the rights of animals. Other religions were more merciful. (Shortly before his death, Cardinal Heenan, the head of the Roman Catholic Church in Britain, wrote to the author a letter which anticipated a more enlightened view — "You will be glad to know that I had already decided to put the question of cruelty to animals on the agenda for the annual meeting of bishops after Easter. Like yourself I feel that the Church has not done enough to draw attention to the unnecessary suffering inflicted on animals. Wishing every success to your efforts and with renewed thanks." 11th March, 1975.)

St. Thomas Aquinas (1225-74) reinforced the view that men were a breed apart from beasts. Men alone had immortal souls, could choose to do good or evil and attain everlasting life. Animals had no souls, no freedom of will and so no salvation. This became the Catholic orthodoxy and one which was reiterated forcefully in the seventeenth century by the theologically-conservative Descartes.

The whole Judeo-Christian tradition gave to man a very special place in the universe. God had created him in his own image and explicitly given him 'dominion' over the animals. They were there principally or solely for his use as food, as clothing, as beasts of burden and as sacrificial victims.

So we can see that ever since European thought has been recorded, there have been, broadly speaking, two opposing ways of regarding other animals — either as fellow-sufferers or as mere objects for use. The first view stresses the similarities between men and animals, whereas the second emphasises real or imagined differences. There is little doubt, however, that the more compassionate tradition has, for centuries, been subordinated to the anthropocentrism of Aquinas. This is hardly surprising, for given that man always has been selfish, conceited and longing for immortality, he has had a strong interest in accepting the latter point of view; it has justified his rapaciousness, flattered his vanity, and held out hopes of a future-life.

It is interesting that man does not seem to be the only animal to show compassion. Elephants, dolphins and whales have been observed attempting to help their stricken comrades. Dogs and other pets have even shown concern for humans in distress. Most mammals will rush to the defence of their children or their mate. In other words, it can be argued that compassionate or protective behaviour can be spontaneous, unlearned, and not uniquely human.

Some modern churchmen have espoused the more compassionate view. In Britain, the Rev. Basil Wrighton, Dr. Edward Carpenter, the Rev. Andrew Linzey, and Dom Ambrose Agius, are outstanding examples, and the Catholic Study Circle for Animal Welfare, through its energetic organisers, has proved to be one of the 'quickest-off-the mark' animal welfare organisations in the United Kingdom and internationally. In their journal *The Ark* (August 1976) Ambrose Agius, in reference to modern cruelties including vivisection, has written —

"Much trouble and concern arises from the fact that Science has been elevated into something so worshipful that no law or consideration may be allowed to stand in its way or in the way by which it acquires the knowledge on which it depends."

In whatever way it operates, it is certain that the view which emphasises that man is different from the animals helps man to dismiss any qualms or scruples he might naturally feel about exploiting them. With the aid of anthropocentric arguments the natural sympathies are gradually suppressed. Man elevates himself above other creatures largely to justify his abuse of them.

In the fifteenth century, Leonardo da Vinci is reputed to have become a vegetarian for humane reasons (E. McCurdy, *The Mind of Leonardo da Vinci,* London, Cape, 1932, p. 78) and to have been disgusted by mankind's cruelty to animals — 'truly man is indeed king of beasts for his brutality surpasses all others'.

In the eighteenth century there are some definite glimmerings of light. In the *Spectator* (No. 120) in 1711, the British essayist and politician, Joseph Addison (1672-1719), condemns a barbarous test of animal love: 'A person who was well skilled in dissection opened a bitch, and as she lay in most exquisite tortures offered her one of her young puppies, which she immediately fell a-licking; and for the time seemed insensible to her own pain; on the removal she kept her eye fixed on it and began a wailing sort of cry which seemed to proceed rather from the loss of her young one than the sense of her own torment.'

Two years later, in the *Guardian,* 21 May 1713, Alexander Pope argued that 'the more entirely the inferior creation is submitted to our power, the more answerable we should seem for our mismanagement of it'. Pope queried the vivisectors' right to cut up dogs: 'How do we know that we have a right to kill creatures that we are so little above as dogs, for our curiosity, or even for some use of us?' He urged that children should be taught to be compassionate but that 'one of the first pleasures we allow them is the licence of inflicting pain upon poor animals; almost as soon as we are sensible what life is ourselves we make it our sport to take it from other creatures. I cannot but believe a very good use might be made of the fancy which children have for birds and insects.'

In 1750 William Hogarth published 'The Four Stages of Cruelty', a series of prints depicting not only cruelty to animals but murder (in part, the outcome of the former), and the dissection of a human corpse. Hogarth wrote of these prints: 'The four stages of cruelty were done in the hopes of preventing in some degree that cruel treatment of poor Animals which makes the streets of London more disagreeable to the human mind than anything whatever, the very describing of which gives pain' (Quoted in Lawrence Gowing, *Hogarth,* London, Tate Gallery, 1971).

When told that his prints were much admired Hogarth replied — 'It gratifies me highly, and there is no part of my works of which I am so proud, and in which I feel so happy because I believe the publication of them has checked the diabolical spirit of barbarity, which, I am sorry to say was once so prevalent in this country' (*Ibid.,* p. 69).

In his *Apology for Painters* he writes 'I had rather, if cruelty has been prevented by the four prints, be maker of them than of the Raphael cartoons'.

Although as late as 1772 an Oxfordshire vicar, James Grainger, could be denounced by his congregation for preaching against cruelty to animals, it is clear that among intellectuals at least, the topic was being discussed.

It is not recorded exactly how or where the redoubtable Dr. Samuel Johnson encountered vivisection. Doubtless he heard the subject being debated over the coffee-tables by the intelligentsia of eighteenth-century London. Accounts of anatomical studies were, even then, being published and circulated among the small and brilliant band of scholars amongst whom Johnson's wit and wisdom were so highly prized. He wrote in *The Idler* (No. 17, 5 August) in 1758:

> Among the inferior professors of medical knowledge is a race of wretches whose lives are only varied by varieties of cruelty; whose favourite amusement is to nail dogs to tables and open them alive . . . and if the knowledge of physiology has been somewhat increased, he surely buys knowledge dear who learns the use of the lacteals at the expense of his own humanity. It is time that a universal resentment should arise against those horrid operations, which tend to harden the heart and make the physicians more dreadful than the gout or the stone.

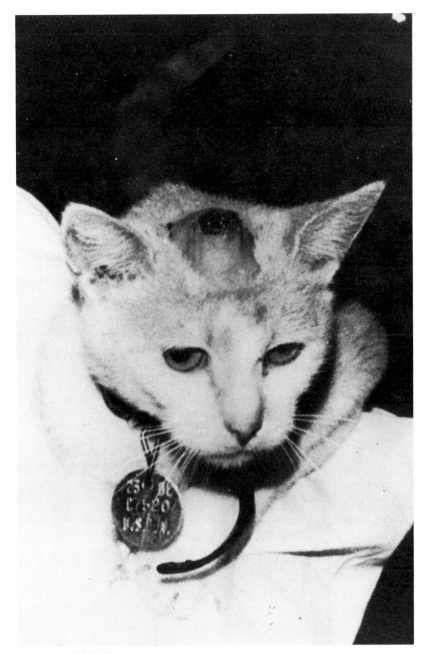

ILLUSTRATION 10.
This cat, incarcerated in a small cage, has an electrode implanted in its brain. By means of a battery the researcher can create an electrical discharge in order to ascertain at what anatomical point an electrical contact will stimulate fear, aggression and other behaviours. (New York).
Photograph by Jon Evans ©

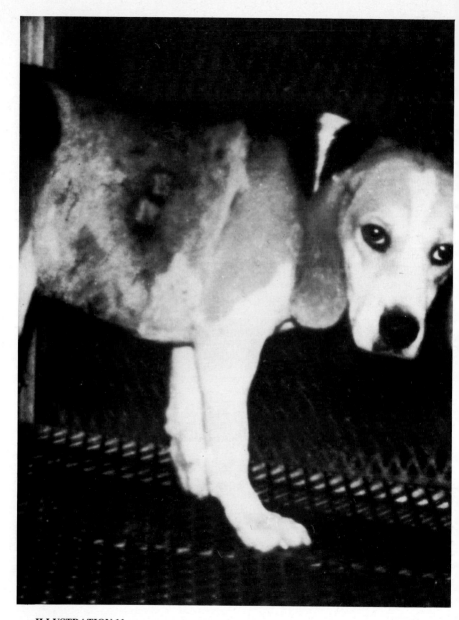

ILLUSTRATION 11.

Picture was taken in a New York University training hospital. The protuberances on the shaved right hand side of the dogs' body (Tumour implants) were produced as a result of an experiment from which the animal will die. The beagle cowered when approached and showed signs of great stress. The sides of the cage and floor are constructed from steel mesh. Nothing was included for the animal's comfort, not even a blanket.

Photograph by Jon Evans ©

Johnson recalled the scene in Shakespeare's *Cymbeline* (Act 1, Scene V) in which the Queen orders poisons ('Movers of a languishing death') and announces her intention of testing their effects upon animals, whereupon she is rebuked by Cornelius: 'Your Highness shall from this practice but make hard your heart.'

In France the answer to Descartes came from no less than Voltaire himself (*Dictionnaire Philosophique, 'Bêtes', 1864*):

"How pitiful, and what poverty of mind, to have said that the animals are machines deprived of understanding and feeling . . ."

Poets such as Blake, Thomson, Cowper and Burns voiced their sense of one-ness with Nature and passionately defended animals. Cowper wrote in 1785: 'I would not enter on my list of friends (though graced with polished manners and fine sense yet wanting sensibility) the man who needlessly sets foot on a worm.'

By the end of the century some of the most politically influential writers were alluding to the question of cruelty to animals. Jeremy Bentham wrote in his *Introduction to the Principles of Morals and Legislation* (1789): 'The day may come when the rest of the animal creation may acquire those rights which never could have been witheld from them but by the hand of tyranny.' In arguing the discrepancy between themselves and brute creation men tended to point to their own rationality or their use of language — 'But a full grown horse or dog is beyond comparison a more rational, as well as a more conversable animal, than an infant of a day, of a week, or even a month old. But suppose the case were otherwise, what would it avail? The question is not, can they *reason*? Nor, can they *talk*? but can they *suffer?*' In his *Principles of Penal Law,* Bentham predicts 'Why should the law refuse its protection to any sensitive being? The time will come when humanity will extend its mantle over everything which breathes . . .'

In 1796, gentleman farmer, John Lawrence, reiterated this idea of Bentham's (*Philosophical and Practical Treatise on Horses*): 'No human government, I believe, has ever recognised the *jus animalum* which surely ought to form a part of the jurisprudence of every system founded on the principles of justice and humanity . . . I therefore propose that the Rights of Beasts be formally acknowledged by the State and that a law be framed upon that principle to guard and protect them from acts of flagrant and wanton cruelty, whether committed by their owners or others.' Other notable examples include Humphry Primatt's *"A Dissertation on the Duty of Mercy and Sin of Cruelty to Brute Animals"* of 1776.

In England this gradually increasing sense of injustice towards animals finally reached the level of the legislature when, in the House of

Commons on 3 April 1800, Sir William Pulteney sought leave to bring in a Bill to prohibit the practice of bull-baiting. He described the practice as 'cruel and inhuman'. The motion was seconded by Sir Rowland Hill and a Mr. Baker, in support, added that cock-fighting should also be abolished. Richard Sheridan added his spirited and witty endorsement.

The Bill failed to become law on account of opposition from the Secretary for War, William Windham, who asked why bull-baiting had suddenly become so alarming. It was no new practice and it served to cultivate the qualities of certain species of dogs. Was there not also cruelty in hunting? Besides, bull-baiting was one of the few pleasures enjoyed by the poor.

The Bill against bull-baiting was eventually re-introduced by a Mr. Dent, and although he was supported by William Wilberforce — 'wretched indeed must be the condition of the people of England if their whole happiness consisted in the practice of such barbarity' — the Bill was again defeated.

On 9 June, 1809, Lord Erskine managed to pass through the Lords a Bill designed to prevent wanton cruelty to animals. This stipulated that any person maliciously wounding or cruelly beating any horse, mare, ass, ox, sheep or pig, should be found guilty of a mis-demeanour and sentenced, on first offence, to not less than one week and not more than one month in prison. Sir Charles Bunbury, with William Wilberforce once more in support, then tried to pass the Bill through the Commons but it was defeated by thirty-seven votes to twenty-seven, much to the disgust of the *Gentlemen's Magazine* whose editorial stated: 'Surely few subjects in the whole compass of moral discussion can be greater than the unnecessary cruelty of man to animals which administer to his pleasure, his consolation and to the very support of his life!'

Not for another twenty-three years did any attempted reforms on behalf of animals finally become law.

In 1821 Erskine joined forces with the redoubtable Richard Martin, MP, and on 18 May, Martin printed his Bill proposing 'that if any person or persons having the charge, care or custody of any horse, cow, ox, heifer, steer, sheep or other cattle, the property of any other person or persons, shall wantonly beat, abuse or ill-treat any such animal, such individuals shall be brought before a Justice of the Peace or other magistrate'. It was amended in Committee to include mares, geldings, mules and asses, and then triumphantly passed through the Commons on 1 June, by forty-eight votes to sixteen. In the Lords, however, Lord Erskine had less luck and the Bill was defeated.

Undismayed, Martin and Erskine reintroduced their Bill the

following year, and it passed through the Commons in May and then through the Lords.

On 22 July 1822, it finally received the Royal Assent and became the first law anywhere in the world passed by a majority of elected legislators which dealt primarily with cruelty to animals. *

The same year as the passing into law of Richard Martin's Act, a priest of the Church of England, the Reverend Arthur Broome, had abortively tried to start an organisation to prevent cruelty to animals. Two years later, in 1824, he tried again and on the 16 June the first meeting of what was to become the Royal Society for the Prevention of Cruelty to Animals (RSPCA) was held at Old Slaughter's Coffee House, St. Martin's Lane, London. Those present included Richard Martin, and the two great opponents of black slavery, Thomas Foxwell Buxton and William Wilberforce. The Society immediately got down to business and during its first year of existence it brought nearly 150 prosecutions under Martin's Act and published several pamphlets, one of which criticised the practice of 'dissecting animals alive'. The Society was formed to pursue legislation, prosecution and education.

By 1848 and echoing Bentham half a century earlier, that other great political philosopher John Stuart Mill wrote (*The Principles of Political Economy*):

> The reasons for legal intervention in favour of children apply not less strongly to the case of those unfortunate slaves and victims of the most brutal part of mankind — the lower animals. It is by the grossest misunderstanding of the principle of liberty that the infliction of exemplary punishment on ruffianism practised towards these defenceless creatures has been treated as a meddling by government in things beyond its province; an interference with domestic life. The domestic life of domestic tyrants is one of the things which it is the most imperative on the law to interfere with.

A decade later, in 1859, Charles Darwin published *The Origin of*

---

* Emily S. Leavitt has produced evidence that in 1641, the Puritans of the Massachusetts Bay Colony published "The Body of Liberties". Liberty 92 and 93 prohibit cruelty to any domestic animal—"no man shall exercise any Tirranny or Crueltie towards any brute Creature which are usuallie kept for man's use". These statutes were compiled by Nathaniel Ward (c. 1578-1652) who was born in Haverhill, England. I am indebted to Christine Stevens for drawing my attention to this information contained in *Animals and their Legal Rights*. (See Bibliography.) Even earlier, however, in 1635 there had been a British legal reference to "The cruelty used to the beasts": 10 and 11 Charles 1, Dublin.

Species, a bombshell which blasted man's arrogant assumption that he was in a superior and separate category to all other animals. Once man had reluctantly accepted that he was just one species among many others, and that despite his greater intelligence he was biologically similar to other creatures and indeed shared kinship with them, then one of his main pretexts for abusing them was blown to pieces. He could no longer justify an entirely separate moral status for himself. If there was biological kinship then why not a moral kinship also?

In 1865, Henry Bergh, at one time Consul at the American Legation in St. Petersburg, visited John Colam, Secretary of the RSPCA. The following year Bergh proceeded to found the American SPCA in New York and became, with Norman Angell of Boston, a prime mover behind the animal welfare legislation in America. Bergh went on to help form the New York Society for the Prevention of Cruelty to Children and through Bergh's association with the RSPCA this idea came back to London. Colam and the RSPCA Committee did all they could to set up a similar organisation in Britain, and in 1884 the National Society for the Prevention of Cruelty to Children was formed. The Reverend Benjamin Waugh, usually regarded as the founder of the NSPCC, acknowledged his debt to the RSPCA when he said 'Your society, the RSPCA, has given birth to a kindred institution whose object is the protection of defenceless children'.

This connection between these two Societies is yet another example of the association of humanity to animals with humanity to humans.

During the latter part of the century several acts were passed to protect wild birds and in 1911 the Protection of Animals Act was passed which consolidated much of the previous legislation.

It seems that for the first half-century or so of organised animal welfare, the reformers were primarily concerned with those forms of cruelty that were openly visible in the streets, markets and cock-pits around them.

Only in about 1860 does experimentation upon live animals begin to come into the forefront of the picture, with reports appearing in British newspapers concerning the terrible experiments conducted in the veterinary school at Alfort near Paris.

Among those members of the British public who felt revulsion at the Alfort revelations was the writer and welfare-worker, Frances Power Cobbe, destined to become one of the most doughty and effective anti-vivisectionists of all time. Her reaction was to write an essay entitled *The Rights of Man and the Claims of Brutes* in the 1863 November issue of *Fraser's Magazine.*

In the same month that this essay was published Frances Cobbe travelled to Florence and there happened to hear of the activities of a vivisector called Professor Schiff. In particular she was impressed by the evidence of Dr. Appleton from Harvard University who 'told us that he himself had gone over Professor Schiff's laboratory, and had seen dogs, pigeons, and other animals in a frightfully mangled and suffering state'.

Those in the neighbourhood of Schiff's laboratory had begun to make complaints about the disturbance caused by the 'cries and moans of the victims'. Frances Cobbe decided to organise this body of feeling and composed a petition addressed to the professor urging him to spare his animals as much pain as possible. This Memorial was signed by 783 people, including many eminent and aristocratic Florentines. Among the English signatures was that of Walter Savage Landor, who, according to Frances Cobbe, 'added some words so violent that I was obliged to suppress them'. This document constitutes some of the first evidence of organised opposition to the cruelty of vivisection.

In the ensuing decade, the issue remained before the public largely owing to the reforming efforts of men like Richard Hutton, editor of the *Spectator* (See *Anti-vivisection and Medical Science in Victorian Society* by Richard D. French, Princeton, 1975). Then in 1874 the habits of French vivisectors once again caused an outcry in Britain. At a Congress of the British Medical Association held at Norwich, Eugene Magnan, an erstwhile pupil of Magendie, shocked some of his British medical colleagues by publicly operating on some dogs in order to demonstrate the effects of alcohol and absinthe which he injected into them. Among those who left the meeting in protest were Samuel Haughton of Trinity College, Dublin and the President of the Royal College of Surgeons in Ireland, T. Jolliffe Tufnell, the latter angrily cutting loose one of Magnan's dogs before he departed.

The RSPCA instituted proceedings against Magnan, and Sir William Fergusson, called as a witness, described the 'ghastly scene', the 'groaning of the dogs' and 'their writhing agony'.

This action by the RSPCA was under the only Act for the protection of animals which existed at that time, the amended form of Richard Martin's Act of 1822. Magnan swiftly withdrew to his own country and the prosecution failed. Nevertheless, these events caused some important publicity and it was in the ensuing public agitation that Frances Cobbe was once more drawn into the issue and drew up another Memorial expressing general concern over the increasing number of experiments being performed in Britain, which was signed by seventy-eight medical practitioners, by many peers and bishops, and by such illustrious men as Cardinal Manning, Lord Shaftesbury, Thomas Carlyle, Alfred Lord

Tennyson, Robert Browning* and John Ruskin (who in 1884 was to resign his chair at Oxford in protest against the establishment of a vivisection laboratory at the university — 'in flaming wrath and sick at heart' (see pp.137-8).

It was while Frances Cobbe was working on her Memorial, in June 1874, that the President of the RSPCA, Dudley Ryder (Earl of Harrowby), received a letter from Queen Victoria's Private Secretary expressing the Queen's concern over the treatment of animals in science and enclosing a donation to the Society's funds. If the Society needed any encouragement, this was it. It is impossible to say how influential this letter must have been, but the knowledge that the Queen was especially interested in the subject must, to some extent, have permeated through the clubs and smoking-rooms of the Victorian professorial and ruling-classes. After nearly forty years on the throne, Queen Victoria was a deeply respected figure and it would be rash to underestimate the force of her influence upon respectable opinion.

At this juncture, a momentous letter appeared in the *Morning Post* of 1 February 1875, written by Dr. George Hoggan, the English physician who had for four months been an assistant to Claude Bernard (see pp.123-4). In it, Hoggan described and condemned the practices of the Paris School. Cobbe forthwith joined forces with Hoggan, and with support from various Parliamentarians and others, among them Robert Lowe (Home Secretary, 1873-3), Sir Frederick Elliot and Lord Chief Justice Coleridge, and with the approval of the Government, a Bill for Reguiating the Practice of Vivisection was introduced into the House of Lords by Lord Henniker on 4 May 1875.

On the 12th of the same month, however, a much weaker Bill was read in the House of Commons by Dr. Playfair, probably at the instigation of those determined to maintain the almost complete freedom of vivisectors.

As a result of these two Bills seeming contradictory, the Government decided to appoint a Royal Commission of Enquiry in June 1875 under the chairmanship of Edward Cardwell, which duly reported that a total ban on vivisection would be unreasonable, since such research sometimes mitigates human suffering and furthermore it would result in scientists emigrating to Europe, so producing no real benefit to animals. Nevertheless they found a case for State licensing for both original research and for teaching demonstrations.

---

*   On 28 December, 1874 Browning had written to Miss Cobbe thus: 'This I know, I would rather submit to the worst of deaths, so far as pain goes, than have a single dog or cat tortured on the pretence of sparing me a twinge or two.'

With the publication of this Report, on 8 January 1876, both sides of the argument set about drafting new Bills.

Frances Cobbe and George Hoggan meanwhile had founded the first anti-vivisection society, (originally named the Victoria Street Society) with the Earl of Shaftesbury as its eminent Vice-President.

Shaftesbury several times chaired the meetings of the Victoria Street Society and he led an important delegation from the Society to see the Home Secretary on 20 March 1876. This deputation, which included Cardinal Manning, was favourably received and invited to submit suggestions for legislation. These were swiftly drafted into a Bill which was introduced into the Lords by the Colonial Secretary, the Earl of Caernarvon, and received its second reading on 22 May.

The Bill received support from the RSPCA and had a good reception in the press. It proposed to implement all the Recommendations of the Royal Commission except the appeal against the revocation of licence. Unfortunately, Lord Caernarvon was, at this juncture, called away from London to attend his mother who was ill and died on the 26 May.

Taking advantage of the temporary interruption of Lord Caernarvon's political life, the General Medical Council, armed with the signatures of some 3,000 members of the medical profession, hurriedly made representations to the Home Secretary, Richard Assheton Cross, petitioning him to modify the Bill. Apparently this 'active malignity of the scientific men', as Shaftesbury subsequently described it in a letter to Frances Cobbe, persuaded the hard-pressed Home Secretary to give way and he introduced a new Bill on 10 August which received the Royal Assent only five days later.

So was born the Cruelty to Animals Act of 1876, which made provision for nearly all its ostensibly humane restrictions to be annulled by means of special certificates issued to experimenters by the Home Office.

The reformers felt they had been cheated by this Act, and with some cause, for it allowed the vivisector, now protected against prosecution by licence and certificate, to continue to inflict severe pain upon his experimental animals.

Nevertheless in the years immediately following the passing of the 1876 Act, Home Secretaries frequently refused applications for licences on the grounds either that they involved too much pain or were for dubious purposes. William Harcourt wrote to one applicant — "the Secretary of State does not wish it to be taken for granted that the discovery of every new poison is to be the reason for instituting a set of vivisection experiments . . .". (French, p. 188) — a comment highly pertinent to the modern situation.

Although no further reforms were to be achieved, the opposition to vivisection continued, not least in the old universities.

At Oxford, Charles Dodgson (Lewis Carroll) had joined in the controversy in 1875 by publishing an attack on vivisection in the *Fortnightly Review* which he entitled 'Some Popular Fallacies about Vivisection'. His biographer, S. D. Collingwood *(The Life and Letters of Lewis Carroll,* London, Fisher Unwin, 1898, pp. 165-71) records that:

> Mr. Dodgson had a peculiar horror of vivisection. I was once walking in Oxford with him when a certain well-known professor passed us. 'I am afraid that man vivisects' he said, in his gravest tone. Every year he used to get a friend to recommend him a list of suitable charities to which he should subscribe. Once the name of some Lost Dogs' Home appeared in this list. Before Mr. Dodgson sent his guinea he wrote to the secretary to ask whether the manager of the Home was in the habit of sending dogs that had to be killed to physiological laboratories for vivisection. The answer was in the negative, so the institution got the cheque. He did not, however, advocate the total abolition of vivisection — what reasonable man could — but he would have liked to see it much more carefully restricted by law.

We will never know for certain who was the well-known professor that Dodgson passed in an Oxford street, but it may have been Dr. John Burdon-Sanderson who had been appointed Waynflete Professor of Physiology at Oxford in 1882. Dr. Burdon-Sanderson had been a staunch supporter of vivisection when it had been opposed in the Convocation of the University of London in 1874. Furthermore he was the editor of the *Handbook of the Physiological Laboratory* which had been discussed in some detail by the First Royal Commission in 1875. It was admitted that the book contained descriptions of painful experiments and John Colam, secretary of the RSPCA, had pointed out that the preface stated that the book was aimed at instructing beginners in research. The Chairman of the Commission (Viscount Cardwell) had read from it descriptions of experiments on animals paralysed with curare —'Rabbits . . . die before the end of the first day. Dogs live longer; often two to three days.' Burdon-Sanderson had been forced to confess to the Commission that the use of anaesthetics whenever possible 'ought to have been stated much more distinctly at the beginning of his book'.

Dr. Burdon-Sanderson's appointment of 1882 began a series of protests and arguments among Oxford scholars. The two outstanding supporters of the new professor were Sir Henry Acland (Regius Professor of Medicine from 1857 till 1894), and the Very Reverend Henry George Liddell (the Dean of Christ Church). The three leading opponents of vivisection at Oxford became Charles Dodgson, John Ruskin and Canon Liddon (the Bishop of Oxford).

Charles Dodgson (1832-98) as Lewis Carroll was not only the famous author of *Alice through the Looking Glass* and *Alice in Wonderland,* he was also a respected mathematician and it is ostensibly on logical grounds that he attacked vivisection. Collingwood records a letter he received from Dodgson dated 29 December 1891. In it, Dodgson criticises an attempt by Collingwood to justify 'killing animals for the purpose of scientific recreations', not by commenting on his conclusions but by shooting holes in the logic of the 'poor little essay' (Collingwood, *op.cit.*, p. 299)

At some earlier date Charles Dodgson had written to the *Pall Mall Gazette* upon the subject: 'Is the anatomist, who can contemplate unmoved the agonies he is inflicting for no higher purpose than to gratify a scientific curiosity, or to illustrate some well-established truth, a being higher or lower in the scale of humanity, than the ignorant boor whose very soul would sicken at the horrid sight?'.

The interest provoked by the subject in Oxford can, perhaps, be gauged by the attendance at successive Convocations where grants were to be voted for the new professor. In 1883 the vivisectors were eighty-eight against the anti-vivisectors' eighty-five. In 1884 it was 188 to 147.

Three years after Burdon-Sanderson had got his chair the arguments about granting funds for vivisection reached a climax. Dodgson notes in his diary for 10 March 1885:

'A great Convocation assembled in the theatre, about a proposed grant for physiology, opposed by many (I was one) who wished restrictions to be enacted as to the practice of vivisection for research. Liddon made an excellent speech against the grant, but it was carried by 412 to 244.'

This result precipitated the most dramatic of all the anti-vivisection protests at Oxford; John Ruskin's resignation as Professor of Art.

Ruskin first had been appointed Slade Professor of Art at Oxford University in 1869. On 9 December 1884, Bishop Liddon held a meeting of the new Oxford branch of the Victoria Street Society at which Professor Ruskin attacked vivisection. For him, he declared, the object of education was the teaching of gentleness to the students — 'their noblest efforts and energies should be set upon protecting the weak and informing the ignorant of things which might lead them to happiness, peace and light, and above all other things the relation existing between them and the lower creation in this life'.

On 17 March 1885, a week after the University had voted further funds for the setting up and equipping of the physiology laboratory,

Ruskin wrote in his diary: 'A lovely and delightful day, yesterday, getting Lilias' and Goodwin's sketches and doing quantities of good work myself, but put in a passion by Acland's speech on vivisection after dinner and slept ill, waking at two to think whether I would resign professorship on it' (Evans and Whitehouse (Eds.) *The Diaries of John Ruskin*, Oxford, Oxford University Press, 1959, p. 1102).

Five days later, on 22 March, the melancholic Ruskin resigned his chair. In his opinion vivisection experiments 'were all carried on in defiance of what had hitherto been held to be compassion and pity and of the great link which bound together the whole creation from its Maker to the lowest creature'.

It has been alleged that the Vice-Chancellor declined to read his letter of resignation to Convocation as Ruskin had asked him to do, that the *University Gazette* refused to publish the reasons for his resignation and that the rumour was deliberately put about that Ruskin had resigned on account of age (Annabel Williams-Ellis, *The Tragedy of John Ruskin*, pp. 378-9).

It is clear that feelings were running high at Oxford and the professors were at each others' throats over the vivisection issue. Two weeks after his resignation, in his diary for 5 April 1885, Ruskin refers to the two main supporters of vivisection — 'tired and angered fiercely yesterday by Acland and Liddell'.

The principal antagonists had known each other for years and most had connections with the same college — Christ Church — where Dean Liddell's influence had for so long been paramount. Charles Dodgson's friendship with Liddell's rather rebellious daughter Alice had been the inspiration for his famous stories. But Ruskin, too, had once had tea with the 'delightful' young Misses Liddell together with the Archbishop of Canterbury (on 24 October 1873) and, indeed, had a perplexing dream the following night that he had 'starved a hermit-crab whom I had packed away in his shell'. Was this vivisectional nightmare a premonition of the battle he was to fight with old Liddell, or was the dream a sign that Ruskin was titillated by young Alice in the same way that Dodgson was? Freudians could interpret it as a masterpiece of symbolic repression: 'The metaphysics of this'. Ruskin notes, '— which came to looking at the starved creature and wondering if I could revive it — are highly curious.'

There is a final ironic twist to this story. Shortly before Liddell, Dodgson and Ruskin all died (at the end of the nineteenth century), E. G. T. Liddell was born. Some forty years later he was to take Burdon-Sanderson's old chair as Waynflete Professor of Physiology at Oxford which had been so fervently advocated by his famous namesake, and became in due course the only man in Britain to be successfully prosecuted for cruelty to laboratory animals in the first three quarters of the century.

Meanwhile, abroad, things had stirred just a little. In Paris, the world's capital of vivisection, a young Englishwoman, Anna Kingsford, had managed to qualify in medicine without the use of animals. This achievement took her six years of study from 1874 till 1880 and she had to fight with her professors every inch of the way. They considered vivisection as a necessary ingredient in the training of any medical student; Anna Kingsford demonstrated that they were wrong.

The first President of the new French anti-vivisection society was the great poet and novelist Victor Hugo who when invited to the presidency had at once accepted, adding:

"Your society is one that will reflect honour on the nineteenth century. Vivisection is a crime, the human race will repudiate these barbarities" (*The Zoophilist,* December 1884).

But the French society had no success equivalent to its British counterpart. The laws of France remain unaltered to this day. Perhaps if Anna Kingsford had not died in the same year as its foundation, her neurotic energies might have driven it forward to achieve greater things. In Germany, Baron von Weber had founded an anti-vivisection society in Dresden. It is reported that Bismark lent a sympathetic ear to its pronouncements as transmitted to him through one of its members, Dr. Grizanowski, who was a friend. One of the staunchest supporters of this society was Richard Wagner, who wrote of vivisected animals in an open letter to von Weber:

> The thought of their suffering penetrates with horror and dismay into my bone; and in the sympathy evoked I recognise the strongest impulse of my moral being, and also the probable source of all my art . . .

In America, also, well-informed criticisms of the vivisection system were published. In his book *The Vivisection Controversy* (1908), Dr. Albert Leffingwell recounted some of the atrocious demonstrations he had had to witness as a medical student, which included regular repetition of some of Magendie's most cruel experiments. Such demonstrations of well established facts were being done entirely for teaching purposes — they 'had no conceivable relation to the treatment of disease'. In Leffingwell's opinion there was more suffering being regularly inflicted upon animals in a single medical college in New York than in the whole of the United Kingdom.

The battle to legislate in America has continued fitfully throughout this century. Two such Bills which failed, produced some sickening evidence which was laid before the House of Representatives in September

1962. (See p. 206, 1st ed.) The following are excerpts, being wholly eye-witness accounts:

'In those windowless, sub-basement rooms, hundreds of dogs flung themselves against the bars of their cages piled tier on tier. They were barking, screaming, whining. A few were mute — and dropped their heads in the dark corners. Others circled ceaselessly in their cages . . . These dogs, mostly beagles, are used primarily for testing food additives. Some remain in their *cages for seven years.*'

'Most pitiful were those whose painful and debilitating surgery prevented them from rising, and who were soaking and shivering in the bottoms of the wet cages, from which they would never be taken again unless it were for further experimentation or as carcasses.'

'All dogs caged, never released for exercise. Three emaciated dogs curled up and uninterested even though most of the dogs were barking furiously. A grey poodle with incredibly matted fur, with food and filth stuck to it . . . did not respond in any way, but stood mute and motionless in its cage. When standing the dog's back was rubbing against the top of the cage. The university refused to build cages any bigger despite urgent requests . . . Post-operative room: many were too sick to rise, and some had had two operations. One heart surgical case was emaciated, had a tremor, and lacked one eye from which red flesh extruded . . . apparently this did not deter its use for heart surgery.'

'One very sick dog had traces of recent surgery on his right side. I stopped and spoke to the dog, and he made an effort to get up in response. As he did so, large quantities of a bloody, pus-like substance extended from his nostrils and he coughed so hard that he was not able to stand.'

'In any class of medical students you can always spot a certain number with sadistic tendencies . . . medicine provides an opportunity to express these tendencies.'

'I am a student studying veterinary medicine. This is a cry and a plea from a young person still holding on to a few ideals I have grown up to believe in — and I am beginning to wonder if there is any real humane goodness among humans.'

'Trying to produce convulsions in dogs is terrible. I know they wouldn't let you see that, though. Shock experiments, removal of organs, blocking intestines, or the urine outlet so the bladder ruptures are only run of the mill . . . you'd be surprised to hear what professors and some students can think up.'

'At night I keep thinking about the dogs. Sometimes I have to walk away, I feel so sick about the dogs.

'Imagine, after you have major surgery and you are between life and death . . . your little square of cold, draughty, cement flooring is cleaned by having a hose of cold water squirted over you. The dogs are soaked by this cold water — dogs right after recovering from surgery. No wonder most of the dogs die. But no one cares. If they live, within a couple of days or a week, they are used for different experiments. One dog survived seven experiments.'

'At Columbia University as many as a thousand blows on each leg of dogs were administered by a rawhide mallet to induce shock. Nervous depression, gasping, thirst and vomiting — not to mention the agonizing pain of crushed muscles, nerves and bones — were some of the effects of the beatings. The researcher who performed this experiment stated that three dogs which survived shock resulting from the beating suddenly expired the following day when they were again placed on the animal-board.'

'A *Symposium on Burns* (National Research Council, November 1950) describes some of the variety of ways in which animals are burned: by gasoline, flame-throwers, burning irons, and for internal burns, hot dry air and steam . . . we do not know of any practical method of irradiating these dogs and burning them at the same time in the laboratory, which is a goal we would like to achieve.'

'Most of the suffering never comes to light. The only people who know about it are those who are responsible for it.'

In Britain, the topic again received public attention some thirty years after the passing of the Act, when the so called 'Brown Dog affair' caused sporadic publicity over a number of years. In 1906 the International Anti-vivisection Council, with the consent of Battersea Council, erected a statue of a dog in Battersea Park with the following inscription appended:

In memory of the brown Terrier Dog done to death in the laboratories of University College in February 1903 after having endured vivisection extending over more than two months and having been handed over from one vivisector to another till death came to his release. Also in memory of the 232 dogs vivisected in the same place during the year 1902. Men and women of England: How long shall these things be?

The account of the experimentation done on this dog was one story among many published in 1903 in a book entitled *The Shambles of Science* written by two Swedish girls, Leisa Schartau and Louise Lind-af-Hageby. These two friends had begun to study medicine in London where they were, according to their teacher of physiology, 'very advanced and intelligent students'.

Appalled by the vivisection they saw at King's and University Colleges they wrote their book as 'an indictment against the system'. This book received considerable publicity and general acclaim. Its accuracy was never seriously questioned, even by its opponents.

A year after it had been unveiled by the Mayor of Battersea, the bronze statue of the Brown Dog was damaged by medical students of University College. Summonses, angry meetings and further disturbances ensued. Pressure was brought upon the Battersea Borough Council to have the statue removed or the inscription deleted. Stalwartly they refused to do either.

Demonstrations were large and violent. On 10 December 1907, about 100 medical students attempted to remove the memorial. From five o'clock in the afternoon until midnight they were opposed by growing numbers of local citizens who successfully defended their statue. Finally a large body of mounted police managed to disperse the mob. Suddenly, in the spring of 1910, the statue disappeared, never to be seen again. A protest meeting in Trafalgar Square was attended by several thousand people and was addressed by Louise Lind-af-Hageby.

Although the Brown Dog had gone, in the seven years since its death it had become a martyr and had gained more publicity for the humane anti-vivisection point of view than had ever been previously achieved.

The speeches and the meetings and the riots stimulated considerable discussion in the press and the widespread popular reaction demonstrated once again that whenever the issue is clearly presented to the public, the majority opinion is fervently and overwhelmingly opposed to the infliction of unnecessary suffering in the name of science.

While all this was happening, and perhaps influenced by the widespread sympathy shown for the little Brown Dog, the second Royal Commission on Vivisection (1906-12) was sitting to consider the practice, and the administration of the law relating to it. The Commission reported in 1912. Its main recommendations led to the attachment to licences of the unsatisfactory Pain Condition and the establishment of the Home Office's Advisory Committee on the administration of the 1876 Act. It had heard some startling evidence from the Hon. Stephen Coleridge. Coleridge had charged 'the Home Office officials with having placed themselves in improper confidential relations with a private society composed of supporters of vivisection'. The society he alluded to was an unstatutory body calling itself the Association for the Advancement of Medicine by Research. Under cross-examination by the Commission the Home Office Chief Inspector, Mr. Byrne, had admitted that his department had been in continuous consultation with this shadowy organisation from which it had regularly accepted advice 'in regard to applicants for licences and certificates'. Stephen Coleridge had done some good detective work.

The cause of anti-vivisection has always been well supported by the most eminent of men. In nineteenth-century Britain, Tennyson (who was a Vice-President of the National Anti-Vivisection Society), Browning, Carlyle, Ruskin, Cardinal Manning and Shaftesbury were all actively involved. As the twentieth century was born, writers as different from one another as John Galsworthy, Thomas Hardy and Colette expressed their conviction that kindness to others should mean kindness to all sentient creatures, not only to our fellow men and women. Albert Schweitzer wrote 'Until we have drawn the animal into our circle of happiness, there can be no world peace'. In discussing his motives for writing *Animal Farm*, George Orwell stated — "Men exploit animals in much the same way as the rich exploit the proletariat."

One voice in particular joined in eloquently and wittily on the side of the animals: George Bernard Shaw, in his *May Lectures*, in the Preface to his play *The Doctor's Dilemma*, and in his *The Adventures of the Black Girl in Her Search for God* puts the humanitarian argument very strongly. His earliest brush with the vivisectionists appears to have been when, with rollicking chivalry he attacked Professor Sir Victor Horsley for calling Frances Cobbe a liar:

'I at once took the field against Horsley. "The question at issue", I said, "is not whether Miss Cobbe is a liar, but whether you as a vivisector are a scoundrel". Horsley's breath was taken away. He refused to debate what seemed to him a monstrous insult.'

In 1927 Shaw's old friend H. G. Wells wrote a defence of vivisection in the *Sunday Express*. Wells, to his eternal discredit, put forward the old cliché that because vivisection was not, in his opinion, the *greatest* cruelty inflicted by mankind, it was thus in some way justified — the 'two-wrongs-can-make-a-right' argument. Shaw replied in the *Sunday Express* of 27 August 1927:

"But Mr. Wells has another shot in his locker . . . 'There is a residuum of admittedly painful cases, but it is an amount of suffering infinitesimal in comparison with the gross aggregate of pain inflicted day by day upon sentient creatures by mankind'.

This defence fits every possible crime from pitch-and-toss to manslaughter. Its disadvantage is that it is not plausible enough to impose on the simplest village constable. Even Landru, and the husband of the brides in the bath, though in desperate peril of the guillotine and the gallows, had not the effrontery to say: 'It is true that we made our livelihood by marrying women and burning them in the stove or drowning them in the bath when we had spent their money; and we admit frankly and handsomely that the process may have involved some pain and disillusionment for them; but their sufferings (if any) were infinitesimal in comparison with the gross aggregate of pain inflicted day by day upon sentient creatures by mankind.' Landru and Smith knew what Wells forgot: that scoundrels who have no better defence than that have no defence at all . . .''

(A. W. S. Robinson has pointed out to me that in view of his polemical novel, *The Island of Dr. Moreau,* it may be that Wells' *Sunday Express* article was intended to be satirical, consisting as it does of bogus argument expressed in clichés.)

Between the wars, other men of letters were to join Shaw in attacking experiments upon animals. Prominent among these was John Cowper Powys who made the subject central to his novel *Morwyn, or The Vengence of God,* and he touches on it elsewhere, as for instance in *Jobber Skold.*

A few medical men, too, dared to follow Dr. George Hoggan in risking their careers by voicing open criticisms of the system. Criticisms of vivisection were made by medical men before the first Royal Commission in 1875. Sir William Fergusson, FRS, Sergeant-Surgeon to Queen Victoria and President of the British Medical Association was posthumously denigrated for questioning the validity of much of the animal research that was being performed.

One surgeon who continued to support Fergusson's view was Robert Lawson Tait (1845-99), a well-known surgeon of his day and a pioneer of aseptic methods and several new and successful techniques in abdominal surgery (see Wilfred Risdon, *Lawson Tait,* NAVS, 1967). His independence of mind enabled him to question contemporary orthodoxies and he was closely associated with the movement to allow women admission to the medical profession on equal terms with men. He outspokenly opposed vivisection on four grounds — moral, political, religious and scientific (in a paper to the Birmingham Philosophical Society, 20 April 1882). He respected the moral view 'that we have no right to inflict sufferings on others that we ourselves may benefit.'

In the twentieth century too there have been medical opponents of animal experimentation. Outstanding contemporary medical reformers have been Dr. Dallas Pratt, Dr. Louis Goldman, Dr. Kit Pedler, Dr. J. D. Whittall and Lord Platt (President of the Royal College of Physicians 1957-1962).

Dr. Kenneth Walker wrote in the *British Medical Journal,* 10 February 1945: 'I have always felt in the age-long dispute between the vivisectionists and the anti-vivisectionists Mr. Bernard Shaw stood on the firmest ground when he stated simply that knowledge could be purchased at too great a cost, and that the knowledge gained from vivisection was an example of this.'

Dr. M. B. Bayly was a doctor who wrote several short books against vivisection during the two decades following the Second World War. These were mostly published by the NAVS and are accounts of cruel and unnecessary animal research. Dr. D. MacD. Fraser was closely associated with the RSPCA's campaign to improve the administration of the 1876 Act and so also was Dr. R. F. Rattray (the Society's vice-chairman). But of all medics involved in the movement, none was more involved than Dr. Walter Hadwen (1854-1932), a medical man who became utterly opposed to the vivisection system. Not only did he criticize it, he advocated its total abolition. Hadwen had, as a medical student, been one of the most brilliant of his generation, winning almost every prize obtainable. Instead of taking up an illustrious career in Harley Street or as a researcher, he became a respected general practitioner in Somerset, and was for thirty years the president of Frances Cobbe's British Union for the Abolition of Vivisection. Hadwen was, however, an absolute purist. His refusal to allow that a step-by-step approach to reform might be more effective in the long run than campaigns for total abolition, aggravated the differences between the two schools of thought.

In 1909 there had been two large international congresses held in England. The first had been under the auspices of Louise Lind-af-Hageby's society and the second was organised by the World League Against Vivisection. The former advocated the gradualist approach supported by, among others, Sir George Kekewitch, Stephen Coleridge and the two ladies from Sweden, while the latter, notably under Hadwen's influence, proposed nothing short of total abolition.

Such schisms are nearly always a waste of effort and a waste of time in any campaign of reform. This rift in the anti-vivisection movement sapped much of its energies up till the time of the Second World War, and may have been responsible for alienating serious and realistic men from having much to do with the cause.

In 1909 the movement had seemed poised for great things. In Britain it had always received substantial backing from the old ruling class and in addition it had attracted the support of the new Labour party. Sir George Kekewitch could claim: 'A new party, the Labour Party, has arisen in Parliament; and every member of that party is on our side.' Forty-four members of the House of Commons had attended the World League Against Vivisection's congress, among them four future Labour Cabinet Ministers — Ramsay Macdonald, Philip Snowden, Arthur

Henderson and J. R. Clynes. In the same year, 175 members of the French Chamber of Deputies signed a protest against vivisection and pledged their support to Louise Lind-af-Hageby's international congress.

Then came the First World War and in the silence that followed the last barrage a deafness settled upon the politicians and the legislators.

The first Labour Government came to power in 1929, and those four Vice-Presidents of the World League who had earnestly and with apparent sincerity pledged their support to the anti-vivisection cause twenty years before, found themselves with the power in their hands to reform or to abolish vivisection — and they did absolutely nothing.

The decade before the Second World War was one of absolute frustration for the anti-vivisection movement and by 1939 the total number of experiments performed annually in Britain alone had almost reached the million mark.

During the war years, Nazi doctors performed experiments upon hundreds of human guinea-pigs, infecting them with typhus, exposing them to poison gas, deliberately wounding them, castrating, decompressing, freezing and asphyxiating. Some of the scientists who did this work had been well-established and socially respectable figures before the war. Very often their human experiments were carried out in conjunction with on-going animal research which was conducted in the same concentration camps. When tried for their lives at Nuremburg their excuse was the same as that used by vivisectors throughout history — they desired to save life through the knowledge they hoped to gain.

Such events demonstrate yet again how fragile is the harness of convention which prevents sincere and ordinary men from becoming monsters of cruelty.

The history of social reform suggests that war has a cauterizing effect upon conscience. Certainly, periods of warfare and their immediately succeeding years have been times of stagnation in the progress of the recognition of animals' rights, although outstanding warriors have not themselves always been inactive in humane causes. The man whose foresight as much as any other's saved Britain from Nazi invasion, Air Chief Marshal Lord Dowding, was pre-eminent in championing the protection of laboratory animals. After the war, out of thirty-three speeches he made in the House of Lords twenty-seven dealt with aspects of animal welfare.

Towards the end of the 1950's the RSPCA again took an interest in animal experimentation and after some years of campaigning by animal welfare organisations, on November 30th 1962 the Home Secretary (Henry Brooke) announced his decision to set up a departmental committee under Sir Sidney Littlewood to inquire into the working of the 1876 Act, and two years later, on February 19th, 1965, their report was ready. Since that date the report's eighty-three recommendations for reform have scarcely been debated by Parliament and no new legislation has resulted. It is true that the Home Office have trimmed administrative practices in some instances to bring them in line with Littlewood, but they have also used selected excerpts from the report to bolster the status quo.

While international complacency reigned in official circles, there began the spate of serious writings about the rights of animals that can only be matched by those published in England during the last quarter of the eighteenth century. C. S. Lewis wrote several leaflets for the National Anti-Vivisection Society in the 1950's and in 1964 Ruth Harrison's *Animal Machines* opened the eyes of the world to the horrors of factory farming. In the same year E. S. Turner brilliantly summarised the history of the welfare movement in *All Heaven in a Rage.* In 1965 Brigid Brophy was given space by the *Sunday Times* (10 October) to put the moral case, and John Vyvyan published his history of animal experimentation in two volumes entitled *In Pity and in Anger* (1969) and *The Dark Face of Science* (1971). *Animals, Men and Morals* ed. Godlovitch and Harris (Gollancz 1971; New York, Taplinger 1973) provided the first collection of philosophical essays on the subject of animals' rights. Antony Brown's *Who Cares for Animals* joined two previous histories of the RSPCA in 1974.

Such publications reflected a growing awareness among intelligent people and, in some cases, a rising impatience, about mankind's tyrannical exploitation of the animal kingdom. This feeling was, to a large extent, consistent with the conservation movement and the new concern for the environment; where it differed was in the conviction that non-humans should be protected, not merely for the benefit of future generations of humans but for their own sake, and that the well-being of the individual animal mattered as much as the survival of a species.

During the early 1970's the anti-vivisection societies (notably the National Anti-Vivisection Society of London) had placed new emphasis upon the replacement of animals by alternative humane techniques and had established funds for giving grants to scientists who used them. British organisations, such as the Air Chief Marshal Lord Dowding Fund, and the Fund for the Replacement of Animals in Medical Research (FRAME) were pioneers and achieved a great deal by making scientists aware of alternative techniques and encouraging their use. The NAVS and its then General Secretary Colin Smith, were also responsible for founding the American Fund for Alternatives to Animal Research and encouraged the establishment of similar groups in other parts of the world.

In the U.S.A. the pleas of reformers such as Christine Stevens of the Animal Welfare Institute in Washington were joined by new voices. Helen Jones of the Society for Animal Rights, Eleanor Seiling of United Action for Animals Inc. (UAA) and Henry Spira began to adopt tough tactics. During the early 1970's UAA published searing reports of American experiments that truly can be called atrocities: crash-research, weapons testing, and psychological torture. Particularly disturbing were the accounts of veterinary involvement in the poisoning of dogs, sheep, pigs and ponies with substances ranging from weed-killer to anti-freeze. UAA could claim publicity successes such as the revelation that the U.S. Air Force was planning to de-bark 200 beagle puppies prior to forcing them to inhale concentrated aviation fumes, and the winning of a libel action following their condemnation of the tormenting of the pathetic monkey Bonny fired into space in 1969.

However, at the levels of legislation and official administration little was changed. Hopes turned to despair and to angry frustration. Right across the spectrum of animal exploitation — from blood-sports to vivisection — opposition became more militant. Disillusioned by the failure of Governments to take imaginative action, some people took the law into their own hands and others sought new approaches. The rapid events of 1975 and the ensuing years are the eruption of these pressures. The story is too recent and too rich to be yet told in detail. An outline must suffice.

During 1973-1974 there were discussions by various interested people as to how entry to the large industrial laboratories could be effected legally, and on January 26th 1975 the *Sunday People* published its first revelations about the beagle dogs being forced to smoke tobacco-substitutes by Imperial Chemical Industries Ltd. (I.C.I) near Maccles-field. This story was obtained by one of the newspaper's reporters who had taken a job at the laboratories as an assistant.

The following week, as the *Sunday People* continued its revelations, *Victims of Science* was published in Britain and received considerable attention from the press, radio and telivision. Public concern can be gauged by the fact that during the two years following publication I was to receive well over three thousand letters from well-wishers eager to help the movement: I answered these by sending practical suggestions for action and outlining reforms that I considered necessary (See Appendix B).

By the end of February, the *Sunday People* had collected petitions signed by over 300,000 people and on March 24th 1975, another event served further to amplify public awareness of the issue. Two men, Ronald Lee and Clifford Goodman, appeared at Oxford Crown Court charged with causing more than £50,000 worth of damage to equipment at various vivisection laboratories and breeding establishments in England and Wales during the preceding two years. Lee said in court —"My intentions were to prevent suffering. I ask for justice for those animals". Both men were jailed for three years (see *The Sun*, 25th March and 29th March). Direct sabotage of laboratories continued, however, conducted by an organisation first calling itself the Band of Mercy and later the Animal Liberation Front. During the summer of 1975, I.C.I.'s laboratories were among those broken into and three dogs were removed. Illegal action persisted into the 1980's and included a mass break-in at an agricultural research centre at Babraham near Cambridge which was filmed and shown nationwide on television. The police eventually dropped all charges against the seventeen defendants (*Daily Telegraph,* August 28th 1980).

Public demonstrations and protests were organised in 1975 by many people notably Joan Latto, Ruth Plant and Clementina Narborough. Lady Parker, the widow of the Lord Chief Justice, lent her support. I.C.I. shareholders at their Annual General Meetings voiced their disapproval of the company's methods. A mammoth petition was raised by Berkshire Councillor Bill Brown, and sections of the National Council for Women and the Women's Institutes expressed their concern about cosmetics tests on animals.

In response to such public pressures activity intensified in Parliament. Parliamentary Questions were asked, and two Early Day Motions were signed by over 200 M.P.s. William Hamilton, A. J. Beith, Andrew Bowden, Sir John Eden, Ivor Clemitson and other "newcomers" gave support to established campaigners such as William Price, Ronald Russell, Marcus Lipton, Richard Body and Kenneth Lomas.

Philip Whitehead introduced a Bill to ban the use of animals where other research methods were available and Baroness Phillips presented a Bill to prevent the testing on animals of non-medical cosmetics. Both Bills failed to make progress — as had Douglas Houghton's and one drafted by Mary Rose Barrington introduced by Lord Willis in 1973 — due to Government opposition. A Bill introduced by Ivor Stanbrook suffered a similar fate.

In the House of Lords the campaign was fought with special vigour by Lord Houghton of Sowerby (who as Douglas Houghton had been a Cabinet Minister and Chairman of the Parliamentary Labour Party) and Lord Platt (at one time President of the Royal College of Physicians).

At last a few concessions were made by the Government: four lay persons were appointed to the Home Office Advisory Committee on the administration of the 1876 Act; an undertaking was given to examine "stress" in experiments; the question of the amount of official informa- tion provided about experiments would be reviewed; the effectiveness of the contact between Inspectors and experimenters would be considered. (*Hansard*, May 14th, 1975). Furthermore, Roy Jenkins, the Home Sec- retary, ordered the Advisory Committee to investigate the specific case of the I.C.I. Beagles. On December 11th, 1975 the Government accepted the Committee's recommendation that further *smoking* experiments on *dogs* should be disallowed. All these were minor advances.

It now became apparent that in the United Kingdom at least, a large body of scientific opinion itself was in favour of reforms. Overt defence of the status quo was limited almost entirely to the Research Defence Society (founded after the disbandment of the criticised Association for the Advancement of Medicine by Research see p. 142), which claimed membership among only five per cent of licensed experimenters in physiology departments and medical schools and increasingly appeared to represent only a minority view among scientists in general.

During 1975 a group had formed around Lord Houghton which could bring pressure directly on the Home Office. This body was an off- shoot of the RSPCA's Animal Experimentation Advisory Committee and its original active members besides Houghton, were Lord Platt, Dr. Kit Pedler, William Jordan (RSPCA Deputy Chief Veterinary Officer), Clive Hollands (Chairman of Animal Welfare Year) and myself. This group composed a document which came to be known as the Houghton- Platt Memorandum which put forward detailed proposals for reform and was submitted to the Secretary of State in May 1976. Its central pro- posal was the complete transformation of the existing Home Office Ad- visory Committee from being an inert body without initiative into a vigorous and widely representative watchdog: other reforms should then flow from this. These six people visited the Home Office on August 4th and on the exact centenary of the 1876 Act nine days later, the Memoran- dum was published.

Three members of the House of Commons, Janet Fookes, Frederick Burden and Kenneth Lomas, had signed their support to the Memoran- dum and towards the end of the year, the further membership of representatives from the principal British anti-vivisection organisations was enlisted, notably Sidney Hicks of the British Union for the Abolition of Vivisection (143, Charing Cross Road, London, W.C.2.) and Jon Evans of the National Anti-Vivisection Society (51 Harley Street, London, W.1.). The group now named itself the Committee for the Reform of Animal Experimentation (CRAE).

On February 15th 1977, after many months of public and private pressure, members of CRAE at last met with the Home Secretary himself, Merlyn Rees, to discuss their recommendations. In the event, this meeting proved a further step forward in overcoming what had hitherto been the bureaucracy's initial resistance to reform. Rees' attitude was sympathetic and constructive.

In many countries, 1976 had been an active year for the humane movements. Jon Evans of the International Association Against Painful Experiments on Animals (IAAPEA) pursued the Association's aims with vigour and in Finland, Germany and other parts of the world conferences were held to promote the development and use of humane techniques which can replace animals in research. Professor Bruce Ames' *in vitro* method for assessing mutagenicity and carcinogencity proved revolutionary in some fields and an I.C.I. team endorsed its usefulness. (I.F.H. Purchase et al. *Nature,* vol. 264, December 16th 1976).

One of the main messages of *Victims of Science,* that many experiments on animals are no longer for strictly medical or therapeutic purposes, was taken up in many countries; in particular, opposition to cosmetics-testing using animals became one of the main planks of the reform platform, very much assisted internationally by Lady Dowding's "Beauty without Cruelty" movement.

In several Scandinavian countries public exhibitions and protests increased. At a conference organised in London by the Universities Federation for Animal Welfare (30th September 1976), speakers from the Netherlands, Denmark, Sweden and Canada described how the pressures of public opinion had led to the setting up in their countries of ethical committees which include animal welfare spokesmen. Science at last was being made answerable to the community at large and its divinity seemed to be under question.

In the USA the Summer of 1976 saw the organisation of mass picketing of the American Museum of Natural History in protest against the use of cats in so-called sex experiments (*Science,* 8 October 1976, 194, No. 4261). The following year saw America's first Animal Liberation trial occur at which two men, Kenneth Levasseur and Steve Sipman were accused of liberating dolphins used for research. (*New Scientist,* 15 December, 1977). In Michigan two months later a protest group succeeded in stopping car crash experimenters on baboons (*Guardian,* 8 February 1978).

Britain probably remained the most politically active (although not always the most progressive) country in this field. During the year, vain attempts were made to improve controls over the breeding and exporting of animals for laboratory use, and to force experimenters to obtain animals only from properly licensed and inspected dealers. Hugh Jenkins joined those M.Ps who sought reforms; during the months of October and November alone he asked more than thirty Parliamentary Questions, many of them about the use of animals in the testing of weapons and riot control devices.

In the English language, the spate of serious publications continued. Outstanding among these was Peter Singer's *Animal Liberation* which was published in New York in 1975 and in London the following year. This book is one of the most powerful books ever written about man's treatment of the other animals. Singer, a university philosopher, attacks speciesism as "a prejudice no less objectionable than prejudice about a person's race or sex". Other important books were *The Civilised Alternative* by Jon Wynne-Tyson (Centaur 1972), *Animals Rights* by Andrew Linzey (SCM Press 1976), *Animals Rights and Human Obligations* ed. Regan and Singer (Prentice Hall 1976) and *The Moral Status of Animals* by Stephen Clark (Clarendon 1977). Later there was to be *Animals Are Equal* by Rebecca Hall (Wildwood 1980).

The subject of animal experimentation became established in the media as one that was of interest, and it began to be featured regularly on radio, television and in the newspapers. One such piece, Ena Kendall's in the *Observer* of 13 June 1976, included statements by several laboratory workers critical of the Home Office administration. Shortly after the appearance of this article, Angela Walder, a Senior Laboratory Technician, was dismissed from her job at the Mount Vernon Hospital, despite support from one of the senior scientists at the establishment, Dr. Harold Hewitt. Through the media, Walder expressed her concern about the welfare of laboratory animals under the British system, and became established in ensuing years as one of the most effective campaigners.

Not only non-technical writers but also leading science journalists such as Louis Goldman and Donald Gould had espoused the humane cause and, in particular, Bernard Dixon, editor of the increasingly influential journal *New Scientist,* became a champion for reform. Open-minded scientists — such as David Sperlinger and Alice Heim (see her Presidential Address to the British Association for the Advancement of Science 5 Sept. 1978 and the author's letters in the British Psychological Society Bulletin e.g. March 1978) — began to motivate changes from within. In January 1979, the British Psychological Society published its report on the use of animals by psychologists which recommended reforms. Subsequently the Society established its own ethical advisory Committee.

In Britain, direct behind-the-scenes intervention by senior politicians — men like Lord Houghton, Evan Luard and even Sir Harold Wilson — was of importance in penetrating the barriers of the bureaucracy: a feature perhaps lacking in the reform movements in other countries. The influence of the redoubtable Lord Houghton cannot be overestimated in this context.

During the culmination of Animal Welfare Year in 1977 and largely as a result of the work achieved by Clive Hollands, CRAE continued to do good business with the Home Office and administrative reforms were put in hand. In August, the world's first academic Conference on Animals' Rights was held at Trinity College, Cambridge by the RSPCA and scores of people, including philosophers and theologians, signed a declaration against speciesism. (In 1979 these proceedings, entitled *Animals Rights — A Symposium,* and edited by David Paterson and Richard D. Ryder, were published by Centaur Press.)

The year closed with several further heartening developments. Richard Adams' brilliant book *Plague Dogs* was published and disseminated to a huge readership its moving plea for compassion.

Following a visit by Muriel Lady Dowding and Jon Evans, the Prime Minister of India, Morarji Desai, announced a ban on the export of Indian monkeys used for research. And on December 8th, 1977, in reply to persistent questioning by Members of Parliament, the Prime Minister of the United Kingdom, James Callaghan, indicated that it would be his Government's policy to "move to alternatives to animal experiment as quickly as possible". (*Hansard,* Column 1644).

Following my own pressure upon the Secretary of State in 1978, he issued an exhortation to all British experimenters to use humane alternatives techniques wherever possible, and he facilitated further meetings between himself, CRAE and Home Office officials. Various small reforms were achieved: the Inspectorate was slightly increased; the LD 50 procedure was officially investigated; the Returns under the 1876 Act were updated along the lines suggested by CRAE; and the controls on pain were put under review. For the first time for many years a British scientist was successfully prosecuted for cruelty to laboratory animals and two were deprived of their licences. Furthermore, Home Office responsibility for encouraging the use of humane alternative techniques was agreed by the Prime Minister and the reconstitution of the Advisory Committee was promised by the Secretary of State.

Such developments, and the increasingly constructive approach adopted by Government officials, have heartened many animal welfare workers.

During 1978, under Lord Houghton's Chairmanship, a new committee was formed for the express purpose of putting animals into politics; not in order to make them a contentious issue between the political parties, but to persuade parties and Governments to take the subject of animal welfare far more seriously than at any time in the past. This General Election Co-ordinating Committee for Animal Protection (GECCAP) made approaches to all the major political parties in Britain, and all responded favourably. In July 1978, the governing Labour Party published some historic proposals entitled *Living Without Cruelty,* covering all the main areas of animal abuse and pledging widespread reforms for laboratory animals, specifically proposing to limit experiments "to proven medical research where it can be demonstrated that no alternative method is available".

After negotiations between myself and the Chairman of the Conservative Party, Lord Thorneycroft, and after I had met with Charles Bellairs of the Conservative Research Department in 1978, Bellairs published in 1979 a forward-looking booklet ("Animal Welfare", *Politics Today,* No. 13, Sept. 17th 1979) suggesting reforms. The Liberal Party responded by setting up its Liberal Animal Welfare Group which, motivated by its founder and convenor Basil Goldstone, rapidly made the Liberal Party the most active of the four major parties in the whole field of animal welfare. The history of this period is well told by one of its key figures, Clive Hollands, in his book *Compassion is the Bugler* (Macdonald, 1980).

One of the most hopeful features of these campaigns was that British scientists began to show a growing and often genuine concern for the treatment of animals in research — a concern not yet reflected by most colleagues in North America, Australia or elsewhere. Even the Chairman of the Research Defence Society in Britain, the late Professor D. H. Smyth, published some constuctive proposals (*Alternatives to Animal Experiments,* Scolar Press, 1978). In July 1978 the Royal Society itself published a report implicitly critical of much animal testing — "toxicology" it stated "is not adequately supported as an academic discipline; it is swamped by routine tests of limited value and governed by regulations rather than by rational thought". (*Long Term Toxic Effects.* p. 13)

A campaign initiated by the International Association Against Painful Experiments on Animals to persuade Amnesty International to cease their so-called "torture experiments" on animals, which had been started in Denmark, was also successfully concluded in 1978 following meetings between Amnesty and a deputation including Brigid Brophy (its leader), Maureen Duffy, myself, and others.

The worsening economic situation worldwide led to slight reductions in the number of animals being employed but again roused fears that the use of stolen pets, cheaper than specially bred animals, was on the increase. Four Doncaster men, for example,were convicted of stealing animals for sale to laboratories and were sent to prison. (*Doncaster Evening Post,* 1st December 1978).

The following year saw the introduction by Congressman Frederick Richmond of the Research Modernisation Act in the U.S. House of Representatives. This Bill aimed to set up a Government backed centre for Alternative Research. In Britain, two full length Parliamentary Bills which contained far greater detail than any previous legislative attempts, were introduced into the British Parliament.

On 16th July 1979, the Earl of Halsbury (President of the Research Defence Society) published his Laboratory Animals Protection Bill. The contents of this Bill met with little approval from the animal welfare societies. Peter Fry's Protection of Animals (Scientific Purposes) Bill was introduced on 27th June and also failed to attract full-hearted support. The RSPCA (which had become more progressive during the late 1970's and was officially opposed to any experimentation or confinement likely to cause suffering of any sort) criticised both Bills on the grounds that they failed to provide sufficient advances on four cardinal points of reform:

    (a)   increased public accountability (e.g. through a Goverment Advisory Committee where "users" and welfarists are equally represented)

    (b)   proper controls over pain and distress

    (c)   constraints upon experimenters to use humane alternative techniques wherever feasible, and

    (d)   restriction of experiments to worthwhile medical purposes.

After much opposition from the scientific lobby the Fry Bill failed through lack of time. But Lord Halsbury's Bill was referred to a Select Committee of the House of Lords under the chairmanship of Lord Ashby which published its Report on 24th April 1980 suggesting radical alterations to the Bill. The Select Committee's central recommendation was that experimentation on animals should be controlled largely through regulations imposed by the Secretary of State on the advice of a statutory Advisory Committee. This proposal did not meet with the approval of the Government although it was already pledged in its Election Manifesto to "update" the law in this field. Lord Belstead, on behalf of the Government, said that the Government would introduce its own legislation only when it knew the final form of the Council of Europe's Convention on the Protection of Laboratory Animals (see *Hansard,* 20th June 1980) and criticised the amended Halsbury Bill on a number of counts, most notably that its control over pain was insufficiently stringent because it gave discretion to the Secretary of State to waive protection. Lord Belstead, in referring to the standard pain condition attached to licences under the 1876 Act said — "we believe the experience of the past 100 years or so shows that the pain condition should be an inviolate provision, and that it could therefore be embodied in a new statute." He also hinted that the Government wanted a clearer definition of the purposes for which live animal experimentation should be permitted.

The amended Halsbury Bill (so extensively altered by the Select Committee that Lord Houghton suggested jokingly that it should be called "the Ashby Bill") was re-introduced in the House of Lords and received a new second Reading on 18th December 1980 at which Lord Belstead reiterated the Government's opposition to the Bill. And it still failed to meet with approval from most animal welfare societies. Although respect for Lord Houghton enabled him to hold together for some months a precarious strategic alliance between Lord Halsbury and the moderate welfare camp, the National Anti-Vivisection Society left CRAE in 1980 and came out in total opposition to the amended Halsbury Bill. The NAVS found themselves aligned with Animal Aid and the Scottish Anti-Vivisection Society (of Glasgow) against the traditionally more extreme British Union for the Abolition of Vivisection (BUAV) which temporarily gave the impression of suport for the Bill, while the RSPCA concentrated its activities elsewhere believing that the Bill was destined for extinction. In December 1980 the progressive ginger group Co-ordinating Animal Welfare (CAW), after a monumental struggle through the law courts, succeeded in gaining control of the BUAV, and Fay Funnell, Margaret Redgrave, Margaret Manzoni, Kim Stallwood and its other leaders immediately brought this body also into direct opposition to the Bill. Radical amendments to the Bill were proposed in the Lords itself by welfare-minded peers, notably Lord Beaumont.

Several themes now united all British welfare groups. One was that any Government proposing legislation in this field which did not radically improve the protection of laboratory animals (especially as regards the infliction of pain and distress) would find itself on the receiving end of a massive publicity campaign which would certainly affect in the country at large its reputation for compassion.

Another unifying concern was the determination of welfarists to be fairly included on any official government advisory committee associated with the administration of the relevant legislation. Although the Government itself had acknowledged that animal welfare was one of the two major public interests involved, it still showed a remarkable reluctance to give the welfare point of view proper representation on the

Home Office Advisory Committee. For many years this Committee had led a moribund existence and was composed largely of elderly scientists. After prolonged pressure the Government began to appoint to the Committee a few "lay" people, selected mysteriously by the civil service from the Parole Board list and other sources. As a result of the campaigns of the late 1970's the new Conservative Government entirely reconstituted the Committee in 1979. Invitations for nominees were sent by the Government to a range of scientific, industrial and welfare bodies and although CRAE and the RSPCA sent in a list of nominees, all with scientific backgrounds, not one of them was acceptable to the Government. In contrast, virtually all the nominees put forward by the industrial and scientific organisations were appointed. Such unwarranted discrimination did little to inspire confidence in the Government's intentions in welfare circles. The Committee as it was reconstituted consisted of a Chairman (Mrs. Mary Warnock), five scientists, two veterinarians, one experimental psychologist, two lay people and only two drawn from the field of animal welfare. Although the two latter were good candidates (Dr. Judith Hampson and Mr. T. G. Field-Fisher Q.C.) the composition itself remained highly controversial. If there are two main public interests involved, why should one interest have at least six members on the Committee when the other has only two — and not even the two that it nominated? If the law is concerned to prevent cruelty to animals then why is animal welfare so inadequately represented on the relevant Committee? The Home Office has provided no satisfactory answer to these questions. In Sweden, Australia and elsewhere, Governments have shown themselves to be less afraid of the welfare lobby. In Sweden the local ethical committees (which have statutory powers) are composed of one third scientists, one third animal care experts and one third local animal welfare people, and these committees have worked well.

This drive to have the welfare lobby properly recognised by Governments is an international phenomenon and one that will have to be resolved during the 1980's.

The abolition of all pain, distress and other forms of suffering in experiments was an aim shared by the RSPCA and other groups. Pain, the RSPCA argued, was not only morally objectionable, but scientifically undesirable since its widespread physiological effects (such as the release of hormones) interfered with experiments often contaminating them to a greater extent than would the use of anaesthetics and pain-killers.

Meanwhile at Strasbourg the Council of Europe's Convention continued to make only slow progress throughout the early months of 1981. Although suggesting protection for animals while being bred and kept for research, as well as for animals actually under experiment, the Convention contains protective measures only of the most general sort. It will provide a useful raising of standards in some member states which have been backward in introducing their own humane legislation, but it will not represent a model or inspiration for countries which already lead the world in animal protection.

In America, much valuable publicity for the movement was created when Donald Barnes, a psychologist employed at the Brooks Air Force Base, San Antonio, Texas, talked to the press about the treatment of animals in these laboratories (e.g. *The Globe,* 27th May 1980). He alleged that dogs, monkeys and other animals had been irradiated, shocked and blinded by lasers in a series of horrifying experiments, and photographs were produced to illustrate his claims. Later in the year he participated in a massive "Liberate Animals from Laboratories Rally" in Los Angeles, organised by the Fund for Animals and Helen Jones of the Society for Animals Rights, and co-sponsored by 35 other humane societies. The rally was addressed by scientists and philosophers such as Professor Charles Magel whose great bibliography on the subjects of animal protection and animal rights was published in 1981. Barnes told his audience — "In over 16 years of research I can cite you no examples of anyone even suggesting to use an anaesthetic on an experiment with animals . . . when I asked myself how much good the research that I was involved in did, the answer was none".

Throughout 1980 Henry Spira of New York and Jean Pink of the British group Animal Aid collaborated in a campaign against the Draize Test as used by the cosmetics giant Revlon. Their efforts were rewarded with considerable success. On December 23rd 1980 Revlon announced a donation of $750,000 to fund a research project at Rockefeller University, New York, to search for an alternative to the Draize Test. This campaign was aided by direct action groups in France which demonstrated against Revlon in Paris.

The previous year laboratory kennels near Auxerre had been broken into and a large number of dogs had been liberated and in March 1981 a group called Katpat released animals from a laboratory at Nogent-sur-Marne.

Similar action had occurred in America on March 4th 1979 when a body calling itself Animals in Distress had rescued five animals from the New York University Medical Centre. On December 4th 1980 a group entitled the International Animal Liberation Front released 60 gerbils and 32 rats from a laboratory of the University of South Florida. This group has also been active in Montreal and Toronto in 1981.

January 4th 1981 saw a further major offensive by the original British Animal Liberation Front (ALF) which, in actions co-ordinated in

London, Oxford and Cambridge, painted anti-experimentation slogans on researchers' cars and houses, and in February the ALF raided the Wickham Research Laboratories in Hampshire — a commercial testing laboratory run largely by members of the British veterinary profession.

The 1970's had seen the birth of a new international movement of young people against speciesism. Its origin was in the Hunt Saboteurs Association (HSA) which was started in Britain in 1963 by John Prestidge and subsequently led for more than a decade by David Wetton. A scrupulously non-violent offshoot of this was the Animal Liberation Front (ALF) which began in 1973 and chose as its principal targets laboratories and factory farms; unlike the HSA on occasions the ALF broke the law. Separate from the ALF was the Northern Animal Liberation League, chiefly responsible for the large Babraham raid in 1980 and responsible in 1981 for the release of a stolen black labrador "Blackie" from the Lodge Moor Laboratories in Sheffield; Blackie was subsequently returned to its owners (see Lord Houghton's Question in the House of Lords 14 May 1981.) But none of these groups, contrary to the paranoid fantasies of huntsmen, farmers and vivisectors, had ulterior political motives or were linked with any political party. There was no sinister conspiracy among the founders of this movement. Quite simply they were united in their sense of outrage and compassion. They saw that Governments had done little to respond to ordinary democratic pressure to curb the worst excesses of speciesism. Like those fighting sexism and racism, out of desperation they chose direct tactics. One of their bibles eventually became Singer's *Animal Liberation,* and June 1979 saw the first publication by John May of the movement's excellent newspaper *Beast.*

The reform of established animal welfare and humane societies was heralded by the RSPCA Reform Group in Britain and led by Stanley Cover, John Bryant and Brian Seager in the 1960's and 1970's. This culminated in the RSPCA revival of 1975-79. The author also played a part in the successful movement of 1977-79 to put animals into national politics. Both these trends are appearing in other countries as well, and are helping to add weight to the anti-vivisection movement.

In Canada, possibly more than in any other western country, most politicians have seemed indifferent to the fate of animals and to pressures from concerned public opinion. A worldwide outcry about the annual slaughter of seals in the St. Lawrence Bay area, has found little sympathy in Ottawa, despite the brave campaigns of Brian Davies, Paul Watson and others. Similarly, the state of laboratory animals in Canada, and the legislative inadequacy of controls over their use must remain matters for concern. Despite public outrage Canadian authorities continued experiments on the feeding of crude oil to polar bears. Of three bears immersed in oil, one died, one had to be destroyed and one survived after considerable suffering.

The slowness of reform has disillusioned many in the movement. Nor have the endless discussions, the postponements, and the ambiguous promises of politicians satisfied those, such as the National Anti-Vivisection Society, who want total abolition. The decade of the 1980's has seen the continued growth of direct action, both legal and illegal. Jean Pink's Animal Aid, an organisation committed to peaceful protest has, in only a few years, attracted a large membership and organised thousand-strong protest marches in University towns such as Oxford and Cambridge, in Birmingham and at Porton Down.

In Australia also, the pressures for reform have increased, inspired by campaigners such as Rosemary Bor, Elizabeth Ahlston (of the Australian Association for Humane Research in Sydney) and by their growing Animal Liberation Movement founded by Peter Singer and Christine Townend. The support of politicians such as Senators Jacobi and Puplick and M.P. Tim Moore was utilised to ask Parliamentary Questions in Canberra and elsewhere.

We have seen some encouraging progress in worldwide awareness among politicians, commentators and even exploiters. It was particularly significant when a report was published in London by the Office of Health Economics in May 1980 which argued that regulations requiring animal testing are now dangerously delaying the development of new drugs. The Office of Health Economics was set up in 1962 by the Association of the British Pharmaceutical Industry, so its comments must carry some weight. The report argues that "the predictive value of studies carried out in animals is uncertain" and goes on —

"The statutory bodies such as the Committee on Safety of Medicines which require these tests do so largely as an act of faith rather than on hard scientific grounds.

With thalidomide, for example, it is only possible to produce the specific deformities in a very small number of species of animal. In this particular case, therefore, it is unlikely that specific tests in pregnant animals would have given the necessary warning: the right species would probably never have been used. Even more strikingly, the practolol adverse reactions have not been reproducible in any species of animal except man. Conversely, penicillin in very small doses is fatal to guinea pigs. If it had been tested in those animals before it being given to man, its systemic use in humans might well have been considered too hazardous and unethical.

Hence the first problem in minimising risks with new medicines is the difficulty inherent in trying to predict adverse reactions in man from studies in experimental animals. The present tendency is to ask for more and longer animal tests merely in the hope that they may somehow make medicines safer. It has to be remembered that in addition they do three things. First they will in some cases rule out the human use of medicines which would in fact be safe and valuable. Second, more predictably, they delay the introduction of all new medicines. Thirdly, they add enormously to their cost. Perhaps the mere price to be paid is relatively unimportant. However, the more fundamental economic costs of delay will be discussed shortly.

As far as delays are concerned, there are only estimates and impressions of the total effect of current measures to maximise safety. In the 1950's it was generally accepted that it took three or four years at the longest for a newly synthesised medicinal compound to emerge in the pharmaceutical market as a new medicine. Now in the 1980s it is *expected to take more than 10 years* (my emphasis). New chemicals being synthesised and first tested today may not be available as new medicines until well into the 1990s unless more rational attitudes can be made to prevail. Returning to the principles, it has been argued that the administrative delays of the Food and Drug Administration in the United States saved the American public from general exposure to thalidomide. It is certainly true that it took so long to process the application that the first evidence of nerve damage (not deformities) had emerged before thalidomide was ready for US approval. Once these reports began to appear, the American authorities became nervous and further delayed approval.

The key point, however, is that the evidence that thalidomide had unexpected adverse effects had only come to light because it was being widely used in clinical practice in other countries. It was not more elaborate laboratory testing which first indicated the potential dangers. Thus, in principle, delay in one country has been shown to be of value only in a case where the medicine was already in use elsewhere. There is no evidence from the United States experience with thalidomide that more prolonged testing as such would have avoided the human tragedy.

On the other hand the effect of delay can be measured realistically in terms of benefits withheld.''

(*A Question of Balance: the Benefits and Risks of Pharma-*

ceutical Innovation. George Teeling-Smith. Office of Health Economics 1980).

Five years earlier, on the first publication of *Victims of Science,* I had been vigorously opposed by spokesmen of the drug industry when I made these points. How encouraging it is to find that some of my old opponents now agree with me.

The report goes on to cite the example of chlorothiazide (a heart drug), maintaining that if the drug had been discovered in 1973 (and not, as it was, in 1957), because of animal testing requirements it would have taken an extra seven years to become available during which period an estimated "20,000 patients would have died needlessly".

The year 1982 saw even greater interest in animals' rights being displayed by the media. On British television, five nationwide programmes dealt with the issue within a matter of weeks. Starting with Anglia Television in September, in the following month there came BBC's "Rabbits Don't Cry" and LWT's "Credo", and, in November, "The Animals' Film" (already shown in many cinemas throughout Britain) was shown on the new Channel 4 television. These programmes made an impression upon public and politicians alike, and on November 30th, David Steel, the first leader of any political party to do so, devoted a whole speech to animal rights. This was reprinted in *Liberal News* (December 14th 1982) and established the seriousness of the Liberal Party's commitment to the cause, reinforced on January 20th 1983 by the publication of Liberal policies on animals, including the resolution, passed at the Liberal Assembly, pledging prohibition of all experiments causing "stress or cruelty". Such prohibition could stop most of the five million or so experiments performed annually in the United Kingdom.

Reformers in America were encouraged by the conviction of Dr. Edward Taub in Maryland District Court on six counts of animal cruelty for failure to provide adequate veterinary care, and, by the end of 1982, seven Federal Bills pertaining to the humane treatment of laboratory animals and the development of non-animal research methods were pending.

In Strasbourg, the Council of Europe's Convention was publicly debated at a Parliamentary Hearing in December 1982. The author, representing CRAE, accused the commercial interests of watering down the Convention's pain-control provisions. But the near completion of the Convention allowed the UK Government to announce that its plans for new legislation will be published in 1983.

Whether the humane movement can finally outstrip the opposing forces of convention, commercialism, technology and the ill-informed demands for consumer protection — or find ways round these powerful forces — remains to be seen. History will, in my opinion, judge that the struggle against speciesism ranks alongside the battles against slavery, poverty, racism, sexual discrimination and the denial of human rights generally.

I will conclude with the words of the Declaration signed at Trinity College, Cambridge, on August 19th 1977 (see *Animal Rights: A Symposium,* ed. Paterson and Ryder, 1979 Centaur Press) and which express the ideals we strive ultimately to attain:

THE RIGHTS OF ANIMALS
A Declaration Against Speciesism

Inasmuch as we believe that there is ample evidence that many other species are capable of feeling, we condemn totally the infliction of suffering upon our brother and sister animals, and the curtailment of their enjoyment, unless it be necessary for their own individual benefit.

We do not accept that a difference in species alone (any more than a difference in race) can justify wanton exploitation or oppression in the name of science or sport, or for food, commercial profit or other human gain.

We believe in the evolutionary and moral kinship of all animals and we declare our belief that all sentient creatures have rights to life, liberty and the quest for happiness.

We call for the protection of these rights.

References

French, R. D. *Antivivisection and Medical Science in Victorian Society,* Princeton University Press 1975.

Hampson, Judith. *Animal Welfare — A Century of Conflict,* New Scientist, 25th Oct. 1979, pp. 208-282.

Hollands, C. *Compassion is the Bugler,* Macdonald 1980.

Report of the Departmental Committee on Experiments on Animals (Chairman: Sir Sydney Littlewood). H.M.S.O. 1965. Cmnd. 2641.

Report of the Royal Commission on the Practice of Subjecting Live Animals to Experiments for Scientific Purposes, H.M.S.O. 1876. Cmnd. 1397.

Report on Royal Commission on Vivisection, H.M.S.O. 1912. Cmnd. 1397.

Ryder, R. D. *"The Struggle against Speciesism"* in *"Animals Rights — A Symposium,"* Centaur Press, 1979. Paterson, D. and Ryder, R. D. (eds).

Ryder, R. D. *"Experiments on Animals"* in *"Animals, Men and Morals,"* Godlovich, S and R, and Harris, J. (ed) Gollancz, 1971.

Ryder, R. D. *Victims of Science,* Davis-Poynter 1975.

Singer, P. *Animal Liberation,* Cape 1976, Paladin 1978.

Sperlinger, D. (ed) *Animals in Research,* John Wiley 1981.

Smyth, D. H. *Alternatives to Animal Experiments,* Scolar Press 1978. (see especially Appendix 4).

Vyvyan, J. *In Pity and In Anger,* Michael Joseph 1969.

Vyvyan, J. *The Dark Face of Science,* Michael Joseph 1971.

14. Summary of Main Findings

(1) There is abundant and growing evidence that other animals can suffer in a way similar to humans.

(2) This century there has been a rapid increase in the use of living animals for research.

(3) Many experiments entail considerable suffering for the animals involved.

(4) It is probable that at least 100 million animals die each year in laboratories throughout the world.

(5) It is known that about four and a half million vertebrates annually are experimented upon while alive, in British laboratories. About eighty-two per cent of the experiments are without anaesthetic, although many of these do not entail severe pain.

(6) It is probable that most experiments on animals are now performed for *commercial* purposes.

(7) An increasingly large proportion of painful experiments upon animals, all over the world, are of a *non-medical sort,* and so cannot be justified on the grounds of medical necessity.

Examples are:

(a) The toxicity-testing of inessentials such as toiletries and cosmetics; non-nutritive food additives; weedkillers and insecticides; and other commercial products, such as detergents, oven-cleaners and fire-extinguishers.

(b) Research on behaviour.

(c) Agricultural research.

(8) Many animals die in the experimental testing of weapons.

(9) Even ordinary routine laboratory life entails considerable suffering for many animals.

(10) There is a growing 'laboratory-animal industry' whose vested interest is in maintaining the use of animals for research.

(11) Many of man's closest evolutionary relatives are being used for experiments; about 200,000 apes and monkeys die annually in the laboratories of the world, and, partly on account of this trade, several species are threatened with extinction.

(12) Nowhere in the world is there legislation which provides adequate protection for laboratory animals. Even the British Law still allows the infliction of severe pain.

(13) Immediate reforms should include:

(a) The prohibition of all painful and non-medical experiments.

(b) Governmental backing for the development of alternatives to animals in research. (see Appendix B.)

(c) Greater public accountability.

(14) Much animal research is scientifically invalid: nowhere is this more evident than in the vast field of the so-called safety testing of drugs and other commercial products.

(15) Promising alternatives to the use of animals for research already exist and could be further developed; in some cases such alternatives are considerably cheaper than animals.

(16) Many great reformers of human society have also shown an interest in animal welfare; in recent years there has been a re-awakening of concern among politicians, scientists and laymen.

(17) One main motive for the enormous use of animals in research is not the relief of human suffering but commercial profit. A secondary motive is career-ambition.

(18) There is no sound logical reason for ignoring the rights and interests of other species. Selfish speciesist prejudices are even unlikely, in the long run, to promote the worthwhile survival of man himself.

Appendix A: The Cruelty to Animals Act, 1876

An Act to amend the Law relating to Cruelty to Animals
(15th August 1876)

Whereas it is expedient to amend the law relating to cruelty to animals by extending it to the cases of animals which for medical, physiological, or other scientific purposes are subjected when alive to experiments calculated to inflict pain:

Be it enacted by the Queen's most Excellent Majesty, by and with the advice and consent of the Lords Spiritual and Temporal, and Commons, in this present Parliament assembled, and by the authority of the same, as follows:

1. This Act may be cited for all purposes as "The Cruelty to Animals Act, 1876".

2. A person shall not perform on a living animal any experiment calculated to give pain, except subject to the restrictions imposed by this Act.

3. The following restrictions are imposed by this Act with respect to the performance on any living animal of an experiment calculated to give pain; that is to say,

(a) The experiment must be performed with a view to the advancement by new discovery of physiological knowledge or of knowledge which will be useful for saving or prolonging life or alleviating suffering; and

(b) the experiment must be performed by a person holding such a licence from one of Her Majesty's Principal Secretaries of State, in this Act referred to as the Secretary of State, as in this Act mentioned, and in the case of a person holding such conditional licence as is hereinafter mentioned, or of experiments performed for the purpose of instruction in a registered place; and

(c) The animal must during the whole of the experiment be under the influence of some anaesthetic of sufficient power to prevent the animal feeling pain; and

(d) The animal must, if the pain is likely to continue after the effect of the anaesthetic has ceased, or if any serious injury has been inflicted on the animal, be killed before it recovers from the influence of the anaesthetic which has been administered; and

(e) The experiment shall not be performed as an illustration of lectures in medical schools, hospitals, colleges, or elsewhere; and
(f) The experiment shall not be performed for the purpose of attaining manual skill.

Provided as follows, that is to say,
(1) Experiments may be performed under the foregoing provisions as to the use of anaesthetics by a person giving illustrations of lectures in medical schools, hospitals or colleges, or elsewhere, on such certificate being given as in this Act mentioned, that the proposed experiments are absolutely necessary for the due instruction of the persons to whom such lectures are given with a view to their acquiring physiological knowledge or knowledge which will be useful to them for saving or prolonging life or alleviating suffering; and,

(2) Experiments may be performed without anaesthetics on such certificate being given as in this Act mentioned that insensibility cannot be produced without necessarily frustrating the object of such experiments; and,
(3) Experiments may be performed without the person who performed such experiments being under an obligation to cause the animal on which any such experiment is performed to be killed before it recovers from the influence of the anaesthetic on such certificate being given as in this Act mentioned that the so killing the animal would necessarily frustrate the object of the experiment, and provided that the animal be killed as soon as such object has been attained; and,
(4) Experiments may be performed not directly for the advancement by new discovery of physiological knowledge, or of knowledge which will be useful for saving or prolonging life or alleviating suffering, but for the purpose of testing a particular former discovery alleged to have been made for the advancement of such knowledge as last aforesaid, on such certificate being given as is in this Act mentioned that such testing is absolutely necessary for the effectual advancement of such knowledge.
4. The substance known as urari or curare shall not for the purposes of this Act be deemed to be an anaesthetic.
5. Notwithstanding anything in this Act contained, an experiment calculated to give pain shall not be performed without anaesthetics on a dog or cat, except on such certificate being given as in this Act mentioned stating, in addition to the statements hereinbefore required to be made in such certificate, that for reasons specified in the certificate, the object of the experiment will be necessarily frustrated unless it is performed on an animal similar in constitution and habits to a cat or dog, and no other

animal is available for such experiment; and an experiment calculated to give pain shall not be performed on any horse, ass, or mule except on such certificate being given as in this act mentioned that the object of the experiment will be necessarily frustrated unless it is performed on a horse, ass, or mule and that no other animal is available for such experiment.

6. Any exhibition to the general public, whether admitted on payment of money or gratuitously, of experiments on living animals calculated to give pain shall be illegal.

7. The Secretary of State may insert, as a condition of granting any licence, a provision in such licence that the place in which any experiment is to be performed by the licensee is to be registered in such manner as the Secretary of State may from time to time by any general or special order direct; provided that every place for the performance of experiments for the purpose of instruction under this Act shall be approved by the Secretary of State, and shall be registered in such manner as he may from time to time by any general or special order direct.

8. The Secretary of State may licence any person whom he may think qualified to hold a licence to perform experiments under this Act. A licence granted by him may be for such time as he may think fit, and may be revoked by him on his being satisfied that such licence ought to be revoked. There may be annexed to such licence any conditions which the Secretary of State may think expedient for the purpose of better carrying into effect the objects of this Act, but not inconsistent with the provisions thereof.

9. The Secretary of State may direct any person performing experiments under this Act, from time to time to make such reports to him of the results of such experiments, in such form and with such details as he may require.

11. Any application for a licence under this Act and a certificate given as in this Act mentioned must *be signed by* one or more of the following persons; that is to say,

> The President of the Royal Society;
> The President of the Royal Society of Edinburgh;
> The President of the Royal Irish Academy;
> The Presidents of the Royal Colleges of Surgeons in London, Edinburgh, or Dublin;
> The Presidents of the Royal Colleges of Physicians in London, Edinburgh, or Dublin;
> The President of the General Medical Council;

The President of the Faculty of Physicians and Surgeons of Glasgow;*

The President of the Royal College of Veterinary Surgeons, London, but in the case only of an experiment to be performed under anaesthetics with a view to the advancement by new discovery of veterinary science;

+ and *also* (unless the applicant be a professor of physiology, medicine, anatomy, medical jurisprudence, materia medica, or surgery in a university in Great Britian or Ireland, or in University College, London, or in a college in Great Britain or Ireland, incorporated by Royal Charter) by a professor of physiology, medicine anatomy, medical jurisprudence, materia medica, or surgery in a university in Great Britain or Ireland, or in University College, London, or in a college in Great Britain or Ireland, incorporated by royal charter.

Provided that where any person applying for a certificate under this Act is himself one of the persons authorized to sign such certificate, the signature of some other of such persons shall be substituted for the signature of the applicant.

A certificate under this section may be given for such time or for such series of experiments as the person or persons signing the certificate may think expedient.

A copy of any certificate under this section shall be forwarded by the applicant to the Secretary of State, but shall not be available until one week after a copy has been so forwarded.

The Secretary of State may at any time disallow or suspend any certificate given under this section.

22. This Act shall not apply to invertebrate animals.

---

*   Now the "Royal Faculty of Physicians and Surgeons of Glasgow".

+   The Secretary of State is advised that in consequence of Article 2 of the Irish Free State (Consequential Adaption of Enactments) Order, 1923, the term "Ireland" where used in this paragraph must now be regarded as meaning "Northern Ireland".

Appendix B:

Experiments on Animals: Suggested Reforms
(This is the author's broadsheet circulated following the first publication of *Victims of Science* in 1975).

My book *Victims of Science* draws attention to the widespread use of animals in experiments which are *not for strictly medical purposes*. Most research on animals is no longer done in hospitals. There has been a trend toward trivial and commercial uses. We now know that *about two-thirds of the over 5 million* U.K. licensed experiments each year, are done for "commercial undertakings". Some 17,000 dogs and 13,000 cats die in British laboratories each year. 30% of these may have come from private ownership (1975 figures).

More than 100,000 animals die in British laboratories each week.

I have had so many letters written to me after the publication of the book asking what action can be taken, that I have drawn up this list of suggestions.

May I say that I am very grateful for all the kind things that have been said and I hope all those who have written will take up the cause and *press the Government for action,* and keep on pressing for years if necessary until we can achieve substantial reforms. These should include:-

(1) *The existing Home Office Advisory Committee should be revitalised*
This committee should become an active standing committee representing a wide range of scientific, veterinary and animal welfare interests. It should be a professionally staffed body with real powers. It should consider the justification for experiments and publish its own reports. It should have access to public opinion.

(2) *Strengthening the Home Office Inspectorate*
There should be 25 Inspectors of whom the majority should be veterinarily qualified. (At present there are only 14 Inspectors to control about 18,500 licence-holders). (1975 figures).

(3) *Channelling funds into the further development of the humane alternatives to research animals.*
A central office (perhaps a Medical Research Council sub-committee) should collate and disseminate information; this body should communicate regularly with the new Advisory Committee (1). Development-units should be established in existing laboratories. (Humane alternatives

mostly are in their infancy, but in some cases are already cheaper and safer than using animals.)

(4) *Improving Home Office Information to the Public*
M.P.s and the tax-payer (who sponsors much of the research being done) receive very little information. According to the Littlewood Report (p. 164) "there has been an appearance of secrecy about the practice of animal experimentation". The tax-payer has some right to know just how many of the over 5,000,000 licensed experiments on animals each year are for strictly medical purposes and how many are for other purposes such as the testing of cosmetics, toiletries, weed-killers, oven-cleaners and fire-extinguishers. Animals are being poisoned to death with such substances, and are being used in the testing of weapons, and in behavioural and "stress" experiments, which are not always medical.

(5) *New and up to date legislation*
This should encourage humane practices such as anaesthesia, analgesia (pain-killing) and euthanasia. (The present law (the Cruelty to Animals Act, 1876) allows the infliction of "severe pain" and the wholesale use of animals in tests which are not truly medical. The Danish, Swedish and German laws are, in some respects, more humane and up to date; Britain needs to catch up.)

Any increased funds required for the implemention of these reforms could be derived from licence fees and registration fees.

The most important action of all is to write to M.P.s: write short letters asking a few technical questions like e.g. "How many animals are experimented on each year by the Ministry of Agriculture?" "How many animals are experimentally poisoned to death with cosmetics/weed-killers/oven-cleaners?" "How many die in weapon-ballistic tests?" Ask your M.P. what he will do to improve the situation.

Other things to do include joining or supporting R.S.P.C.A. (Horsham, Sussex), British Union for Abolition of Vivisection, (143, Charing Cross Rd., W.C.2), National Anti-Vivisection Society (51 Harley St., W.1.), FRAME (5b The Poultry, Bank Place, Nottingham) Scottish Society for the Prevention of Vivisection (10 Queensferry St., Edinburgh) and other welfare organisations, getting other bodies (such as womens' Societies and local political organisations) to *bring pressure on the Government (especially on the Home Secretary, c/o House of Commons, London S.W.1)*, getting in touch with commercial firms that use animals in research, and writing short, factual letters to the newspapers and to radio and television.

It is really, however, only the Government which can change things. In 1965 the Littlewood report urged 83 Recommended Changes to the Cruelty to Animals Act 1876 and its administration; but successive

Governments have almost entirely ignored this report. They have ignored also the wishes of the majority of the British electorate. In 1974 the R.S.P.C.A. announced the result of an Opinion Survey carried out by N.O.P. Market Research Ltd., which revealed that 73% of the electorate disapproved of the testing of cosmetics on animals, and 74% disapproved of using animals in weapons' testing. Only 13% actually said they approved of these procedures.

People who are concerned about this issue should try to inform themselves of the facts. A useful source is the Home Office list of Premises Registered under the Cruelty to Animals Act 1876, obtainable from the Home Office, Queen Anne's Gate, London S.W.1., (Tel: 01-213-3000) — cheques for about £7.00 made payable to "The Accounting Officer, Home Office". This list will show laboratories in your locality where you can, quite legally, write for further information. Each summer H.M. Stationery Office, London, publishes the annual Returns under the 1876 Cruelty to Animals Act — this can be useful too.

Women could well write to the various cosmetics firms (and the manufacturers of other household products) asking them if they use animals in testing, whether this involves force-feeding the animals to death, how many animals and of what species. (I would be interested to see the replies obtained.) Boots Ltd., have publicly stated that they do *not* test cosmetics on animals. So if they don't, why do other firms do it? Shareholders have a right to know how their money is being spent and so should lobby firms and press them to spend money on the search for alternatives. Shareholders also have a right to attend meetings and ask searching questions.

Thank you again. I hope my book will be a reliable source of evidence for those interested in animal welfare.

Richard D. Ryder

P.S. The British Veterinary Association, 7 Mansfield St., London, may also be able to supply information; but nowadays some vets are, unfortunately, themselves involved in commercial research on animals.

Essential Reforms, 1983

As a step towards completely stopping the exploitation of non-humans in laboratories, the following intermediary reforms are called for:-

(i) banning trivial and unnecessary experiments completely.

(ii) abolishing pain and distress altogether in the remaining experiments.

(iii) allowing laboratories only to obtain animals from dealers who are officially licenced (rather than from unscrupulous dealers who may be supplying stolen pets).

(iv) completely reconstituting Government Advisory Committees on animal experimentation so as to represent fairly animal welfare and lay interests, and giving them powers of investigation and a duty to publish their reports.

(v) licensing as experimenters only those who are trained in anaesthetic, analgesic, euthanasic, tranquillising and animal-care techniques.

(vi) Governments should do far more to develop and encourage the use of alternative research techniques which do not involve any suffering at all.

R.D.R.

Appendix C:

A letter from one of the original discoverers of the dangers of thalidomide

"Daily Telegraph   January 13th, 1973."
LETTERS TO THE EDITOR
DRUG DANGERS FOR THE UNBORN
Sir,

I have refrained from taking part in the thalidomide compensation wrangle but recent events have prompted me to point out some relevant facts.

Prior to November 1961, I know of only one drug company in the world who tested their new products for teratogenicity; even that company would not have detected the teratogenic effects of thalidomide as they did not use the susceptible animal species in their routine testing.

It took many months even after I suspected thalidomide as the cause of congenital anomalies in June, 1961 to substantiate these findings in the New Zealand white rabbit then, later still in monkeys.

In 1961 it was a new concept that a non-toxic drug, particularly one that had no lethal dose, could produce severe congenital anomalies. The abnormalities were so diverse that it was, and still is difficult to explain how thalidomide could produce them. How could it produce a child with six fingers on each hand? Indeed the first three babies that I saw with the thalidomide syndrome in May and June of 1961 did have this type of deformity.

Eleven years later we know little about the action of drugs on the foetus, so that it is not surprising that I had great difficulty in 1961 convincing anyone for some months that thalidomide was indeed the cause of these abnormalities and I confess that at times I had doubts myself if this theory was correct.

Many distinguished obstetricians, pathologists, paediatricians, teratologists and editors were reluctant to accept my hypothesis that thalidomide did cause abnormalities, particularly as I could not confirm it in laboratory animals.

Surely if we have a sense of justice we must accept that thalidomide was the first non-toxic drug developed which produced severe abnormalities in the unborn child. Two other related compounds in the same group are non-teratogenic.

Secondly, this was bound to happen as teratologists thought it impossible for non-toxic substances to affect the unborn child.

Thirdly, thalidomide does not affect the foetuses of the normal laboratory rodents or indeed most animals.

Many people, including myself, feel that we will have more thalidomide-type tragedies in the future, perhaps not on such a large scale, but as man is different from other animal species it is likely that, no matter how thoroughly new drugs are tested on animals, species differences or synergistic actions will occasionally betray us. *

One wonders if the best method of compensation for individuals such as the thalidomide children would be the payment of life pensions by the company concerned.

Payment of a lump sum has many disadvantages. Few people have the expertise to invest it wisely, and with the depreciation of money surely a pension adjusted periodically by a court would be much more satisfactory to all concerned, and it would seem only fair that such compensation should not be subjected to taxation either by the company or the recipient. Surely if we are to tax individuals or companies on their profits we must exempt them from their liabilities.

We must face the fact that thalidomide-type tragedies may occur in the future and that a just method of compensation should be devised. As most new drugs are developed by large corporations, if any indemnity is required on any of their products, surely a pension would be preferable to a lump sum payment, and such payments must be legitimate business expenses.

WILLIAM McBRIDE, M.D., F.R.C.P.G.,
Sydney

* My italics, R.D.R.

Appendix D:

Some Animal Protection Organisations to support
   United States
American Anti-Vivisection Society, Suite 204 Noble Plaza, 801 Old York Road, Jenkintown, PA 19046, USA.
American Fund for Alternatives to Animal Research, 175 West 12th St., New York, 10011.
Animal Welfare Institute, P.O. Box 3650, Washington, D.C. 20007.
Fund for Animals Inc., 140 West 57th Street, New York, N.Y. 10019.
Humane Society of the United States, 2100L Street N.W., Washington, D.C. 20037.
International Fund for Animal Welfare, P.O. Box 193, Yarmouth Port, MA 02675.
Society for Animal Rights Inc., 421 South State St., Clarks Summit, Pa 18411.
United Action for Animals Inc., 205 East 42 Street, New York, N.Y. 10017.
Animal Rights Network, Inc., P.O. Box 5234, Westport, CT 06881.
   Australia
Australian Association for Humane Research, P.O. Box 356, Broadway, New South Wales, 2007.
Animal Liberation, 22 Elgin Rd., Gordon, N.S.W.
Anti-Vivisection Union (SA) Inc., P.O. Box 77, Marden, South Australia.
   Canada
Society for Animals in Distress, 603 St. Clair Ave West, Toronto, M6C 1A3.
Canadian League for Animal Rights, P.O. Box 5201, Station B, Victoria, British Columbia, V8R 6NR.
   Britain
Animal Aid, 111 High Street, Tonbridge, Kent.
Beauty Without Cruelty, 11 Limehill Road, Tunbridge Wells, Kent.
         (Promotes sale of cruelty-free furs and cosmetics)
British Union for the Abolition of Vivisection, 143 Charing Cross Road, London W.C.2.
Coordinating Animal Welfare (CAW), P.O. Box 61, Camberley, Surrey.
Fund for the Replacement of Animals in Medical Experiments (FRAME), 5b The Poultry, Bank Place, Nottingham.
Hunt Saboteurs Association, P.O. Box 19, London SE22.
            (Direct Action; main concern is wildlife)
National Anti-Vivisection Society, 51 Harley Street, London W.1.

Royal Society for the Prevention of Cruelty to Animals (RSPCA), Causeway, Horsham, Sussex.
Scottish Anti-Vivisection Society, 121 West Regent Street, Glasgow C.2.
Scottish Society for the Prevention of Vivisection, 10 Queensferry Street, Edinburgh.

International
International Association Against Painful Experiments on Animals, 51 Harley Street, London, W1N 1DD.
International Fund for Animal Welfare, P.O. Box 193, Yarmouth Port, Massachusetts, U.S.A.
World Federation for the Protection of Animals, Dreikönigstrasse 37 -CH - 8002 Zurich, Switzerland.
Royal Society for the Prevention of Cruelty to Animals (RSPCA), Causeway, Horsham, Sussex, U.K.
International Primate Protection League, P.O. Drawer X, Summerville, S.C. 29483, U.S.A.

Bibliography

Adams, Richard: *The Plague Dogs* (novel) Penguin, 1977.

Agius, Dom Ambrose: *God's Animals* C.S.C.A.W. 1970. 2nd Ed. 1973.

Amory, Cleveland: *Man Kind? Our Incredible War on Wildlife,* New York, Harper and Row. 1974.

Aspinall, John: *The Best of Friends*, Macmillan, London. 1976.

Bayly, M. Beddow: *More Spotlights on Vivisection*, National Anti-Vivisection Society, 1960.

Brown, Anthony: *Who Cares for Animals? 150 Years of the R.S.P.C.A.* Heinnemann, 1974.

Clark, Kenneth (Lord Clark): *Animals and Men*, Thames and Hudson, 1977.

Clark, Stephen, R. L.: *The Moral Status of Animals*, Clarendon Press, 1977.

Cobbe, Frances Power: *The Anti-Vivisection Question*, 1884 pub. The Victoria Street Society.

Coleridge, Stephen: *Great Testimony against Scientific Cruelty*, pub. John Lane, 1918.

Fairholme, Edward and Pain, Wellesley: *A Century of Work for Animals*, pub. John Murray, 1924.

Fox, Dr. Michael: *Between Animal and Man,* Blond and Briggs, London 1977.

French, Richard D.: *Anti-Vivisection and Medical Science in Victorian Society*, pub. Princeton University, 1975.

Godlovitch, Stanley, Godlovitch, Rosalind, and Harris, John (eds.): *Animals, Men and Morals*, Gollancz, 1971.

Hall, Rebecca: *Animals are Equal*, Wildwood 1980.

Hammerton, Canon H. J. *Kingdom of Neighbours*, pub. Crusade Against All Cruelty to Animals Ltd., 1970.

Harrison, Ruth: *Animal Machines* Vincent Stuart, London 1964.

Hollands, Clive: *Compassion is the Bugler*, Macdonald 1980.

Hutchings, Monica M., and Caver, Mavis: *Man's Dominion: Our Violation of the Animal World*, Rupert Hart-Davis, 1970.

Kotzwinkle, William: *Doctor Rat*, pub. Aidan Ellis, Oxford, 1976.

Lawick-Goodall, Jane van: *In the Shadow of Man*, Collins, 1971.

Leavitt, E. S. et al: *Animals and Their Legal Rights*, pub. Animal Welfare Institute, Washington, D.C. 1968.

Lind-af-Hageby, L. (ed): *The Animals' Cause,* pub. 1909 by the Animal Defence and Anti-Vivisection Society.

Linzey, Andrew: *Animal Rights,* pub. S.C.M. Press, London, 1976.

Moss, A. W.: *Valiant Crusade—The History of the Royal Society for the Prevention of Cruelty to Animals,* Cassell, 1961.

Paterson, David and Ryder, Richard D., (eds.) *Animals' Rights: A Symposium,* Centaur, 1979.

Paterson, David, (ed.): *Humane Education — A Symposium,* Humane Education Council — 1981.

Paget, G. E. (ed.): *Methods in Toxicology,* Blackwell Scientific Publications, 1970.

Pratt, Dr. Dallas: *Painful Experiments on Animals,* Argus Archives, New York, 1976.

Regan, Tom, and Singer, Peter: *Animal Rights and Human Obligations,* Prentice-Hall, 1976.

Risdon, Wilfred: *Lawson Tait: A Biographical Study,* National Anti-Vivisection Society, 1967.

Ruesch, Hans: *Slaughter of the Innocent,* Bantam 1978.

Ryder, Richard D.: *A Scientist Speaks on the Extensive Use of Animals in Non-Medical Research.* pub. Scottish Society for the Prevention of Vivisection, 1972.

"   *Scientific Cruelty for Commercial Profit* pub. Scottish Society for the Prevention of Vivisection, 1974.

"   *Speciesism: The Ethics of Vivisection* pub. Scottish Society for the Prevention of Vivisection, 1974.

"   "Experiments on Animals" in *Animals, Men and Morals,* ed. Godlovitch and Harris (op.cit)

"   "Experiments on Animals" in *Animal Rights and Human Obligations* ed. Regan and Singer (op.cit).

"   "Psychologische Experimenten met Dieren" in *Dierproeven in de Moderne Samenleving* ed. Smid. pub. Uitgeverij Ankh-Hermes by-Deventer, 1978.

"   "Speciesism — Psychological and Moral Aspects" in *Humane Education — A Symposium* ed. Paterson. 1981. (op.cit.)

"   "The Struggle Against Speciesism" in *Animals' Rights — A Symposium* ed. Paterson and Ryder (op.cit.) 1979.

"   "British Legislation and Proposals for Reform" in *Animals in Research* (ed.). Sperlinger (op.cit.)

"   *Victims of Science,* Davis-Poynter, 1975.

Salt, Henry S.: *Animals Rights,* (1894) republished Society for Animals Rights, 1980 USA, and Centaur Press, UK.

Singer, Peter: *Animal Liberation,* pub. New York Review, 1975, and Jonathan Cape, London, 1976.

Soulairac, A., Cahn, J., and Charpentier, J. (eds.): *Pain,* Academic Press, 1968.

Sperlinger, David (ed.): *Animals in Research*, Wiley, 1981.
Townend, Christine: *In Defence of Living Things*, Wentworth, Australia, 1980.
Turner, E.S. *All Heaven in a Rage*, Michael Joseph, 1964.
Vyvyan, John: *In Pity and in Anger*, Michael Joseph, 1969.
"   *The Dark Face of Science*, Michael Joseph, 1971.
Westacott, E.: *A Century of Vivisection and Anti-Vivisection*, C. W. Daniel Co. Ltd., 1949.
Whittall, Dr. J. D.: *People and Animals*, NAVS, 1981.
Wynne-Tyson, Jon: *Food For A Future*, Abacus, 1976.
"   *The Civilised Alternative*, Centaur, 1972.

Index